WITHDRAWN FROM TSC LIBRARY

PQ
241
.N8

Nurse, Peter
Classical voices

A FINE WILL BE CHARGED FOR EACH OVERDUE BOOK

Classical Voices

TO MY PARENTS

François VI, duc de La Rochefoucauld (1613–1680)
Anonymous seventeenth-century painting

PETER H. NURSE

Classical Voices

*Studies of Corneille,
Racine, Molière,
Mme de Lafayette*

GEORGE G. HARRAP & CO. LTD
London   Toronto   Wellington   Sydney

First published in Great Britain 1971
by GEORGE G. HARRAP *&* CO. LTD
182-184 High Holborn, London, WC1V 7AX

© *Peter H. Nurse* 1971
Copyright. All rights reserved

ISBN: 0 245 50566 0

Composed in Garamond type and printed by
William Clowes and Sons, Limited
London, Beccles and Colchester

PREFACE

The aim of this book is neither to formulate a comprehensive definition of French Classicism, nor to present an exhaustive survey of the work of the four authors who are the subject of the following chapters. It seeks, rather, to capture the characteristic 'voice' of each of these artists, through the study of one or two of their more celebrated creations.

At the same time, while maintaining the individuality of each author as a focus, the perspective is broadened to include a wide range of significant general questions: for instance, the growth of the literary conventions within which the Classical writers worked; the influence of the *moralistes*, especially La Rochefoucauld, who inherited the Sceptic tradition passed on by Erasmus and Montaigne; and the degree to which this climate of moral thought was shaped by the socio-political environment. Also treated are such perennial aesthetic problems as the nature of the 'tragic' and the 'comic', and the ethical function of art, with particular reference to the distinction between Comedy and Satire.

In the case of Corneille, I have limited myself to one play, *Horace*, on the grounds of its reputation as the first great French Classical tragedy, and have reproduced the Introduction to my critical edition (Harrap, 1963). For the Racine chapter, I have concentrated on what seem to me to be the three outstanding masterpieces: *Andromaque*, *Britannicus* and *Phèdre*, seeking primarily to provide a definition of *le tragique racinien*. The Molière chapter is essentially a study of four plays: *L'École des Femmes*, *Tartuffe*, *Dom Juan* and *Le Misanthrope*, which probably represent this author's highest achievement. Finally, the chapter on Madame de Lafayette deals, of course, with *La Princesse de Clèves*; though originally written for this book, it also serves as the Introduction to my critical edition of the novel (Harrap, 1970).

For such qualities as this book possesses, I am indebted to many people. For their encouragement and inspiration, special thanks belong to my wife; to my two *maîtres*, Austin Gill and René Pintard; and, lastly, to Paul Bénichou, whose book, *Morales du Grand Siècle*, so frequently quoted in these pages, remains for me one of the great works of criticism.

P.H.N.

ANALYTICAL TABLE OF CONTENTS

CHAPTER ONE—CORNEILLE

The genesis, performance and reception of *Horace*, p. 13. — The evolution of French tragedy before 1640: Renaissance tragedy, p. 16. — Baroque drama, p. 17. — *La Querelle du Cid*: neo-Classical theory, p. 20. — Corneille's reply to his critics, p. 24. — The Roman source and dramatic framework of *Horace*, p. 27. — The moral conflict of the protagonists: Sabine, p. 31. — Camille and the "coup d'épée inévitable", p. 35. — Curiace and Horace, p. 40 — The Unity of Action in *Horace*, p. 44. — Horace as tragic hero, p. 45. — The sources of Cornelian heroism: the seventeenth-century view of ancient Rome, p. 48. — The aristocratic concept of *générosité* and neo-Stoic philosophy, p. 50. — The moral ambiguity of *gloire*, p. 52. — *Horace* and the seventeenth-century political background, p. 57 — NOTES, p. 60.

CHAPTER TWO—RACINE

The psychology of the tragic emotions, p. 69. — Poetic tonality: *tristesse majestueuse*, p. 70. — Corneille and the heroic tradition, p. 70. — Racine's early work: *La Thébaïde* and *Alexandre*, p. 71. — The social and political background after the Fronde: the threat to heroic status, p. 73. — The poetry of lamentation in *Britannicus*, p. 74. — Hermione, Phèdre and Hippolyte, p. 75. — The theme of fatality, p. 77. — Tragic structure: character and plot, p. 82 — Aristotelian theory and Sophoclean practice, p. 83. — Tragic 'error' in *Phèdre*: Thésée and Hippolyte, p. 86. — Neo-Classical criticisms of Racine, p. 90. — The problem of the morally guilty protagonist: Shakespeare and Racine, p. 91. — Phaedra and Phèdre, p. 93. — *Britannicus* and the question of tragic pity, p. 99. — Character and tragic action, p. 102 — Varieties of tragic meaning, p. 103. — NOTES, p. 106.

CHAPTER THREE—MOLIÈRE

The comic tradition before Molière: Renaissance and seventeenth-century literary comedy, p. 113. — Molière's novelty, p. 114. — The theory of comedy and the nature of *le ridicule*, p. 116. — *L'École des Femmes* and the comedy of the 'solipsist', p. 121. — Arnolphe and the sex-war, p. 123. — Mock-heroic comedy, p. 125. — Arnolphe as *faux dévot*, p. 128. — The theme of love in *L'École des Femmes*, p. 130. — Comedy and moral perspective, p. 131. — Satire and Comedy: "the genius of thoughtful laughter", p. 133. — *Tartuffe*: the historical context, p. 135. — Orgon and Tartuffe: "la poésie de l'imposture", p. 136. — Religion and the Sceptic perspective, p. 139. — Cléante and the problem of the *raisonneur*, p. 142. — Elements of dramatic realism in *Tartuffe*, p. 142. — Tartuffe: a sinister or a comic figure? p. 143. — *Dom Juan*: critical attitudes to the hero, p. 148. — Dramatic structure: Dorimond, Villiers and Molière, p. 149. — Dom Juan as 'seducer' and the theme of *obligations*, p. 151. — Sganarelle as comic foil, p. 154. — A comic Dom Juan? p. 156. — *Le Misanthrope*: the question of ambiguity, p. 159. — Alceste as satirical spokesman? p. 160. — The idealist in a corrupt society, p. 162. — Rousseau on Alceste, p. 163. — Alceste v. Philinte, and the 'scène du sonnet', p. 164. — Alceste in love, p. 167. — Alceste and Célimène, Act IV, scene 3, p. 169. — The ambiguity of Célimène: "chronic liar" or "personnage sans équivoque"? p. 171. — The comedy of *amour-propre*, p. 173. — "La morale de Molière", p. 174. — The comic vision of Scepticism: *Amphitryon*, p. 175. — Conclusion, p. 177. — NOTES, p. 178.

CHAPTER FOUR—MADAME DE LAFAYETTE

La Princesse de Clèves: a tragic novel, p. 187. — Genesis of the novel: the social background of Mme de Lafayette, p. 189. — The *salon* world and psychological analysis, p. 191. — Attitudes to love, p. 192. — The literary tradition: *L'Astrée*, p. 193. — Mlle de Scudéry, p. 196. — *Roman* and *nouvelle historique*, p. 197.

— The historical background in *La Princesse de Clèves*, p. 198. — Reality 'idealised', p. 199. — Social *milieu* and tragic structure, p. 201. — Narrative modes of moral analysis, p. 205. — The moral drama: Pascal, La Rochefoucauld and Mme de Lafayette, p. 208. — "Les désordres de l'Amour", p. 210. — The significance of "les actions involontaires", p. 213. — "La scène de l'aveu", p. 217. — The final encounter of Mme de Clèves and Nemours, p. 218 — Psychological complexity and moral ambiguity, p. 219. — Mme de Lafayette and the Montaigne tradition, p. 221. — NOTES, p. 223.

SELECT BIBLIOGRAPHY — p. 227.

ILLUSTRATIONS

François VI, duc de La Rochefoucauld (1613–1680).
   Anonymous seventeenth-century painting

                                                  frontispiece

Pierre Corneille (1606–1684).
   Engraving by Woolnoth, after a painting by Le Brun

                                                  facing page 13

Jean Racine (1639–1699).
   Painting attributed to Mignard

                                                  facing page 69

Jean-Baptiste Poquelin de Molière (1622–1673)
   Painting by Le Brun

                                                  facing page 113

Marie-Madeleine, comtesse de Lafayette (1634–1693)
   Painting by Antoine Hoerse

                                                  facing page 187

CHAPTER ONE

CORNEILLE

Pierre Corneille (1606–1684)
Engraving by Woolnoth, after a painting by Le Brun

The Genesis, Performance and Reception of "Horace"

By the end of 1636, Pierre Corneille was already, at the age of thirty, one of the leading dramatists in France. Born in Rouen, he had followed the family tradition by training as a lawyer and acquiring official legal functions in the Norman capital which he continued to exercise until at least 1650. At the same time, with the performance in Paris of his first play, *Mélite*, probably in the 1629-30 season, he began a successful career in the theatre which was to produce no less than thirty-two plays before it ended with his death in 1684.

However, it was not until *Le Cid*, his eighth play, staged in the first days of 1637, that Corneille proved his clear superiority over his theatrical rivals, headed by Rotrou, Mairet and Scudéry. It is therefore all the more strange that, in spite of the enormous popular success of *Le Cid*, Corneille should have remained silent for three years, until the performance of *Horace* in 1640. The most obvious cause of this silence[1] lies in the furious controversy that broke out a month or two after his triumph in January 1637: provoked by Corneille's undisguised self-satisfaction and jealous of his success, his rivals launched a series of pamphlets which contested the validity of his achievement, Scudéry leading the attack with the assertion that *Le Cid* breached all the essential rules of drama. But besides the public's verdict, expressed in its enthusiastic reception of the play, Corneille had his own champions to support him in print, and so venomous did the exchanges become that Richelieu had to intervene: alarmed at the disrepute which threatened the theatre which he had done so much to encourage because of the added splendour it gave to the régime he had been promoting since 1624, the Cardinal-Prime Minister ordered an end to the controversy.[2] The newly founded Académie Française, to whom Scudéry had first appealed, was officially commissioned to act as referee, eventually publishing its verdict towards the end of November 1637;[3] it was clearly the relatively unfavourable terms in which he found his play treated that fundamentally discouraged Corneille and brought his creative activity to a temporary halt.

It is impossible to say whether or not Corneille had begun work on *Horace* before the publication of the *Sentiments de l'Académie*, but it seems likely no substantial headway had been made on it by the beginning of 1639. For, on January 15th, Chapelain wrote a letter to Guez de Balzac, containing the following passage:

> Corneille est ici [à Paris] depuis 3 jours et d'abord m'est venu faire un éclaircissement sur le livre de l'Académie pour ou plutôt contre *Le Cid*, m'accusant, et non sans raison, d'en être le principal auteur. Il ne fait plus rien, et Scudéry a du moins gagné cela, en le querellant, qu'il l'a rebuté du métier, et lui a tari sa veine. Je l'ai, autant que j'ai pu, réchauffé et encouragé à se venger, et de Scudéry et de sa protectrice, en faisant quelque nouveau *Cid* qui attire encore les suffrages de tout le monde et qui montre que l'art n'est pas ce qui fait la beauté; mais il n'y a pas moyen de l'y résoudre; et il ne parle plus que de règles et que de choses qu'il eût pu répondre aux académiciens, s'il n'eût point craint de choquer les puissances, mettant au reste Aristote entre les auteurs apocryphes lorsqu'il ne s'accommode pas à ses imaginations.[4]

It is likewise Chapelain's correspondence that provides the principal evidence of the progress of the new subject: a letter addressed to Balzac on February 19th, 1640, confirms that: "Corneille a fait une nouvelle pièce du combat des trois Horaces et des trois Curiaces, où il y a une quantité de belles choses et du même esprit du *Cid*"; and Chapelain adds the comment: "Néanmoins je voudrais pour sa perfection qu'il l'eût inventé et disposé autrement qu'il n'a fait." His knowledge of the play seems to have come from hearing Corneille read it to a private gathering at Boisrobert's house, including himself, Barreau, Charpi and L'Estoile.[5] It is shortly after this that comes the announcement to the effect that *Horace* had its first private performance, in the presence of Richelieu, no doubt in the theatre which the Cardinal had had built in his palace near the Louvre; for, on March 9th, Chapelain again wrote to Balzac:

> Pour le combat des *Horaces*, ce ne sera pas sitôt que vous le verrez, pource qu'il n'a pas encore été représenté qu'une fois devant Son Éminence, et que, devant que d'être publié, il faut qu'il serve six mois de gagne-pain aux comédiens....[6]

Not until May 19th do we hear that the play has just had its first three performances before the general public[7]—probably at the Théâtre du Marais. It was this troupe which had acted all of Corneille's previous works and which was to present those that immediately followed, notably: *Cinna* (1640–1), *Polyeucte* (1642–3) and *Pompée* (1643–4).

It would seem that the reception given to *Horace* disappointed Corneille, since in his *Examen* of 1660, he refers to "la chute de ce poème." In ascribing this failure to the murder of Camille ("Tous veulent que la mort de Camille en gâte la fin"), Corneille confirms the evidence of both Chapelain and d'Aubignac that the real objection to the new play was essentially based on moral scruples: indeed, as with *Le Cid*, it was the very subject which was considered unsuitable material for tragedy.[8] The significance of this judgement cannot be exaggerated and it probably explains the real reason why Corneille had hesitated for three years before going ahead with and putting on his work. It was not, as has so often been suggested, that the poet needed time to assimilate those "rules" which he had been accused of breaking in *Le Cid*, in order to prove in *Horace* his reconciliation to the official "Classical" doctrine set out by the Académie in 1637. On the contrary, Corneille has remained unrepentant on the central issue of the controversy: his play is the defiant rejection of the official conception of what subjects are suitable for tragedy and the reaffirmation of the principles which had produced the excellence of *Le Cid*. The following survey of French tragedy before *Horace* is designed to demonstrate this assertion and to illustrate the original nature of Corneille's genius.

The Evolution of French Tragedy before 1640

It was in 1552-3 that Étienne Jodelle largely set the pattern for French Renaissance tragedy with the performance of his play, *Cléopâtre Captive*. Reflecting the Humanists' enthusiasm for Greco-Roman antiquity, this work and subsequent examples of the *genre* take as the subject of the tragic action the spectacle of man crushed by an inexorable Fate—what Jodelle calls "l'inviolable cours de la fatalité." Divided into five acts, each distinguished by the appearance of a chorus, and written in verse, with the alexandrine rapidly asserting its supremacy, they portray characters of noble origin taken from antique history or legend, or from the biblical story, plunged into misfortune by Destiny, in the form of the gods or human tyrants. Their most striking feature is the absence of true drama: the interest is concentrated on victims who are helpless to resist the blows that befall them in the opening stages of the play and whose lyrical plaints constitute the tragic theme during the subsequent course of the action. Instead of a dramatic conflict of wills and a struggle to dominate Fate, we have in fact a succession of elegiac tableaux that exploit the pathos of human misery. Jodelle's *Didon se sacrifiant*, though poetically inferior to many of the tragedies of later sixteenth-century authors such as Jean de la Taille, Garnier or Montchrétien, is typical of the *genre*.

Here, Fate strikes its victims at the very beginning of the action: Aeneas is ordered by Jupiter to leave Carthage with his warriors and continue his mission of founding a new city of Troy; it is this which provides the tragic theme, for to follow duty he must sacrifice his love and abandon Dido, Queen of Carthage. The Classical theatre of the following century, and notably Corneille's *Horace*, will repeatedly take as its material the clash of love and duty, drawing from the psychological conflict involved a powerful source of tragedy. Yet it is this very conflict which is almost entirely missing in Jodelle's treatment of the theme. Both protagonists accept as immutable the god's decree of eternal separation: their first encounter in the play, at the end of Act II, provides neither a struggle of wills, nor a revolt against Fate, but only a mutual lamentation upon its cruelty. The heroine's suicide, though not carried out till the end of the play, is already decided upon in the second Act, and the intervening matter is purely oratorical. In fact, Faguet was not exaggerating when he described the majority of figures of sixteenth-century French tragedy as "bouches parlantes," rather than real complex characters of flesh and blood.

It is, of course, easy to find faults in the dramatic structure of such plays; but their achievement was considerable in view of the absence of an indigenous tradition of any significance and of an established professional theatre for their performance. Like Shakespeare, the great French dramatists of the seventeenth century had experienced troupes of actors with whom they could test their material and learn the secrets of the *métier*: Corneille mainly at the Théâtre du Marais; Molière with his own troupe; Racine at the Hôtel de Bourgogne. Whether or not Jodelle's *Didon* was ever performed is unknown; but while there were certainly performances of some of these Renaissance tragedies,[9] their appeal was essentially literary rather than dramatic: the work of scholars, they were more often designed to be read than acted. Nevertheless, they established in France a tradition on which the seventeenth-century writers were to build: a tradition, inspired by Classical antiquity, which seeks its tragic impact in the rhetorical elaboration of human misery, rather than in the representation of physical action. It is this which explains the fact that, already in the Renaissance, the Classical unities of Time, Place and Action were, on the whole, observed in practice and became part of the orthodox structure of tragedy, before the neo-Aristotelian theorists of drama imposed their authority in France after 1620.

But, before Corneille gave French tragedy its first masterpiece with *Horace*, this orthodox structure was to undergo a profound evolution. By the last decades of the sixteenth century, a new form of sensibility is unmistakably beginning to affect all the arts in Europe, ushering in a phase known as the Baroque. In literature, one of its distinctive features is the choice of themes evoking violent contrasts of emotion, appealing directly to the senses as opposed to the rational faculties. Where the Classical artist subordinates his material to a formal architecture giving an impression of an ordered, finite world of absolute values, the Baroque artist creates a dynamic impression of disorder and instability. The result, in drama, was the invasion of the stage by characters who energetically affirmed their individuality and gave free rein to instinct, while the incidents of the plot were multiplied in a frenzy of violent action that constantly provided fresh excitement and suspense; and where Jodelle and his fellow Humanists concentrated on arousing pity for the innocent victim of Fate, the new trend turned its chief attention to exciting horror and awe for the agents of the tragic catastrophe. Laudun d'Aigaliers gave voice to this approach when he wrote in his *Art Poétique* of 1597: "Plus les tragédies sont cruelles, plus elles sont excellentes."[10] Torture, sexual assault and murder become stock themes.

The inevitable result was the gradual breakdown of the neo-Classical conventions: thus the traditional messenger, whose function was to relate such events as battles and deaths that the plot demanded but which the elegiac and oratorical formula kept off the stage, disappeared in favour of the direct spectacle of physical violence. When d'Aigaliers himself wrote a tragedy based on Livy's story of the Horace-Curiace brothers, the audience was intended to witness the battle.[11] The unities of Time (generally twenty-four hours), Place (a single geographical locality, rather than a single scene) and Action (one main intrigue, with secondary intrigues strictly subordinated) continued to be technically observed in most cases, but with such laxity that their spirit was killed. It was merely a question of time before tragedy in its accepted sense gave way to a new *genre* that unequivocally rejected the Classical conventions and provided a proper mould for the uninhibited expression of the changing tastes.

The *genre* in question was the *tragi-comédie*, first elaborated by the Italian dramatists of the sixteenth century and virtually introduced to France by Garnier in his *Bradamante* (1582).[12] Taking its themes from modern *romanesque* literature, notably that of Italy and

Spain, it specialised in highly coloured, complex plots that multiplied the *coups de théâtre*; its aristocratic characters were involved in both tragic and comic situations that could extend over a period of years and several widely separated localities.

It was not until after 1627 that the *tragi-comédie* (and its near counterpart, the *pastorale*, which is virtually a *tragi-comédie* with pastoral characters) formally displaced tragedy; but its spirit had triumphed long before its name was officially given to the bulk of dramas being written. It is this time-lag which explains a curious phenomenon: no sooner was tragi-comedy at the height of its vogue in France, between 1627 and 1634, than the neo-Classical rules came into their own again as the result of an increasing interest in dramatic theory, with Aristotle and Horace as the main sources of authority. The moment marking the real beginning of the ascendancy of the theorists over the practising dramatists was the republication of Schélandre's *Tyr et Sidon* in 1628. Although labelled a *tragédie* when first published twenty years earlier, it had nevertheless reflected the spirit of the times with its *romanesque* subject, its mixture of the *genres* and its complex plot, all forced into the framework of the unities. In 1628, following the fashion, it was re-entitled a *tragi-comédie* and the action was spread over two days, instead of the twenty-four hours in the original version. Accompanying the play was a Preface, written by the abbé Ogier, in which he defended the "irregular" drama in the name of realism as demanded by modern taste. With Chapelain's subsequent defence of the rules, invoking the superior experience of what he calls *la judicieuse antiquité*,[13] the drama became the object of a controversy between the so-called Ancients and Moderns, or Regulars and Irregulars, that was to continue throughout the century.

The result was that, as Chapelain's attitude rapidly gained ground, first the *pastorale* and then the *tragi-comédie*, while retaining their *romanesque* themes and predilection for multiple action, began to accept the discipline of the unities; and it was Corneille himself who, with his *tragi-comédie*, *Clitandre* (acted 1631–2), provided the first "regular" example of the *genre* in France. For the circle of evolution to be almost complete, it only remained for tragedy to recapture its ascendancy, with its rejection of all non-tragic material, its choice of themes from antique sources and its exclusion of multiple plots and physical violence. And it was precisely this which was achieved following the performance in 1634 of two such tragedies: Rotrou's *Hercule Mourant* and Mairet's *Sophonisbe*, both drawn from Classical sources, both respecting the unities. But one essential advance had been made which distinguished the new tragedy from its Renaissance predecessors: authors had learned from experience the importance of dramatic conflict and suspense. Instead of deriving this from the direct spectacle of physical action—the method adopted by the *tragi-comédie* at the expense of the rules—their solution was to transfer the conflict into the minds of the characters: the passive, elegiac figures of Jodelle are replaced by heroes who struggle against Fate, whether represented by their own passions or by some external tyranny.[14]

La Querelle du Cid

It was at this stage—following a season (1635–6) in which the number of new tragedies equalled the tragi-comedies (half the latter being "regular" in form)—that Corneille's *Le Cid* made its celebrated appearance. A perfect example of the tragi-comedy in its *romanesque* theme, with two duels and a battle between the Spaniards and the Moors to provide a constant source of excitement, the play also had the essential virtues of Classical tragedy, for while its plot was undoubtedly colourful, almost all physical action was kept off the stage and the real drama based on the psychological conflicts of the two protagonists, Rodrigue and Chimène. The question is therefore: why did the play encounter such opposition from the partisans of neo-Classical theory?

The answer lies principally in the distinction (drawn from Aristotle) between *le vrai* and *le vraisemblable*. Real life, as attested by history, is full of episodes which shock both our moral scruples and our sense of psychological probability; and since the artist's first concern should be to win our complete intellectual and emotional involvement in his subject, he must avoid the extraordinary, whatever its historical credentials, in favour of the universal. Corneille's fault, in the eyes of his adversaries, is precisely his breach of this canon of *vraisemblance*; and Scudéry sums up their view concisely when he writes:

> Il est vrai que Chimène épousa le Cid; mais il n'est pas vraisemblable qu'une fille d'honneur épouse le meurtrier de son père. Cet événement était bon pour l'historien, mais il ne valait rien pour le poète; et je ne crois pas qu'il suffise de donner des répugnances à Chimène, de faire combattre le devoir contre l'amour, de lui mettre en la bouche mille antithèses sur ce sujet, ni de faire intervenir l'autorité d'un roi; car enfin tout cela n'empêche pas qu'elle ne se rende parricide en se résolvant d'épouser le meurtrier de son père; et bien que cela ne s'achève pas sur l'heure, la volonté, qui seule fait le mariage, y paraît tellement portée, qu'enfin *Chimène est une parricide*.[15]

The criticism levelled at all the characters of the play obeys the same principles: the King acts without the dignity befitting his royal estate when he tricks Chimène into confessing her love in Act IV, scene 4[16] and offends our sense of moral propriety by sanctioning the marriage; Chimène's father is excessively ambitious and insolent; and Rodrigue himself acts with "effronterie" when he forces his way into Chimène's private apartments after the duel in which he has killed the Count. On all these points, Scudéry's objections were sustained by the Académie's verdict: the heroine is "une amante trop sensible et fille trop dénaturée," while the hero is unchivalrous: "Dans son transport, il fait des choses qu'il n'était pas obligé de faire, et sans nécessité cesse d'être amant pour paraître seulement homme d'honneur."[17] In other words, Corneille's major error was his "realism"—his sacrifice of *le vraisemblable* to *le vrai*, whereby his characters forfeit our moral respect and strain our credulity.

At first sight, the objections of his critics would seem to be purely of an ethical, rather than aesthetic nature: both Chapelain and Scudéry thus demand that drama pursue a didactic end either by presenting morally superior characters, or by ensuring that vice be punished. Hence the key statement in the *Sentiments de l'Académie*:

> Nous maintenons que toutes les vérités ne sont pas bonnes pour le théâtre, et qu'il en est quelques-unes comme de ces crimes énormes dont les juges font brûler les procès avec les criminels.... Il y a des vérités monstrueuses, ou qu'il faut supprimer pour le bien de la société, ou que, si l'on ne les peut tenir cachées, il faut se contenter de remarquer comme des choses étranges.[18]

In fact, however, there is clearly an aesthetic basis to this apology for didactic tragedy. It rests upon the view that the essential emotion of tragedy is pity and that the key to true pathos lies in depicting innocence victimised by Fate.

What is often implicit in the criticisms of Chapelain and Scudéry is made explicit in La Mesnardière's *Poétique*, published in 1639. What he really wants is a return to the original Humanist conception of tragedy as practised by the Renaissance writers, and the rejection of the Baroque drama, with its concentration on the horror aroused by exceptional criminal figures:

"Le Poète doit tendre principalement à émouvoir la Pitié."[19] Hence the ideal:

> [Il est important que le Héros], qui souffre les infortunes, paraisse bon et vertueux presqu'en toutes ses actions. Je dis simplement presqu'en toutes, car il suffit qu'il commette une faute médiocre qui lui attire un grand malheur, sans qu'il se noircisse encore par un crime détestable, dont même l'exemple est mauvais.[20]

Le Mesnardière is obviously uneasy since the Classical theatre of antiquity has frequently introduced characters such as Œdipus, Orestes, Thyestes or Medea, who have committed great crimes—but he counsels the modern writer to avoid them:

> Mais puisque nous éprouvons que la Commisération est infiniment plus douce, plus humaine et plus agréable que la terreur et l'effroi, je conseille à notre Poète d'introduire rarement de ces criminels détestables....[21]

D'Aubignac, author of a *Pratique du Théâtre*, published in 1657, though already begun in 1640, affirms the same attitude and demands the same exemplary characters in tragedy. In 1663, he came out with an open attack on Corneille for his stubborn attachment to "reality" with all its ethically offensive aspects:

> Je sais bien que la compassion est le plus parfait sentiment qui règne au théâtre.... En France il n'y faut jamais joindre l'horreur des incidents, ni le crime des princes malheureux. *Il y faut tant d'innocence*, quand on veut que nous y compâtissions, que je conseillerais toujours à nos poètes d'éviter ces sujets[22] comme trop difficiles et presque toujours dangereux.[23]

Hence the scornful reference to Corneille:

> Voilà d'ordinaire quels ont été les Héros de M. Corneille: Horace tue sa propre sœur, Cinna veut assassiner Auguste son bienfaiteur et Pompée trahit son amour et viole tous les droits de la nature, des hommes et des dieux.[24]

So great is d'Aubignac's concern for the corruptive influence of certain themes that he speaks of the desirability of creating a Government *Intendant* (similar to our Lord Chamberlain) to supervise and censor the French Theatre, and he concludes with the following words addressed to Corneille:

> Il ne vous aurait pas permis de faire marier Chimène avec le meurtrier de son père, ni de faire tuer Camille par un Héros de nouvelle trempe, son propre frère....[25]

It is this attitude which explains the advice that d'Aubignac had given Corneille when the latter had read *Horace* to the private gathering at Boisrobert's house before the play was ever performed. By deliberately killing his sister, Horace loses that innocence which is essential to the tragic hero and, to avoid this, the circumstances of Camille's death ought to be changed:

> La mort de Camille par la main d'Horace, son frère, n'a pas été approuvée au théâtre, bien que ce soit une aventure véritable, et

j'avais été d'avis, pour sauver en quelque sorte l'histoire, et tout ensemble la bienséance de la scène, que cette fille désespérée, voyant son frère l'épée à la main, se fût précipitée dessus: ainsi elle fût morte de la main d'Horace, et *lui eût été digne de compassion comme un malheureux innocent*; l'histoire et le théâtre auraient été d'accord.[26]

By rejecting this solution, Corneille at once rejected the official doctrine of the Academy as formulated in 1637 and defiantly reasserted the principles that had moulded the greatness of *Le Cid*. In so doing, he not only preserved his own genius but saved French Classical tragedy from the stultifying influence that posed as neo-Classicism. Racine faced the same pressures as Corneille when his *Andromaque* was performed in 1667: Pyrrhus, like Horace, was accused of not conforming to the *romanesque* ideals of the contemporary novel with its exemplary heroes. But it is reasonable to doubt whether Racine would have created *Andromaque* had Corneille bowed before his critics in 1637-40. It is scarcely surprising therefore, in view of the gravity of the issue, that the author of *Le Cid* hesitated for three years before producing his new play.

Corneille's Reply to his Critics

During the *querelle du Cid*, Corneille made no reasoned reply to his opponents and it was only later, notably in the prefaces of subsequent plays, in the *Examens* and the three theoretical *Discours*, first published in the 1660 collective edition, that a detailed statement of his principles is elaborated. Here, one of his main concerns is precisely to repudiate the canon of *vraisemblance* by which Chapelain, Scudéry and d'Aubignac sought to limit the choice of suitable subjects for tragedy. Quoting Aristotle as his authority, he says that the most powerful sources of tragic emotion are to be found in the conflicts between people bound by blood relationship or by personal affection:

> Quand les choses arrivent entre des gens que la naissance ou l'affection attache aux intérêts l'un de l'autre, comme alors qu'un mari tue

ou est prêt de tuer sa femme, une mère ses enfants, un frère sa sœur, c'est ce qui convient merveilleusement à la tragédie.[27]

The very essence of these themes is their *invraisemblance*, for only in the most exceptional cases does a mother kill her children or a brother his sister. Therefore, the dramatist must obtain the "willing suspension of disbelief" in his audience by taking only subjects from history or historical legend, so as to guarantee their authenticity:

> Ces entreprises contre des proches ont toujours quelque chose de si criminel et de si contraire à la nature, qu'elles ne sont pas croyables, à moins que d'être appuyées sur l'une [l'histoire] ou l'autre [la fable]; et jamais elles n'ont cette vraisemblance sans laquelle ce qu'on invente ne peut être de mise....[28]

The same points are made with equal vigour in the *Discours du Poème Dramatique*:

> On est venu jusqu'à établir une maxime très fausse, *qu'il faut que le sujet d'une tragédie soit vraisemblable*; appliquant ainsi aux conditions du sujet la moitié de ce qu'il [Aristote] a dit de la manière de le traiter. Ce n'est pas qu'on ne puisse faire une tragédie d'un sujet purement vraisemblable...mais les grands sujets qui remuent fortement les passions, et en opposent l'impétuosité aux lois du devoir ou aux tendresses du sang, doivent toujours aller au-delà du vraisemblable, et ne trouveraient aucune croyance parmi les auditeurs, s'ils n'étaient soutenus, ou par l'autorité de l'histoire qui persuade avec empire, ou par la préoccupation de l'opinion commune qui donne ces mêmes auditeurs déjà tous persuadés. Il n'est pas vraisemblable que Médée tue ses enfants, que Clytemnestre assassine son mari, qu'Oreste poignarde sa mère; mais l'histoire le dit, et la représentation de ces grands crimes ne trouve point d'incrédules....

This conception of the tragic subject made it inevitable that Corneille should cross swords with those who interpreted Aristotle as saying that the *mœurs* of the characters of tragedy should be essentially virtuous; and it is in this context that he introduces, beside the traditional emphasis on pity as the principal tragic emotion, an aesthetic based on admiration or awe, reminiscent of the Baroque:

> Je ne puis comprendre comment on a voulu entendre par ce mot de « bonnes », qu'il faut qu'elles [les mœurs] soient vertueuses. La plupart des poèmes, tant anciens que modernes, demeureraient en un pitoyable état si l'on en retranchait tout ce qui s'y rencontre de personnages méchants, ou vicieux, ou tachés de quelque faiblesse qui s'accorde mal avec la vertu....
> S'il m'est permis de dire mes conjectures sur ce qu'Aristote nous demande par là, je crois que c'est le caractère brillant et élevé d'une habitude vertueuse ou criminelle, selon qu'elle est propre et convenable à la personne qu'on introduit. Cléopâtre, dans *Rodogune*, est très méchante; il n'y a point de parricide qui lui fasse horreur, pourvu qu'il la puisse conserver sur un trône qu'elle préfère à toutes choses, tant son attachement à la domination est violent; mais tous ses crimes sont accompagnés d'une grandeur d'âme qui a quelque chose de si haut, qu'en même temps qu'on déteste ses actions, on admire la source dont elles partent.[29]

It is this Baroque fascination for the morally ambivalent energy which raises man above his normal human limits that has earned for Corneille his reputation as the poet of Heroism. But not till 1674, when Boileau produced his translation of the treatise attributed to the rhetorician Longinus (A.D. 213–273), did this aspect of Corneille's work get its distinctive term—*le style sublime*. For Longinus, as for Corneille, one of the main sources of the *sublime*, which produces in us "une certaine admiration mêlée d'étonnement et de surprise," is the portrayal of "une certaine élévation d'esprit," reflecting both a *grandeur d'âme* and a *grandeur de courage*.[30]

It was probably Boileau's study of Longinus that helped to shape the views on Corneille which he expresses in a letter to Perrault in 1700:

> Pouvez-vous nier que ce ne soit dans Tite-Live...que M. de Corneille a pris ses plus beaux traits, a puisé ces grandes idées qui lui ont fait inventer un nouveau genre de tragédie inconnu à Aristote? Car c'est sur ce pied, à mon avis, qu'on doit regarder quantité de ses plus belles pièces de théâtre, où, se mettant au-dessus des règles de ce philosophe, il n'a point songé, comme les poètes de l'ancienne tragédie, à émouvoir

la pitié et la terreur, mais à exciter dans l'âme des spectateurs, par la sublimité des pensées et par la beauté des sentiments, une certaine admiration, dont plusieurs personnes, et les jeunes gens surtout, s'accommodent souvent beaucoup mieux que des véritables passions tragiques.

Boileau no doubt underestimates here the rôle of pity and fear in Corneille's tragic genius, but he was certainly right in sensing the novelty and essential modernity of his aesthetic.[31] It is, indeed, this very combination of antique and modern elements that gives Corneille's work its distinctive quality and contributes to make *Horace*—the first of his plays drawn from Livy—a great French Classical tragedy.

The Roman Source and Dramatic Framework of "Horace"

It is Corneille himself who informs us, in the 1648 edition of his work, that his source for *Horace* was Livy's *History of Rome* (*Ab Urbe condita libri*), where chapters 23–7 of Book I provide the essentials of the plot.[32]

Here, Livy tells of the initial quarrel between the two States of Alba and Rome, both of common Trojan stock, so that "war between them would be like father against son." In the reign of Tullus Hostilius—a King full of "lust for action" whose "one object was to find cause for renewed military adventure"—a dispute over cattle thefts rapidly degenerated into a declaration of war, and the armies of both sides were drawn up for battle. At that juncture, the leader of the Alban forces suggested that it was in their mutual interest to avoid a general slaughter since their common enemy, the Etruscans, would profit from their troubles.

It was therefore agreed that, as there were in each army three brothers (triplets), equally matched, these should be chosen as the champions to represent their country: the Horatii for Rome and the Curatii for Alba; the victorious side would then be recognised as the master of the other. The six champions, encouraged by their friends, joined combat: "careless of death and danger, each thought only of his country's fate, of the grim choice between lordship and ignominy." And soon, two of the Romans fell dead to the cheers of the Alban army, "while from their adversaries all hope was gone." But, although this left three Albans against one Roman, they were all wounded, while their opponent was unhurt. With this in mind, Horatius fled before them, and when they were separated by their unequal speed of pursuit, he turned round and killed them one by one.

It was as he returned to the city at the head of the Roman army that Horatius met his sister (not named by Livy), who had been betrothed to one of the Curatii. She immediately recognised on her brother's shoulders a cloak which she herself had made for her lover; and, overcome by this sight, "she loosed her hair and, in a voice choked with tears, called her dead lover's name. That his sister should dare to grieve at the very moment of his own triumph and in the midst of national rejoicing filled Horatius with such uncontrollable rage that he drew his sword and stabbed her to the heart."

Arrested and charged with treason by order of the Roman King, Horatius is convicted. When he appeals, "the decisive factor was the statement of Horatius's father, to the effect that his daughter deserved her death." And so the story ends with the pardoning of the hero: "The young man's courage, in the face of this peril as of all others, no less than his father's moving appeal, had its due effect. Though he was guilty in law, popular admiration of his quality obtained his acquittal."

It is immediately evident from this brief analysis that Livy's narrative supplied merely a framework of events and that Corneille's major achievement lies in the psychological and moral orchestration of his source; in other words, in the true Classical manner, the action has been transferred into the minds of the characters. Yet before studying these characters, it is significant to note the extreme theatrical skill with which Corneille has handled the plot.

In its first phase, that is up until the victory of Horace, the play is based on a perfect Renaissance-type tragic situation: Fate, in the guise of the State and the gods, has chosen as its victims two families bound by strong ties of affection and forced them, in spite of themselves, to destroy each other in the name of duty. But where the sixteenth-century formula was to give us elegiac lamentation upon a virtual *fait accompli*, Corneille reflects the modern tradition of the tragi-comedy by his careful attention to maintaining suspense—concentrating on what one of his modernist contemporaries called "des accidents qui sont hors d'attente." Hence the series of *coups de théâtre* which keep the audience curious as to what will happen next. First, the calling off of the general battle, related by Curiace (Act I, scene 3); then the choice of the Horace brothers as the champions of Rome (Act II, scene 1); then the designation of the Curiace brothers to oppose them (Act II, scene 2); then the news that both armies have rebelled against the inhumanity of the combat and the decision of the King to postpone it till he has consulted the gods (Act III, scene 2); then the announcement that the fight has begun, following the gods' approval (Act III, scene 5); then the apparent defeat of Rome, when we hear how Horace, his brothers dead, has fled before the three Albans (Act III, scene 6); and finally, in Act IV, the emergence of the real truth: the Curiace brothers have been slain and Rome has triumphed.[33]

Yet, for all the excitement derived from this technique of suspense, the real impact of the play lies in its exploration of the moral conflict in the protagonists and here Corneille owed virtually nothing to Livy. While the latter certainly provides a striking picture of the fierce patriotism of Ancient Rome which Corneille develops mainly in the figures of Horace and his father, the only suggestion of a clash of duty with personal emotions lies in the bare fact that the hero kills his sister for grieving over a private loss at a moment of national triumph. By emphasising the ties of affection between the combatants, with the invention of Horace's marriage to an Alban—Curiace's own sister, Sabine—and by making the moral conflict a central issue with the novel conception of Sabine, Curiace and Camille as victims and critics of the Roman ethos, Corneille has given the subject a new tragic dimension, in which pity plays a major rôle.[34]

It is, moreover, this same concentration of the drama in the minds of his characters that enables Corneille to handle with such ease the Unities of Time and Place: the whole sequence of events takes place within one day and involves no change of set. Yet Corneille was no slave to these rules which some of his contemporaries exalted with almost superstitious reverence, for he understood the true nature of dramatic illusion. If the dramatist knows his job, he can capture the imagination of his audience in such a way that they will not count the hours or question the exact location of the action. Writing of the Unity of Time, Corneille thus says:

> Surtout je voudrais laisser cette durée à l'imagination des auditeurs, et ne déterminer jamais le temps qu'elle emporte, si le sujet n'en avait besoin, principalement quand la vraisemblance y est un peu forcée comme au *Cid*, parce qu'alors cela ne sert qu'à les avertir de cette précipitation.[35]

It is this same principle which undoubtedly explains his handling of the Unity of Place in *Horace*, where there is a single set: a room in Horace's house. He knows that it is not strictly probable that all the characters would always congregate in the same place;[36] but by giving his set an abstract character,[37] the spectator's imagination is not distracted by questions of exact locality:

> Pour le lieu, bien que l'unité y soit exacte, elle n'est pas sans quelque contrainte. Il est constant qu'Horace et Curiace n'ont point de raison de se séparer du reste de la famille pour commencer le second acte, et c'est une adresse de théâtre de n'en donner aucune, quand on n'en peut donner de bonnes. L'attachement de l'auditeur à l'action présente souvent ne lui permet pas de descendre à l'examen sévère de cette justesse, et ce n'est pas un crime que de s'en prévaloir pour l'éblouir, quand il est malaisé de le satisfaire.[38]

A remark of d'Aubignac seems to confirm in fact that, in writing the play, Corneille had no explicit intention of observing the exact unity of place:

> Quand l'*Horace* de Corneille fut vu dans Paris, je crus que la scène était dans la salle du palais du père, comme tout s'y peut assez bien

accommoder: mais l'auteur m'assura qu'il n'y avait pas pensé, et que si l'unité de lieu s'y trouvait observée, c'était par hasard.[39]

The Moral Conflict of the Protagonists

Sabine

While in a sense all the characters of Corneille's play are of his own invention, it is Sabine who is most literally his creation, for, as has been seen, she has no counterpart in the Roman source. Corneille himself considered her part to be "assez heureusement inventé," and his contemporaries were here in agreement with him: Balzac, writing to him in 1643, described her as the "principal ornement" of the play; and again, in d'Aubignac's *Pratique du Théâtre* (1657), she is frequently cited with approval as a noble tragic figure. On the other hand, it is probably Sabine who has fared worst at the hands of later critics, who have tended for the most part to find her too passive, H. C. Lancaster going so far as to refer to "the useless and somewhat ridiculous rôle of Sabine" and to the "absurdity of her three requests that she be put to death, although she never had any reason to suppose that her offer would be accepted."[40]

Corneille is ready to admit in 1660 that Sabine "ne sert pas davantage à l'action que l'Infante à celle du *Cid* et ne fait que se laisser toucher diversement, comme elle, à la diversité des événements." But, if her part never affects the course of the action, it contributes immeasurably to the moral texture of the play. As an Alban by birth and a Roman by marriage, Sabine is forced to face the same problem of allegiance that confronts the other three protagonists of the drama: it is her steady refusal to accept a solution in a situation that admits of none in accordance with her conscience that gives her rôle its tragic grandeur and its dramatic value.

In this severe Roman world, where personal feelings are constantly repressed in the name of duty to the State, Sabine puts forward the most sustained plea for the rights of the private conscience. As the play opens, when the battle between the two opposing armies is imminent after two years of skirmishing, she finds her earlier attempts to settle her allegiance on the side of her husband a betrayal of her full humanity:

> L'hymen me fait de Rome embrasser l'intérêt,
> Mais il tiendrait mon âme en esclave enchaînée
> S'il m'ôtait le penser des lieux où je suis née.
>
> (26-8)

She cannot accept as morally legitimate an *engagement* of her will which, since it offends every natural human instinct, she brands as an *impiété*.

The full sense of this attitude that has reduced her in Act I to a temporary passivity ("[Je] serai du parti qu'affligera le sort"), is brought out in her second appearance, in Act II, scene 6, after her husband and brother have been picked as champions of their countries, when she makes the first of her three bids to sacrifice herself. To write this off as absurd—as did Lancaster—is to miss the whole significance of the episode, for her speech (ll. 613-62) is at the same time ironic and tragic. Her irony is unmistakable as she lulls the men's suspicions of her intentions (*cf.* Curiace's lines, 609-12), by praising the unshakable "fermeté de ces grands cœurs" of which they boast; unmistakable, as she prepares to drop her bombshell by the apparent innocence of her request:

> Pourrais-je toutefois vous faire une prière
> Digne d'un tel époux et digne d'un tel frère?

For her real target is nothing less than to unmask this very concept of "dignity" and "honour", which is their sole justification for seeking each other's death, and to undermine the foundations of their courage. And so she makes her monstrous proposal that one of them kill her and provide a legitimate motive for their duel:

> Achetez par ma mort le droit de vous haïr:
> Albe le veut, et Rome: il faut leur obéir.
> Qu'un de vous deux me tue, et que l'autre me venge:
> Alors votre combat n'aura plus rien d'étrange
> Et du moins l'un des deux sera juste agresseur,
> Ou pour venger sa femme, ou pour venger sa sœur.
>
> (629-34)

Not for a moment does Sabine doubt the monstrosity of this suggestion and her purpose is achieved when the two warriors recoil in horror: it is with a cry of triumph that she seizes on the proof of her argument that their *fermeté* is an offence against every sacred human instinct:

> Quelle peur vous saisit? Sont-ce là ces grands cœurs,
> Ces héros qu'Albe et Rome ont pris pour défenseurs?
>
> (665–6)

By ironically equating their combat ("un coup si noble") with her own murder ("un digne sacrifice à vos chères patries"), she believes she has stripped the patriotic notion of *gloire* of its false splendours and demonstrated the barbarity of an ethic which glorifies killing in cold blood.

But, if this first intervention of Sabine is ironic, it is also deeply tragic. Its aim was to shake the resolution of the warriors and make impossible a "combat plein de crimes," at complete variance with her notion of divine law (l. 828); to prevent it, she was prepared to descend into the arena and throw herself between the combatants. Yet when we see the collapse of her hopes—when Horace regains his self-control and receives moral support from his father—we appreciate how profound was her vision of the tragedy that awaits her and how desperate was her attempt to avert it:

> Quoi? me réservez-vous à voir une victoire
> Où, pour haut appareil d'une pompeuse gloire,
> Je verrai les lauriers d'un frère ou d'un mari
> Fumer encor d'un sang que j'aurai tant chéri?
> Pourrai-je entre vous deux régler alors mon âme,
> Satisfaire au devoir et de sœur et de femme,
> Embrasser le vainqueur en pleurant le vaincu?
>
> (647–53)

Sabine makes a last effort, in Act III, scene 1, to *régler son âme*, but the Stoic dialectic once more proves its futility against the voice of conscience,[41] and when the ultimate blow arrives, with the gods' sanction for the combat, Sabine's tragic dilemma gets its final dimension: metaphysical despair. The second request for death, after the murder of Camille, is the poignant affirmation of her sense of total isolation in an absurd world, where she nevertheless clings to her own humanity as the one sacred duty:

> Cherche pour t'imiter des âmes plus parfaites.
> Je ne t'impute point les pertes que j'ai faites,
> J'en ai les sentiments que je dois en avoir,
> Et je m'en prends au sort plutôt qu'à ton devoir;
> Mais aussi je renonce à la vertu romaine
> Si pour la posséder je dois être inhumaine.
>
> (1363–8)

Her last speech, in Act V, to plead with the King to let her atone by her own death for Horace's guilt, reveals the tragic consummation of the fears which provoked her first intervention in lines 647–53:

> Sire, voyez l'excès de mes tristes ennuis
> Et l'effroyable état où mes jours sont réduits:
> Quelle horreur d'embrasser un homme dont l'épee
> De toute ma famille a la trame coupée!
>
> (1613–6)

It is these lines, recalling for us Chimène's final outburst in *Le Cid*,[42] which point most clearly to the essential tragic character of Sabine's rôle. She is, of course, above all a figure of pity, forced by circumstances (as was Chimène) to suffer, without—once the gods have sanctioned the combat—any means of escape but death. Hence the apparent passivity of the part and its resemblance to the elegiac figures of Renaissance tragedy. Yet, to deny Sabine heroic stature is to judge her by the Roman standards which she herself rejects; and it is well to recall that what evoked Balzac's admiration in 1643 was precisely her moral strength.[43] Indeed, it is her very refusal to conform to an ethic at odds with her conscience which gives her rôle its nobility; her own notion of *gloire*, to which she remains steadfastly faithful, is in this respect the same as that expressed by Camille:

> C'est gloire de passer pour des cœurs abattus
> Quand la brutalité fait les hautes vertus.
>
> (1241–2)

Camille

In the *Examen* of 1660, where Corneille analyses the structure of *Horace*, he admits that the weakness of the play lies in the death of Camille. But, true to his theory of tragedy, he denies that this weakness has anything to do with the moral offensiveness of the murder (all the more powerfully tragic for being *invraisemblable*), and ascribes it to the lack of sufficient psychological motivation for the fatal clash between Horace and his sister:

> Cette action, qui devient la principale de la pièce, est momentanée. ... Elle surprend tout d'un coup; et toute la préparation que j'y ai donnée par la peinture de la vertu farouche d'Horace et par la défense qu'il fait à sa sœur de regretter qui que ce soit, de lui ou de son amant, qui meure au combat, n'est point suffisante pour faire attendre un emportement si extraordinaire et servir de commencement à cette action.

Yet here, as so often in his subsequent judgements on his work, Corneille was unjust to himself and it is the very inevitability of this *coup d'épée* that has provoked the admiration of later critics.[44] It is therefore with special reference to this tragic climax that Camille's character will be studied, for her rôle is much more closely subordinated to the demands of the plot than that of Sabine.

Generally speaking, Camille's tragic plight, as a victim of Fate caught between impossible alternatives, is the same as Sabine's, as she herself quickly reminds us in her first appearance:

> Comme elle je perdrai dans l'une et l'autre armée:
> Je verrai mon amant, mon plus unique bien,
> Mourir pour son pays ou détruire le mien,
> Et cet objet d'amour devenir, pour ma peine,
> Ou digne de mes pleurs ou digne de ma haine.
>
> (140-4)

But in all other respects, in her nature and in the pressures brought to bear on her, her rôle in the drama is very different.

True to the Classical principle of dramatic concentration, Corneille begins his play at the moment of crisis, so that it covers the few hours in which the conflict between the two rival States comes to a head, leading to the combat and the fateful return of Horace as victor. But in his exposition, he evokes for us the preceding two years during which time Alba and Rome have been cut off from each other by their quarrel. It is here that we learn that Camille had just been officially betrothed to Curiace when she found herself forcefully cut off from all contact with him; and for two years she has lived in constant anxiety, a prey to "éternelles douleurs" (ll. 101–6; 169–86). In this mood of despair, she has consulted the oracles in search of peace of mind, but for all the apparent comfort of their verdict, she remains haunted by nightmares that predict disaster (ll. 216–22). Only by bearing this in mind do we appreciate the profoundly human truth of her reaction when Curiace unexpectedly visits her in Act I, scene 3. For two years she has steeled herself to face the worst and now, suddenly, Fate seems to have produced the promised miracle by reuniting her with Curiace. The thought that he must have deserted his own army and broken his own oaths of allegiance counts for nothing, for, in the flood of happiness that overwhelms her, moral scruples are forgotten.

Already, in the outburst with which she greets Curiace (ll. 243–58), we have all the essential features of Camille's character: in contrast to the more matronly Sabine, with her more balanced elegiac rhetoric, she has the passionate and often rash impetuosity of youth. This contrast is even more apparent in Act II, when both women once again are confronted by the prospect of disaster following the news of the nomination of the champions. Where Sabine proceeds with carefully planned tactics, using a subtle irony to undermine the men's resolve, Camille appeals with all the spontaneity and urgency of young despair for her lover's pity:

> Iras-tu, ma chère âme, et ce funeste honneur
> Te plaît-il aux dépens de tout notre bonheur?
>
> (533–4)

Camille can even accept Curiace's threat to revoke his obligations to her if only he will abandon the decision to fight her brothers, and it is this longing for an innocent, untroubled love that provides some of the most poignant lyrical poetry in the play:

> Ne fais point d'autre crime, et j'atteste les dieux
> Qu'au lieu de t'en haïr, je t'en aimerai mieux;
> Oui, je te chérirai, tout ingrat et perfide,
> Et cesse d'aspirer au nom de fratricide.
> Pourquoi suis-je Romaine, ou que n'es-tu Romain?
> Je te préparerais des lauriers de ma main.
>
> (597–602)

It is the mark of Corneille's genius that, together with the ardent and impetuous sensibility of youth in Camille's character, he has combined a fierce pride, typical of her Roman background: for only this intense pride, or *gloire*, accounts for the fanatical zeal with which she defends her love and defies those who seek to challenge it.

Already in her speech addressed to the *confidente*, Julie, she has revealed a strong resentment at the assumption that her suffering is less profound and less justified than Sabine's:

> Pourquoi fuir et vouloir que je vous entretienne?
> Croit-elle ma douleur moins vive que la sienne,
> Et que, plus insensible à de si grands malheurs,
> A mes tristes discours je mêle moins de pleurs?
>
> (135–8)

The suggestion that she should abandon Curiace for Valère is twice rejected as an affront to her *gloire*, when she asserts the moral and legal sanctity of her love. The first time is in the same scene with Julie:

> Donnez-moi des conseils qui soient plus légitimes,
> Et plaignez mes malheurs sans m'ordonner des crimes...
> Quoi! le manque de foi vous semble pardonnable?...
> D'un serment solennel qui peut nous dégager?
>
> (151–2; 156; 158)

The second occasion is in her exchange with Sabine in Act III, scene 4, where the rights of passion are supported by the same essentially legal justification:

> Vous ne connaissez point ni l'amour ni ses traits:
> On peut lui résister quand il commence à naître,
> Mais non pas le bannir quand il s'est rendu maître,
> Et que l'aveu d'un père, engageant notre foi,
> A fait de ce tyran un légitime roi.
>
> (918–22)

It is these passages which give us the full sense of Camille's reaction when, following the death of Curiace, her father and brother deny her the right to mourn; for in so doing, they have, in her view, broken the unwritten contract whereby, so long as she honoured her moral obligations to Rome (by rejecting marriage to a man who was either "le vainqueur ou l'esclave de Rome"), she retained the right to remain faithful to Curiace.

With the breach of this contract, her father and brother, as well as the Roman State which they represent, have become guilty of tyranny and thereby forfeited all claim to obedience. For Camille, therefore, her revolt is both justified and heroic.[45]

In the famous monologue of Camille in Act IV, scene 4, Corneille has skilfully brought together all these factors to motivate the frenzy of her outburst. The full psychological significance of the constant reversals of Fate is here made clear: besides providing the plot with real suspense, they have acted as an exacerbation of her resentment at being victimised beyond all reason:

> En vit-on jamais un [sort] dont les rudes traverses
> Prissent en moins de rien tant de faces diverses,
> Qui fût doux tant de fois, et tant de fois cruel,
> Et portât tant de coups avant le coup mortel?
> Vit-on jamais une âme en un jour plus atteinte
> De joie et de douleur, d'espérance et de crainte,
> Asservie en esclave à plus d'événements,
> Et le piteux jouet de plus de changements?
> Un oracle m'assure, un songe m'épouvante,
> La bataille m'effraye, et la paix me contente.
> Mon hymen se prépare, et presque en un moment
> Pour combattre mon frère on choisit mon amant;
> Les deux camps mutinés un tel choix désavouent,
> Ils rompent la partie et les dieux la renouent;

> Rome semble vaincue, et seul des trois Albains
> Curiace en mon sang n'a point trempé ses mains.
> Dieux! sentais-je point lors des douleurs trop légères
> Pour le malheur de Rome et la mort de deux frères,
> Me flattais-je point trop quand je croyais pouvoir
> L'aimer encor sans crime et nourrir quelque espoir?
> Sa mort m'en punit bien, et la façon cruelle
> Dont mon âme éperdue en reçoit la nouvelle:
> Son rival me l'apprend, et faisant à mes yeux
> D'un si triste succès le récit odieux,
> Il porte sur le front une allégresse ouverte,
> Que le bonheur public fait bien moins que ma perte;
> Et bâtissant en l'air sur le malheur d'autrui,
> Aussi bien que mon frère il triomphe de lui.
>
> (1203-30)

Camille's revolt, like that of Racine's Oreste, in *Andromaque*, has a metaphysical dimension[46]—inspired by the determination to take control of her own destiny. Hence the decision to defy her father is at the same time a defiance of the gods:

> Oui, je lui ferai voir, par d'infaillibles marques,
> Qu'un véritable amour brave la main des Parques,
> Et ne prend point de lois de ces cruels tyrans
> Qu'un astre injurieux nous donne pour parents.
> Tu blâmes ma douleur, tu l'oses nommer lâche;
> Je l'aime d'autant plus que plus elle te fâche,
> Impitoyable père, et par un juste effort
> Je la veux rendre égale aux rigueurs de mon sort.
>
> (1195-1202)

It is in this sense that Camille is truly a Cornelian character who achieves the *sublime* of heroic self-affirmation against all odds. Her courage evokes that same admiration to which Corneille gave emphasis in his theory and which he had already illustrated in his first tragedy, *Médée*.[47]

Ultimately, Camille's death is the triumph of her will, for it is the voluntarily accepted price of her vengeance. In cursing Rome and provoking her brother to kill her, she achieves her wish and sullies his reputation:

> Puissent de tels malheurs accompagner ta vie
> Que tu tombes au point de me porter envie,

> Et toi, bientôt souiller par quelque lâcheté
> Cette gloire si chère à ta brutalité!
>
> (1291–4)

And it is Sabine who subsequently recognises the full premeditation of Camille's behaviour towards Horace:

> Que Camille est heureuse! elle a pu te déplaire;
> Elle a reçu de toi ce qu'elle a prétendu,
> Et recouvre là-bas tout ce qu'elle a perdu.
>
> (1380–2)

The inevitability of the fatal *coup d'épée* is thus doubly guaranteed, since it is willed by both the assassin and his victim.

Curiace and Horace

Already, in *Le Cid*, Corneille had exploited the tragic theme of a hero faced with a conflict of loyalties and in *Horace* it is above all Curiace whose situation most closely resembles that of Rodrigue: both are more or less officially betrothed when called upon to kill a blood-relative of their loved one, and their inner struggle follows much the same pattern. For, whatever the issue, their personal happiness is doomed; Rodrigue's

> Que je meure au combat ou meure de tristesse

is thus echoed by Curiace's

> Hélas! je vois trop bien qu'il faut, quoi que je fasse,
> Mourir, ou de douleur, ou de la main d'Horace.
>
> (535–6)

Each ultimately realises that there can be no real choice for them and that honour dictates only one course:

RODRIGUE.   Je dois tout à mon père avant qu'à ma maîtresse.
CURIACE.   Avant que d'être à vous [Camille], je suis à mon pays.

In both cases, therefore, it is the irresistible impulse of their *gloire*—a combination of self-respect and the desire for public renown—which provides the necessary resolution to overcome the moral dilemma. Camille's suggestion that Curiace should let somebody else fight for Alba in his place thus releases within him the categorical imperative of patriotic duty:

> Que je souffre à mes yeux qu'on ceigne une autre tête
> Des lauriers immortels que la gloire m'apprête,
> Ou que tout mon pays reproche à ma vertu
> Qu'il aurait triomphé si j'avais combattu,
> Et que par mon amour ma valeur endormie
> Couronne tant d'exploits d'une telle infamie!
> Non, Albe, après l'honneur que j'ai reçu de toi,
> Tu ne succomberas ni vaincras que par moi;
> Tu m'as commis ton sort, je t'en rendrai bon compte,
> Et vivrai sans reproche, ou périrai sans honte.
>
> (551–60)

Yet even this instinctive decision of will is shaken by the pitiful spectacle of Camille's tears, and Curiace is forced to resort to provoking a complete rupture with his love:

> N'attaquez plus ma gloire avecque vos douleurs
> Et laissez-moi sauver ma vertu de vos pleurs;
> Je sens qu'elle chancelle et défend mal la place:
> Plus je suis votre amant, moins je suis Curiace.
> Faible d'avoir déjà combattu l'amitié,
> Vaincrait-elle à la fois l'amour et la pitié?
> Allez, ne m'aimez plus, ne versez plus de larmes,
> Ou j'oppose l'offense à de si fortes armes;
> Je me défendrai mieux contre votre courroux,
> Et pour le mériter je n'ai plus d'yeux pour vous.
> Vengez-vous d'un ingrat, punissez un volage.
> Vous ne vous montrez point sensible à cet outrage!
> Je n'ai plus d'yeux pour vous, vous en avez pour moi!
> En faut-il plus encor? je renonce à ma foi.
>
> (581–94)

The essence of Curiace's tragedy lies in this passage, for he has discovered the human impossibility of his earlier attempt to reconcile the two conflicting allegiances, expressed in the first meeting with Camille.[48] Such is the cruelty of Fate that he can now only solve his dilemma at the expense of his conscience, which recognises the rejection of Camille as a crime:

> Rigoureuse vertu dont je suis la victime,
> Ne peux-tu résister sans le secours d'un crime?

What makes this scene the more profoundly tragic is the underlying irony whereby Curiace is driven to that very sacrifice of humanity with which he had reproached Horace in their encounter after both had been chosen to oppose each other as their countries' champions (Act II, scene 3). For Curiace's final words to Camille ("J'oppose l'offense à de si fortes armes.... Je n'ai plus d'yeux pour vous") unmistakably reproduce the pattern of Horace's attitude to him:

> Albe vous a nommé, je ne vous connais plus.
> (502)

It is this which makes more understandable the recent attempt by a French critic to rehabilitate Horace, who has traditionally fared badly in the inevitable comparison with Curiace.[49] M. Herland's thesis is that Horace is not the insensitive fanatic for which he is commonly taken; that he suffers no less than Curiace at the prospect of having to shed the blood of a man whose friendship he cherishes as dearly as his own life ("un sang qu'on voudrait racheter de sa vie"). If he welcomes the combat as an unrivalled opportunity to display the supreme virtue of self-sacrifice for a patriotic ideal, it is not at the expense of this friendship, for he is equally glad for Curiace that he can share the promised glory ("Une telle vertu n'appartenait qu'à *nous*"). In M. Herland's view, it is Curiace who betrays their relationship by rejecting the impersonal idealism of Horace's attitude and introducing a note of discord; only after the Alban has attacked the barbarity implicit in such *fermeté* and challenged the Roman ethic does Horace respond with a similar tone of provocation, leading to the celebrated line:

> Albe vous a nommé, je ne vous connais plus.[50]

This new interpretation is to be welcomed; argued with skill and subtlety, it provides a salutary corrective to the one-sided denigration to which Corneille's hero has been constantly subjected and which only serves to diminish his tragic stature. For, if we insist exclusively, like Sarcey and others, on the "inintelligente brutalité" of Horace, he forfeits all claim to our sympathy—which is almost certainly not Corneille's intention. In the *Discours de la Tragédie* of 1660, the author specifically includes Horace with Curiace as deserving of pity: "Horace et Curiace ne seraient point à plaindre s'ils n'étaient point amis et beaux-frères." It is an opportune reminder that Horace is subject to the same terrible pressure of conflicting loyalties as his Alban adversary, even if his reaction to it is so different.

Unfortunately, M. Herland is led by this interpretation to overstate his case and to defend Horace at the expense of Curiace,[51] whereas the essential factor is that we are in the presence of two distinct temperaments, two distinct types: Curiace, the realist, like his sister, "songe par quel bras, et non pour quelle cause"; he cannot disguise from himself that behind the exalted generalities of rhetorical patriotism there is a grim human reality:

> Je vois que votre honneur gît à verser mon sang,
> Que tout le mien consiste à vous percer le flanc;
> Près d'épouser la sœur, qu'il faut tuer le frère...
>
> (469-71)

Horace, on the other hand, with all the passion of youth[52] and the same streak of mystic fervour that distinguishes Camille from Sabine, yields to the intoxication of the abstract ideal. Once again, Corneille's genius shows itself at its greatest as Horace succumbs to his own heady rhetoric in the face of an inhuman task. In spite of his affirmations that he is fully conscious of all the terrible truth of Fate, he owes something of his *fermeté* to the abandonment of lucidity:

> La solide vertu dont je fais vanité
> N'admet point de faiblesse avec sa fermeté,

> Et c'est mal de l'honneur entrer dans la carrière
> Que dès le premier pas regarder en arrière.
> Notre malheur est grand, il est au plus haut point;
> Je l'envisage entier, mais je n'en frémis point.
> Contre qui que ce soit que mon pays m'emploie,
> J'accepte aveuglément cette gloire avec joie;
> Celle de recevoir de tels commandements
> Doit étouffer en nous tous autres sentiments.
> Qui, près de le servir, considère autre chose
> A faire ce qu'il doit lâchement se dispose;
> Ce droit saint et sacré rompt tout autre lien.
> Rome a choisi mon bras, je n'examine rien:
> Avec une allégresse aussi pleine et sincère
> Que j'épousai la sœur, je combattrai le frère.[53]

As we have already seen, Corneille's major self-reproach in the *Examen* of 1660 was that the murder of Camille spoiled the play; and the first of his reasons for this view was that Horace's "emportement si extraordinaire" is not sufficiently motivated. The second reason was that the murder constitutes a breach of the Classical unity of Action:

> Le second défaut est que cette mort fait une action double, par le second péril où tombe Horace après être sorti du premier. L'unité de péril d'un héros dans la tragédie fait l'unité d'action; et quand il en est garanti, la pièce est finie, si ce n'est que la sortie même de ce péril l'engage si nécessairement dans un autre que la liaison et la continuité des deux n'en fasse qu'une action; ce qui n'arrive point ici, où Horace revient triomphant, sans aucun besoin de tuer sa sœur, ni même de parler à elle; et l'action serait suffisamment terminée à sa victoire.

In fact, Corneille's definition of the Unity of Action gives us the best argument for defending the structure of *Horace* and for rejecting both the reasons on which the dramatist based his criticism. In the *Poetics*, Aristotle remarks that the essence of tragedy lies in the depiction of the Irony of Fate, whereby a man is cast from good fortune into misfortune by a false step (*hamartia*, or "error"). Had Corneille ended his play with the triumphant return of his Roman hero, this essential irony would have been missed. At the same time, the two perils of Horace are indissolubly linked, and the unity of the tragic action lies precisely in the fact that the "sortie même de ce [premier] péril l'engage si nécessairement dans un autre que la liaison et la continuité des deux n'en [fait] qu'une action."

Already, in steeling himself for the combat, Horace has reached a state of exaltation that brings with it a sense of his own infallibility. The battle has brought this to fever pitch, as Valère's description of the hero's final triumph attests;[54] and it is in this mood that he encounters his sister, bent upon provoking him. As such, the murder constitutes a classical example of *hubris*—that excessive pride which inevitably brings with it the wrath of the gods. Horace's own father provides the appropriate commentary:

> Retirons nos regards de cet objet funeste
> Pour admirer ici le jugement céleste.
> Quand la gloire nous enfle, il sait bien comme il faut
> Confondre notre orgueil qui s'élève trop haut.
> Nos plaisirs les plus doux ne vont point sans tristesse;
> Il mêle à nos vertus des marques de faiblesse,
> Et rarement accorde à notre ambition
> L'entier et pur honneur d'une bonne action.
>
> (1403–10)

In the subsequent trial, the elder Horace defends his son on the grounds that the murder was an unpremeditated impulse, inspired by virtuous zeal:

> Un premier mouvement ne fut jamais un crime,
> Et la louange est due, au lieu du châtiment,
> Quand la vertu produit ce premier mouvement.
>
> (1648–50)

Even while rejecting the view that it automatically exonerates Horace—for the deed is branded as an offence to both gods and men (ll. 1733–40)—the King himself recognises this interpretation of it as a sudden impulse. And there is every reason to believe that this was Corneille's intention: in the *Examen*, he speaks of it as "l'emportement d'un homme passionné pour sa patrie, contre une sœur qui la maudit en sa présence avec des imprécations terribles." He is clearly anxious to maintain Horace's tragic stature as a hero worthy of our sympathy. A passage in the *Discours de la Tragédie* of 1660 adds weight to this evidence:

> Il serait à propos de mettre quelque distinction entre les crimes. Il en est dont les honnêtes gens sont capables par une violence de passion, dont le mauvais succès peut faire effet dans l'âme de l'auditeur. Un honnête homme ne va pas voler au coin d'un bois, ni faire un assassinat de sang-froid; mais s'il est bien amoureux, il peut faire une supercherie à son rival, il peut s'emporter de colère et tuer dans un premier mouvement, et l'ambition le peut engager dans un crime ou dans une action blâmable.[55]

Yet if here again Horace has largely failed to win the sympathy of most critics, the reason lies in his own steady refusal to admit his guilt. Unlike so many of the great tragic figures of Racine, who seem to disintegrate morally as they regain their lucidity after committing the *crime passionnel* and in whom the return of reason brings recognition of the horror of their deed, Corneille's hero stands firm. Just as, at the moment of killing Camille, he claimed to be acting in the name of reason (l. 1319) and to be performing *un acte de justice* (l. 1323), so later he maintains his innocence. The whole tone of his reply to his father in Act V, scene 1, where he offers to submit to punishment, makes it clear that he does not understand or admit the arguments that condemn him:

> Disposez de mon sort, les lois vous en font maître;
> J'ai cru devoir ce coup aux lieux qui m'ont vu naître.
> Si mon zèle au pays vous semble criminel,
> S'il m'en faut recevoir un reproche éternel,
> Si ma main en devient honteuse et profanée,
> Vous pouvez d'un seul mot trancher ma destinée.
>
> (1419–24)

And his reply to the King, for all its profession of humility to sovereign authority, ill conceals a note of defiance: "A quoi bon me défendre?" If he accepts to die, it is not as an expiation, but as the necessary price for preserving his *gloire*:

> Permettez, ô grand roi, que de ce bras vainqueur
> Je m'immole à ma gloire, et non pas à ma sœur.
>
> (1593–4)

Obviously, our reactions in the theatre will depend on how the part is played. Horace can easily be made to appear the *brute féroce* of Sarcey—both before and after the murder: but such an interpretation probably betrays Corneille's purpose. Horace can defend his reputation in Act V with a dignity that commands admiration—while at the same time arousing a pathos proper to tragedy. For the dominant impression he gives as he faces both his family and his accusers is of a man profoundly bewildered by the sudden change in his fate, driven back into a solitude of universal incomprehension from which death is the only release:

> D'autres aiment la vie, et je la dois haïr.
> (1546)

His reflections upon the inability of the common people to understand the true quality of heroism echoes a disabused realisation that the *renommée* to which he had aspired (l. 452) is illusory. Even the death that he now seeks, in order to save his honour, is too late to serve its full purpose:

> ... pour laisser une illustre mémoire
> La mort seule aujourd'hui peut conserver ma gloire:
> Encor la fallait-il sitôt que j'eus vaincu,
> Puisque pour mon honneur j'ai déjà trop vécu.
> Un homme tel que moi voit sa gloire ternie
> Quand il tombe en péril de quelque ignominie.
> (1579-84)

The play ends with the King's pardon being granted to Horace; but there is little comfort for him in this verdict, dictated by reasons of expediency: namely, that the State needs him for its defence. For, as Corneille reminds us in the *Examen*, the murder of Camille has cast Horace into "un péril infâme, *dont il ne peut sortir sans tache.*"

That is why the dénouement does not in any way compromise the tragic quality of the play. Indeed, in a sense it gives it its final irony: once more, it is to Roman imperialism, in which lay the origins of his crime, that Horace is sacrificed.[56]

It is largely by virtue of this irony that Horace maintains his place as the central figure of the drama, for in his character and fate are focused all the elements of the tragedy. Without it, one is led to seek elsewhere the pivot of the action—hence the opinion that the real hero is the elder Horace.[57] Undoubtedly, it is a rôle which, though introduced late in the action, grows in stature and moves us deeply in the final act as he fights to save his son and the honour of the family name. But his suffering remains only one facet of a tragedy, at the centre of which stands his son. More intelligible is the suggestion that we should recall the title by which the play was commonly known in the seventeenth century—*Les Horaces*— for this evokes more fully the perspective of a tragic action in which the triumph of the Roman State entails the disintegration of a whole family.[58]

The Sources of Cornelian Heroism

In the foregoing analysis of the main protagonists of *Horace*, we have seen the dual nature of Corneille's aesthetic of tragedy, combining both the pity and fear of Aristotelian theory as well as the admiration which Boileau picked out as its distinctive originality. It is above all this latter element which has become traditionally associated with his work, and the adjective "Cornelian" evokes for us, as for Saint-Évremond, "l'expression d'une grandeur d'âme héroïque."[59]

Horace is the first of a long series of tragedies in which Corneille turns to Roman history for his subject. This choice was no doubt partly prompted by contemporary fashion, since Mairet's *Sophonisbe*, acted with such success in December 1634, had re-established ancient Rome as a favourite source of plots among his fellow dramatists.[60] At the same time, Corneille's consistent preoccupation with Rome is to be explained by the unrivalled richness of material which it offered to a writer fascinated by the spectacle of *la fermeté des grands cœurs*.

Perhaps the best testimony to the prestige enjoyed by the ancient world in Corneille's day is to be found in the work of his contemporary, Guez de Balzac; in particular, the dissertation entitled

Le Romain, addressed to Madame de Rambouillet, gives us the measure of Corneille's inspiration for the character of Horace himself. For Balzac, "Rome était la boutique où les dons du Ciel étaient mis en œuvre et où s'achevaient les biens naturels"; and he continues by drawing the following portrait of the type who gave this ancient civilisation its greatness:

> Croyant que faillir est le seul mal qui puisse arriver à l'homme de bien, il croit qu'il n'y a point de petites fautes; et, se faisant une religion de la moindre partie de son devoir, il pense qu'on ne peut pas même être négligent sans impiété. Il estime plus un jour employé à la vertu qu'une longue vie délicieuse; un moment de gloire qu'un siècle de volupté....
> Agissant sur ce principe, il est toujours préparé aux entreprises hasardeuses; il est toujours prêt à se dévouer pour le salut de ses citoyens, à prendre sur soi la mauvaise fortune de la république. Et soit que l'oracle le lui donne, soit que l'inspiration vienne de son propre esprit, il remercie les dieux, comme de la plus grande grâce qu'il ait jamais reçue d'eux, de ce qu'ils veulent qu'il soit le général qui sera tué, de l'armée qui gagnera la bataille. Ensuite de cela...il n'est rien qui ne lui soit aisé, et rien qui ne nous doive être croyable. *Il ne connaît ni nature, ni alliance, ni affection, quand il y va de l'intérêt de la patrie; il n'a point d'autre intérêt particulier que celui-là, et n'aime ni ne hait que pour des considérations publiques....* Tout ce qu'il y a dans le monde d'effroyable et de terrible n'est pas capable de lui faire cligner un œil; tout ce qu'il y a d'éclatant et de précieux ne lui peut pas donner une tentation; on ne saurait le vaincre; on ne saurait le gagner.[61]

Almost point for point, this passage reflects the character of Horace with his religious conception of duty to the State, his scorn for death when it is the price of glory (ll. 398–402); his rejection of *nature, alliance, affection*, where they conflict with duty (ll. 443–9) and his unshakable faith in his ability to triumph against all odds when armed with pride in the justice of his cause (l. 385).

Yet if, in *Horace*, Corneille gives us a magnificent historical evocation of antiquity, as it appeared to his contemporaries, his drama equally draws its inspiration from the social, philosophical and political currents that shaped early seventeenth-century France. Essentially an aristocratic civilisation, it believes in the innate moral superiority conferred by noble blood, and the significance of the term *générosité*, used by the Cornelian heroes to describe their ethical ideal, is that it implies at once social and moral nobility. It is typical of the essentially military character of the average male aristocrat's life and education in the period that courage is foremost among the virtues; and when Montaigne asks what are the qualities that distinguish the nobleman from the common people ("Par où s'acquerra l'avantage que nous voulons avoir sur le vulgaire?"), his answer is: "la vaillance, la force, la magnanimité et la résolution."[62] Similarly, when a Cornelian hero uses the word *vertu*, its immediate sense is generally physical and moral courage, as in the following speech of the elder Horace:

> Je sais trop comme agit la vertu véritable:
> C'est sans en triompher que le nombre l'accable;
> Et sa mâle vigueur, toujours en même point,
> Succombe sous la force, et ne lui cède point.
>
> (1067–70)

It is this courage, employed in the service of a duty that transcends a man's private interests, that constitutes *générosité*[63]; hence the explanation given by the elder Horace of his firm resolution in facing the ordeal of the combat in which his sons risk their lives:

> Il [mon esprit] s'arme en ce besoin de générosité,
> Et du bonheur public fait sa félicité.
>
> (981–2)

As has been admirably demonstrated by two modern critics,[64] it was essentially the natural pride of caste in the semi-feudal aristocracy of Corneille's day that promoted this ethic; for, in harnessing its natural worship of physical valour to ideal causes, such as duty to the State (a process which M. Bénichou calls "sublimation" of the natural instincts[65]), the nobility achieved further proof of its claim to moral superiority. In other words, *générosité*, like Chivalry in the Middle Ages, was its *titre de noblesse*.

But, at the same time, there is a profound influence exerted by the philosophical doctrines of the period, strongly marked by the revival of Greco-Roman thought in the Renaissance. Of these, Stoicism was probably the most significant, and its extraordinary vogue in the early seventeenth century—when it provided the basic elements of Descartes's ethic of *générosité*, as formulated in the *Traité des Passions* (1649)—is no doubt partly due to the intellectual justification which it provided for the innate moral idealism of an aristocratic civilisation.

Essentially a rationalist doctrine, Stoicism holds that the natural faculties of reason and free will are sufficiently strong in every man to enable him to conquer all adversity and overcome the inner dissensions and doubts that spring from the passions. Hence the equation of virtue with the energetic pursuit of duty as dictated by reason:

> Le bien donc de l'homme consistera en l'usage de la droite raison — qui est à dire en la vertu, laquelle n'est autre chose que la ferme disposition de notre volonté à suivre ce qui est honnête et convenable.[66]

It is in this sense that Horace enjoins his wife to emulate his own *vertu* (l. 1356), just as he consistently claims that he is pursuing the dictates of a rational conscience. When both he and Curiace opt to follow the call of duty to their country, it is their honour or *gloire* which provides the impetus of will. And it is primarily in the Stoic sense that they use the word, where "honour," as the intuition of reason, is distinguished from "public honours" or "renown," which are condemned as a false motive inspired by the passion of ambition:

> Le vrai honneur est l'éclat d'une belle et vertueuse action, qui rejaillit de notre conscience à la vue de ceux avec qui nous vivons et, par une réflexion en nous-mêmes, nous apporte un témoignage de ce que les autres croient de nous, qui se tourne en un grand contentement d'esprit....
> Composons nos affections de façon que la lueur des honneurs n'éblouisse point notre raison; et plantons de belles résolutions en notre esprit, qui lui servent de barrière contre les assauts de l'ambition. Premièrement, persuadons-nous qu'il n'y a vrai honneur au monde que celui de la vertu; que la vertu ne cherche point un plus ample ni plus riche théâtre pour se faire voir que sa propre conscience.[67]

And, in Horace's first reaction to the news that he has been chosen to represent Rome—with his initial modesty in declaring that others were more worthy of the choice than he, and his firm resolution to give of his best (ll. 371 *et seq.*)—we have the exemplary Stoic character described by Du Vair:

> Si le témoignage de notre vertu, si l'utilité de notre pays, si la faveur de nos amis nous présente quelque charge dont nous soyons capables, acceptons-la modestement et l'exerçons sincèrement, estimant que c'est Dieu qui nous a là posés en sentinelle, afin que les autres reposent sous notre soin.[68]

It is true that, while in Stoic philosophy the distinction between public renown and honour was a categorical one, both Curiace and Horace, like their seventeenth-century aristocratic counterparts, regard the former as a necessary, though not sufficient condition of the latter (*cf.* ll. 452; 551–2; 1583–4). Yet even the fact that the neo-Stoic writers made this distinction between the two aspects of *gloire* did not save them from sustained attacks by those who saw in their philosophy a dangerous apology for self-sufficient pride. It is not surprising that to the fore among these critics were the Augustinian Christians, notably the Jansenists, with their semi-denial of free-will and their belief in the radical corruption of all human instinct following the Fall. Pascal's *Pensées* thus select Stoicism as the major example of the moral pitfalls of rationalism, while Nicole, a leading Jansenist thinker (*circa* 1625–95), directs a bitter invective against those like Corneille who depicted the Roman ethic as a source of *grandeur*:

> Si l'on considère les comédies de ceux qui ont le plus affecté cette honnêteté apparente, on trouvera qu'ils n'ont évité de représenter des objets entièrement déshonnêtes, que pour en peindre d'autres aussi criminels, et qui ne sont guère moins contagieux. Toutes leurs pièces ne sont que de vives représentations de passions, d'orgueil, d'ambition, de jalousie, de vengeance et principalement de cette vertu Romaine, qui n'est autre chose qu'un furieux amour de soi-même. Plus ils colorent ces vices d'une image de grandeur et de générosité, plus ils les rendent dangereux et capables d'entrer dans les âmes les mieux nées.[69]

But it was not only Augustinian apologists who looked with misgivings upon the Stoic ethic and denied its claims to produce superior figures by the subjection of the passions to the rational will. La Rochefoucauld is perhaps the most outstanding of the secular moralists who denounced the impostures of its idealism, methodically exposing in his *Maximes* (first published in 1664–5) the hidden egoism behind such traditional virtues as courage and generosity, and concluding that "à une grande vanité près, les héros sont faits comme les autres hommes."[70]

And at the same time as La Rochefoucauld was composing the *Maximes*, Chapelain wrote his *Dialogue de la Gloire* (1662), presenting in a debate between two speakers the moral issues involved in an ethic based upon *gloire*. One speaker defends the pursuit of honours and reputation as a necessary incentive for men to be virtuous, insisting that we should harness the innate egoism of human nature for the good of society:

> Pour faire de ces bonnes actions, quel motif plus puissant que celui de la Gloire? Il n'est pas jusqu'aux enfants que la crainte du blâme et le plaisir de la louange ne porte à bien faire.[71]

His adversary, however, insists that this is a dangerous philosophy, for it encourages the tyrannical instincts present in man: it is this self-love

> qui le fait soulever contre son espèce de telle sorte qu'il n'y a point d'individu qui ne se fasse un règne en lui-même, qui ne se dresse un tribunal sur tous, qui ne prétende au moins une absolue indépendance de tous, s'il ne se peut établir d'absolu commandement sur tous.

The peculiar interest of this passage is that it has a direct parallel in Act V of *Horace*, where the hero is tried before the King. His main accuser, Valère, uses the same argument, namely that Horace has shown by the murder of Camille that he considers himself above the laws of the State and the sole dispenser of justice:

> Arrêtez sa fureur, et sauvez de ses mains,
> Si vous voulez régner, le reste des Romains...

> Faisant triompher Rome, il se l'est asservie:
> Il a sur nous un droit et de mort et de vie;
> Et nos jours criminels ne pourront plus durer
> Qu'autant qu'à sa clémence il plaira l'endurer.
>
> (1489–90; 1507–10)

In the play, the last word on Horace is spoken by the King when he delivers judgement at the end of Act V, and it seems likely that the essence of Corneille's attitude to his hero is to be found here. The substance of the verdict is that, by the murder of Camille, Horace is guilty of a heinous crime, but he is pardoned since the crime is the product of the same *vertu* which enabled him to triumph over the Curiace brothers; it must therefore be accepted as the inevitable price to be paid for an exceptional force of character which can be of use to the State:

> Ce crime quoique grand, énorme, inexcusable,
> Vient de la même épée et part du même bras
> Qui me fait aujourd'hui maître de deux États...
>
> Vis donc, Horace, vis, guerrier trop magnanime;
> Ta vertu met ta gloire au-dessus de ton crime;
> Sa chaleur généreuse a produit ton forfait;
> D'une cause si belle il faut souffrir l'effet.
>
> (1740–2; 1759–62)

This final line: "D'une cause si belle il faut souffrir l'effet" reminds us again of the verdict expressed by Corneille himself on the character of Cléopâtre in *Rodogune* (1644):

> Mais tous ses crimes sont accompagnés d'une grandeur d'âme, qui a quelque chose de si haut qu'en même temps qu'on déteste ses actions, on admire la source dont elles partent.[72]

This highly pragmatic conclusion, with its realistic acceptance of the moral ambivalence of human nature, at once capable of greatness and of baseness, finds a final echo in a singularly important text written in 1642 by a friend of Corneille. In his *Entre-*

tiens sur Divers Sujets d'Histoire, de Politique et de Morale,[73] the Abbé Nicolas de Campion records the conversation of a circle living in Rouen, and the last topic dealt with is the psychology of heroism. One of the speakers, called upon to sum up the discussion, says that the mistake we make in analysing the great public figures of history is that of over-simplifying their psychological make-up, for man is composed of a complex mixture of humours, and his actions rarely conform to any one consistent pattern.[74] He admits that there are some who are essentially rational minds, in whom virtue predominates, and that others are primarily swayed by their passions, being creatures of vice. But there is a third category, far more complex and interesting, among which we find so many of the great heroes of history, a category which includes "ceux qui sans avoir égard à la raison ni à leurs passions, poussent le plus loin qu'ils peuvent les avantages qu'ils ont reçus de la nature ou de la fortune." They are like giants among ordinary men and their strength comes from what Campion calls a special Genius— "le propre génie." Here is his full explanation of this term, which throws such remarkable light upon both Horace and the whole race of Cornelian heroes:

> Ce que j'appelle le propre génie n'est autre chose que la grandeur et la générosité de certains naturels élevés, que vous diriez être venus au monde avec un droit absolu de commander aux autres. En effet ce génie porte je ne sais quelle impression d'une puissance si absolue sur ceux qui s'y laissent guider, que ce n'est qu'avec effort qu'on s'oppose à ses volontés.
>
> Aussi prétend-il avoir droit d'entraîner toutes choses après lui partout où il croit devoir aller; il se sert bien de la Religion et des lois comme de liens pour attirer les autres à sa suite, mais non point pour se retenir lui-même; de sorte que s'il demande quelquefois conseil, c'est beaucoup moins pour s'y conformer que pour autoriser ses résolutions qui ne sont pour l'ordinaire que des effets de ses premiers mouvements.
>
> Il est certain que ceux qui s'y abandonnent sont capables de grands biens et de grands maux: tout le bien qu'ils font ne vient ni du raisonnement ni de la réflexion sur les obligations auxquelles la vertu ou la raison les engagent; mais du simple mouvement de je ne sais quel noble instinct; tout le mal qu'ils causent ne procède ni d'une mauvaise

> inclination, ni d'une malice affectée, mais d'une certaine impétuosité de nature qui veut détruire tout ce qui s'oppose à eux. Et comme ils prétendent être envoyés ici-bas pour conduire ou pour réformer le monde, sans se mettre en peine des révolutions qu'ils y causent, ils élèvent ce qui leur plaît, ils rabaissent ce qui leur fait ombrage, détruisent tout ce qui leur nuit; persuadés qu'ils ne sont point obligés de rendre d'autre raison de leur conduite que leur mission prétendue pour réduire les choses dans un meilleur état.
>
> C'était ce génie qui poussait Alexandre le Grand à se vouloir rendre maître du monde entier; Cléomènes à se faire tout ensemble Législateur et Roi de la patrie; Alcibiades à se rendre indépendant des lois de son pays. Ce fut le même qui parmi les Romains attira la vénération des peuples à Scipion, qui éleva Sylla à la Dictature, qui mit Sertorius en état de choquer toute la puissance Romaine: enfin qui fit fléchir presque toute la terre sous les armes de Jules-César et depuis sous l'Empire d'Auguste.
>
> Les uns ont plus participé de la vertu comme Scipion, les autres ont plus lâché la bride à leurs passions, comme Sylla; quelques-uns se sont abandonnés à la suite de ce génie comme Alexandre le Grand; les autres, comme César, ont porté le flambeau devant; mais toujours pour marcher du côté que leur impétuosité les poussait.[75]

Horace's character has already been analysed in sufficient detail to make apparent the striking applicability to it of Campion's definition: the natural authority and prestige of the hero's personality; his conviction that he is the arbiter of human justice and the whole spontaneity and impetuosity of his impulses—those *premiers mouvements* in which the King recognised the source of his crime; the immense capacity for good and evil, both on a scale beyond that of ordinary humanity; and finally, the haughty refusal to justify his actions, so sure is he of his sacred mission to "réduire les choses dans un meilleur état."

In Campion's text, the definition is also applied finally to Richelieu himself, and though the Cardinal is repeatedly attacked for his politics, it is obvious that he inspires a mixture of awe and admiration in his critics for the sheer dimensions of his genius. So it is with Corneille's presentation of Horace: inhuman, when judged by the moral criteria of the common man (as Sabine constantly reminds us), he nevertheless forces that admiration which was the avowed aim of the dramatist's tragic aesthetic.

"Horace" and the Seventeenth-century Political Background

When *Horace* was published in 1641, it appeared with a dedication to Cardinal de Richelieu, in which the poet refers to the inspiration he has received from the great statesman:

> Et certes, Monseigneur, ce changement visible qu'on remarque en mes ouvrages depuis que j'ai l'honneur d'être à Votre Éminence, qu'est-ce autre chose qu'un effet des grandes idées qu'elle m'inspire, quand elle daigne souffrir que je lui rende mes devoirs?

In fact, since 1635, Corneille had been in receipt of an annual *pension* from Richelieu, who saw in his patronage of literature a means of extending his prestige and indirectly promoting his own political ideas.[76] The question inevitably arises, therefore, whether in *Horace* Corneille can be said to have written a political drama designed to express the Cardinal's ideas.

There is no doubt that in many respects the situation of Rome in the play corresponds closely to that of France during the Cardinal's Ministry. Richelieu's whole policy was directed to building up the political and military supremacy of his country in Europe, and one is particularly struck for instance by the analogy of his designs with those ascribed to Rome by Sabine in Act I, scene 1:

> Je sais que ton État, encore en sa naissance,
> Ne saurait, sans la guerre, affermir sa puissance;
> Je sais qu'il doit s'accroître, et que tes bons destins
> Ne le borneront pas chez les peuples latins;
> Que les dieux t'ont promis l'empire de la terre,
> Et que tu n'en peux voir l'effet que par la guerre.
> Bien loin de m'opposer à cette noble ardeur
> Qui suit l'arrêt des dieux et court à ta grandeur,
> Je voudrais déjà voir tes troupes couronnées
> D'un pas victorieux franchir les Pyrénées.
> Va jusqu'en l'Orient pousser tes bataillons,
> Va sur les bords du Rhin planter tes pavillons,
> Fais trembler sous tes pas les colonnes d'Hercule.
>
> (39-51)

In almost identical terms, Malherbe extols the territorial ambitions of Richelieu on behalf of France:

L'espace d'entre le Rhin et les Pyrénées ne lui semble pas un champ assez grand pour les Fleurs-de-Lys: il veut qu'elles occupent les deux bords de la Méditerranée et que de là elles portent leur odeur aux dernières contrées de l'Orient.[77]

But before Richelieu's military ambitions could be realised and his armies made powerful enough to secure the French frontiers against the threat of the Spanish-Austrian Habsburgs, he was forced to weld the country into a disciplined unit, where the many conflicting individualities and minorities would be strictly subordinated to the central authority of the Crown. For, when he took over the government of France in 1624, she was split by a host of factious elements: there were the Huguenots with their pretensions to both political and religious independence; there was the Catholic party (known as the *catholiques espagnolisés* or *catholiques ligueurs*), who dreamed of keeping France tied to the Spanish alliance; and finally, there was the semi-feudal nobility, fighting to maintain its political autonomy and privileges against the central government. All these factors of disunity are remarkably well evoked in a memorandum specially drawn up for Richelieu by one of his advisers, Fancan, in 1627:

Étant nécessaire de connaître l'origine des désordres de la France pour sagement y remédier, il faut demeurer d'accord qu'ils procèdent tous des guerres civiles dans lesquelles les étrangères inductions ont jeté les Français, ce qui a mis le Roi et ses sujets de la campagne en l'extrême nécessité où ils sont à présent, en suite de quoi il n'y a aujourd'hui partie de l'État qui soit saine, tout étant altéré par les diverses factions qui ont corrompu non seulement les lois de la monarchie, mais encore les esprits, et tout cela par un abandon général que l'on a fait durant quelques années des maximes solides du gouvernement.

De plus, qui approfondira la disposition présente du royaume, il trouvera que tous les corps des communautés sont malcontents, la Sorbonne, les Parlements, les Universités, les officiers et la plupart des Grands, pareillement les princes du sang éloignés de la Cour, OO en jalousie d'Herman et en assez mauvaise intelligence avec H, les ministres de l'État peu amis, peu unis en leurs sentiments et une bonne partie de ceux-ci assez incapables de leurs charges, tous les bons Français étonnés, les catholiques ligueurs comme aussi tous les huguenots entièrement ulcérés et les peuples incertains si la paix subsistera ou s'ils retomberont en guerre. Ainsi de tous côtés, les désordres sont visibles et pressants.[78]

In France, as in Rome as evoked by Corneille, there were families split by religious loyalties, or even—as in the case of the royal family itself, where the Queen and Queen Mother were Habsburgs—split by different national ties. It was Richelieu's task therefore to promote a sense of national unity and patriotism which could overcome the internal divisions, so that the individual would accept the overriding authority of the State. Fancan again gives us an idea of this aim when he speaks of the duty incumbent on all "bons Français":

> Quant au parti des bons Français, il est sans hasard et tout plein de gloire, c'est celui des gens de bien qui savent aimer leur religion, leur Roi et leur patrie conjointement, dans lequel nul ne peut périr qu'avec l'État et où chacun se peut rendre recommandable, quand par prudence, fidélité et courage il conserve son prince et sa patrie contre ceux qui, pour leurs seuls intérêts, imbuent les Français de fausses maximes par le moyen desquelles ils nous font abandonner notre propre conservation et celle de nos alliés.[79]

As with all totalitarian systems, the political measures taken by Richelieu were often ruthless. Fancan gives the following maxim as that of his master: "Ne pratiquer aucune voie lâche et traînante quand il est question du bien de l'État et de défendre les lois de celui-ci," while the Cardinal himself, in his *Testament Politique*, declares this article of faith:

> Il faut, en certaines rencontres, où il s'agit du salut de l'État, une vertu mâle, qui passe quelquefois par-dessus les règles de la prudence ordinaire.[80]

As we have already seen, the seventeenth-century view of Ancient Rome which Corneille so admirably reproduces in the play closely follows Richelieu's ideas, and one last example is worth quoting to emphasise the point. It is Montesquieu's definition of the Roman conception of *virtus* ("*vertu*"):

> C'est un amour dominant pour la patrie qui, sortant des règles ordinaires des crimes et des vertus, n'écoutait que lui seul, et ne voyait ni citoyen, ni ami, ni bienfaiteur, ni père; la vertu semblait s'oublier pour se surpasser elle-même, et l'action qu'on ne pouvait d'abord approuver, parce qu'elle était atroce, d'après les idées romaines, elle la faisait admirer comme divine.[81]

It is by this same ethic that Horace's crime is judged: at first condemned as *atroce*, and then pardoned since the instinct that produced it is noble.

Corneille himself clearly saw both the arguments for and against such an ethic—for the opposition voiced by Sabine, Camille and Curiace has its own validity. Moreover, a significant variant in one of the later editions of the play reflects Corneille's hesitations. Referring to Horace's *vertu*, the King had said in the original version:

> Sa chaleur *généreuse* a produit ton forfait.

In 1656, this is temporarily changed to:

> Sa chaleur *dangereuse* a produit ton forfait.

This small change shows the dramatist's awareness of the moral dangers implicit in the Genius of his hero, but, like Chapelain, he seems to conclude that ultimately ethics cannot be divorced from pragmatic realities—that is, political realities. For, in the final words of the *Dialogue de la Gloire*, politics is the "science architectonique à laquelle toutes les autres doivent soumettre leurs devis, pour les accommoder aux besoins des hommes."[82]

NOTES

1 L. Herland, in his *Corneille par lui-même*, Paris, 1959, p. 16, gives as an additional reason for Corneille's dramatic inactivity the poet's involvement in a legal dispute lasting from 1638 to 1640.

2 Boisrobert, Richelieu's secretary, wrote to Mairet on October 5th, 1637, of the Cardinal's displeasure at the public spectacle of "injures, outrages et menaces," and ordered them to cease.

3 The *privilège* (printer's licence) of the *Sentiments de l'Académie sur le Cid*, written by Chapelain, is dated November 26th, 1637.

4 *Lettres de Jean Chapelain*, published by Tamizey de Larroque, Paris, 1880, vol. I, p. 367.

CORNEILLE — NOTES

5 It was d'Aubignac who reported this gathering, probably held in late 1639, in his *Troisième Dissertation...Sur la tragédie intitulée « L'Œdipe »*, Paris, 1663, p. 14.

6 The play was not published till early 1641, the *achevé d'imprimer* of the first edition being dated January 15th, 1641. Chapelain's reference to the six months' delay before publication is explained by the fact that the actors who first performed the play only kept their exclusive rights to it as long as it was unpublished.

7 Chapelain writing to Balzac: "Pour les *Horaces*, les comédiens, qui ne les ont encore représentés que 3 fois au peuple et qui en sont les maîtres parce qu'ils les ont payés, ne souffriront pas qu'on les imprime si tôt...."

8 In another letter to Balzac, November 17th, 1640, Chapelain said that opinion was unanimous (among the *doctes*, no doubt) that the play's ending was "brutale et froide." D'Aubignac's more detailed strictures will be considered below.

9 For details, see G. Lanson: *Esquisse d'une Histoire de la Tragédie française*, Paris, 1954 edition, pp. 32–5.

10 Ed. Dedieu, Paris, 1909, p. 160. *Cf.* R. Lebègue: "Le Théâtre baroque en France," *Bibliothèque d'Humanisme et Renaissance*, 1942, p. 161 *et seq.*, where the author remarks on p. 177: "Dès la fin du seizième siècle, le peuple demande au théâtre tragique des émotions fortes. L'horreur morale ne lui suffit pas, il lui faut l'horreur matérielle, visible. Aux récits ampoulés d'un Garnier il préfère les combats et les meurtres sur la scène, et les exhibitions de cadavres, de têtes coupées, de cœurs et autres débris macabres."

11 *Les Horaces*, 1593. I have found no evidence of the play's having been performed.

12 In fact, there are three earlier French tragi-comedies: *Daniel* (1561), *Geniévre* (1564) and *Lucelle* (1576), but their influence cannot be compared to that of *Bradamante*.

13 *Lettre sur la Règle des Vingt-Quatre Heures*, 1630.

14 Already in the work of Alexandre Hardy (who died in 1632) the dramatic conflict is well developed. It is instructive to compare his version of *Didon* (written before 1608) with that of Jodelle: the suspense is maintained and the figures of Aeneas and Dido are far more complex.

15 "Observations sur Le Cid," in *Œuvres de Corneille*, ed. Marty-Laveaux, 1862, vol. 12, pp. 441–2. The italics are mine.

16 "[Corneille] devrait traiter avec plus de respect la personne des rois, que l'on nous apprend être sacrée" (*Ibid.*).

17 *Op. cit.*, p. 473.
18 *Op. cit.*, p. 468.
19 p. 86.
20 *Op. cit.*, p. 18.
21 *Op. cit.*, p. 19.
22 Subjects such as Œdipus, with its theme of incest and parricide, treated by Corneille in 1658–9. My italics.
23 *Remarques sur Œdipe*, 1663, p. 54.
24 *Deux Dissertations concernant le Poème Dramatique, en forme de Remarques sur deux tragédies de M. Corneille, intitulées: « Sophonisbe » et « Sertorius »*, Paris, 1663, second dissertation, pp. 73–4.
25 Fourth dissertation, 1663, p. 170.
26 *Pratique du Théâtre*, Paris, 1657, p. 82. My italics.
27 *Discours de la Tragédie.*
28 *Discours de la Tragédie.*

29 *Discours du Poème Dramatique*. Furetière gives the following definition of *admiration*: "Action par laquelle on regarde avec étonnement quelque chose de grand et de suprenant."

30 Corneille's definition of *bonté* in the character of tragic heroes closely parallels Longinus: "Cette bonté nécessaire aux mœurs, que je fais consister en cette élévation de leur caractère" (*Discours du Poème Dramatique*). He instances Homer's Achilles, whose *emportements de la colère* are intensely dramatic and exciting.

31 A. Adam, in his *Histoire de la Littérature française au XVIIe Siècle*, vol. I, pp. 473–5, reminds us appropriately that Corneille's early literary affiliations are essentially with writers known for their modernist outlook: "Mais surtout, les relations de Corneille avec l'Hôtel de Liancourt éclairent l'attitude qu'il adopte dans la grande querelle qui oppose alors partisans des règles et défenseurs de la liberté. Ami de Saint-Amant, vivant dans un cercle où la leçon de Théophile reste vivante, Corneille est résolument moderniste."

32 Quotations are from the excellent translation of Livy's *Early History of Rome* by A. de Sélincourt (Penguin Classics).

33 It is possible that the suggestion for two of these twists in the plot, designed to increase suspense, came from a later history: the *Roman Antiquities* of Dionysius Halicarnassus. The temporary calling-off of the combat may have been prompted by Dionysius's remark that, at the sight of the combatants, "all the spectators melted into tears and accused both themselves and their leaders of insensibility in confining the combat ... to kindred blood" (III, 18). And the false supposition that Horace had fled is adumbrated by Dionysius in the phrase: "And the Romans reproached their combatant with cowardice" (III, 20).

34 Here again, the Greek historian of Rome, Dionysius, may well have guided Corneille's hand, for in the *Roman Antiquities* the moral problem is given more prominence than in Livy. According to Dionysius, the Horace and Curiace brothers are first cousins, their mothers having been twin Alban girls, one married to a Roman, the other to an Alban. Moreover, before the designation of the Horatii as the representatives of Rome is finally confirmed, the advisability of the choice is questioned by King and Senate, who ultimately leave the decision to the combatants. The latter weigh the issue in family council and decide to "prefer their virtue to their affinity" (III, 17).

35 *Discours des Trois Unités*.

36 The point is discussed with reference to *Horace* in the *Discours de la Tragédie*, *Œuvres*, ed. Marty-Laveaux, vol. I, pp. 85–6.

37 The available evidence suggests that the set was probably decorated with the conventional furnishings of a typical contemporary French palace: it was "abstract" only in the sense that it had no connection with any particular plot or locality. Cf. J. Vanuxem: "Le Décor de Théâtre sous Louis XIV," *XVIIe Siècle*, 1958, p. 197: "L'idée de jouer sur un plateau dénudé n'est jamais venue à quiconque au xviie siècle; si misérable fût-elle, la représentation s'entourait de tapisseries, de toiles peintes, et les acteurs s'efforçaient avec des moyens parfois sommaires d'évoquer un certain faste de costumes. A la cour ou à Paris, le décor était de la plus grande richesse, ainsi que les costumes des comédiens."

38 *Examen d'Horace*.

39 Quoted by A. Adam, *op. cit.*, p. 522, note 3.

40 *A History of French Dramatic Literature in the Seventeenth Century*, Part II, vol. I, pp. 302–12.

41 Montaigne considers the same problem in *Essais* II, 16, and concludes: "Toute personne d'honneur choisit de perdre plutôt son honneur que de perdre sa conscience."

42   Si Rodrigue à l'État devient si nécessaire,
De ce qu'il fait pour vous dois-je être le salaire,
Et me livrer moi-même au reproche éternel
D'avoir trempé mes mains dans le sang paternel?

(1809–12)

43 Referring to Sabine and Émilie (in *Cinna*), Balzac wrote, in a letter to Corneille of January 17th, 1643: "Et qu'est-ce que la saine Antiquité a produit de vigoureux et de ferme dans le sexe faible, qui soit comparable à ces nouvelles héroïnes que vous avez mises au monde, à ces Romaines de votre façon?"

44 *Cf.* Jules Lemaître, *Impressions de Théâtre*, 1888: "[Corneille] a conçu le caractère de Camille et celui d'Horace de façon à rendre inévitable le coup d'épée de la fin."

45 P. Bénichou, in his *Morales du Grand Siècle*, p. 29 *et seq.*, gives a brilliant analysis of this conception of contract in terms of the aristocratic feudal society that still existed in early seventeenth-century France. *Cf.* p. 30: "Le pacte féodal fixe le point jusqu'où la domination est légitime et la révolte criminelle, et au delà duquel la première est abusive et la seconde héroïque.... Tel se flattera de servir celui à qui il s'est donné, parce qu'il se démentirait s'il y manquait; pour la même raison, s'il se voit opprimé par lui, il le désavouera, le défiera devant l'opinion, opposera l'orgueil à la force, cherchera à lui faire honte. Cinna, Émilie et tous leurs pareils ne font pas autre chose." Camille's revolt is precisely of the same nature.

46 *Cf. Andromaque*, Act III, scene 1:

Mon innocence enfin commence à me peser.
Je ne sais de tout temps quelle injuste puissance
Laisse le crime en paix et poursuit l'innocence.
De quelque part sur moi que je tourne les yeux,
Je ne vois que malheurs qui condamnent les Dieux.
Méritons leur courroux, justifions leur haine...

47 A good example is Médée's speech in Act I, scene 5:

L'âme doit se raidir plus elle est menacée,
Et contre la fortune aller tête baissée,
La choquer hardiment, et, sans craindre la mort,
Se présenter de front à son plus rude effort.
Cette lâche ennemie a peur des grands courages,
Et sur ceux qu'elle abat redouble ses outrages.

Her *confidente* then says to her:

Votre pays vous hait, votre époux est sans foi:
Dans un si grand revers que vous reste-t-il?

And Médée gives her famous reply:

...Moi,
Moi, dis-je, et c'est assez.

48 *Cf.* ll. 265–70. Here, too, there is a striking parallel with the hero of *Le Cid*: in the *Stances*, Rodrigue attempts to harmonise dialectically love and honour by evolving the notion that to be worthy of Chimène's love he must fight her father (ll. 323–4, 1637 version). But finally, it is only by completely

rejecting the claims of love that he can acquire the necessary impetus of will to resolve the dilemma:

> Respecter un amour dont mon âme égarée
> Voit la perte assurée!
> N'écoutons plus ce penser suborneur
> Qui ne sert qu'à ma peine.
>
> (335–8)

Only after the duel does Rodrigue claim that his motive in fighting was *specifically* to prove himself worthy of Chimène's love (ll. 895–6), confirming Bénichou's remark: "La gloire commande, l'intelligence invente pour elle et justifie après elle" (*op. cit.*, p. 50).

49 L. Herland: *Horace ou Naissance de l'Homme*, Paris, 1952.

50 *Op. cit.*, p. 114: "Pas un instant Horace n'avait pensé à leurs patries rivales: il ne pensait pas qu'il parlait à l'homme du camp ennemi, il pensait seulement qu'ils étaient appelés l'un et l'autre à un sacrifice sans exemple et il le conviait à cette lutte à mort avec des yeux illuminés d'une amitié fraternelle. Et l'autre lui répond en Albain: incapable de dominer la situation et de concilier les devoirs contraires du soldat et de l'ami, et d'ailleurs irrité contre Horace parce qu'il le sent plus fort que lui; déjà il ne voit plus en son vieux camarade que l'Ennemi." It is interesting to note that, according to tradition, the actor Baron attempted, even in Corneille's life-time, to play Horace with this vein of humanity: the "je ne vous connais plus" was spoken more in sorrow than in anger!

51 *Op. cit.*, p. 116: "Curiace incarne tous les mensonges que depuis cent ans on nous a appris à vénérer: les bellicistes déguisés en pacifiques agneaux, et la guerre du droit, et la France soldat de l'idéal en face de la barbarie teutonique." Also p. 120: "Curiace n'offre que le tragique de la souffrance refusée, Horace seul celui de la souffrance âprement, farouchement, victorieusement assumée dans sa plénitude et son intégrité."

52 A. Adam (*op. cit.*, p. 527) is perfectly right in insisting on the importance of having Horace played by a young actor: "Rodrigue n'a guère que vingt ans et le jeune Horace n'en a guère davantage. Tout le sens des drames où ils sont mêlés s'affaiblit si on les imagine plus âgés. Qu'ils aient seulement trente ans, et Rodrigue tombe dans la sentimentalité romantique, et Horace n'est plus qu'une brute." One thinks also of Molière's Alceste, whose rôle changes completely when played (as so often at the Comédie Française) by an actor nearer sixty than twenty!

53 ll. 485–500. *Cf.* Herland, *op. cit.*, p. 121: "Le secret de sa force, c'est qu'il s'interdit d'arrêter à l'avance son esprit sur ce qui pourrait le faire chanceler." Hence M. Herland's admission that Horace resorts to "de beaux mensonges héroïques." Here seems to be the major flaw in this critic's logic: "Horace se grisait de pures idées.... Curiace refuse de se payer de mots et regarde la réalité en face. C'est donc qu'il est capable d'en soutenir la vue, c'est donc qu'elle ne lui fait pas peur autant qu'à Horace" (p. 117). In both cases, *donc* seems to me to introduce a purely gratuitous deduction.

54 *Cf.* l. 1130: C'est peu pour lui de vaincre, il veut encor braver.

55 By emphasising here Horace's loss of self-control as the source of his tragedy, we are going against the old view that the Cornelian hero is free from irrational impulses (*Cf.* G. Lanson: "Le Héros cornélien et le « généreux » selon Descartes," *Revue d'Histoire Littéraire de la France*, 1894, p. 401: "L'on ne trouve point chez Corneille un seul *passionné* qui soit purement un *passionné*, un *impulsif* qui soit vraiment un *impulsif*.") Yet Corneille specifically describes the

tragic subject as one in which the clash is between the '*impétuosité* des passions' and the 'tendresses du sang' (*Discours du Poème Dramatique*).

56 *Cf.* W. G. Moore: "Corneille's *Horace* and the Interpretation of French Classical Drama," *Modern Language Review*, 1939, p. 393: "Rome could not have been saved, no state can be saved, unless it be by men who will put aside other considerations and risk all for it. Like so many, he willed to be blind, on that issue, and his one-sidedness was the condition of his strength. But it was also the cause of his downfall, as a human being. The man who was a hero on the field proved himself a savage in the home, and for the same reason."

57 *Cf.* Géruzez: *Histoire de la Littérature française*: "Quoique Corneille l'ignore, le pivot de l'action n'est-ce pas le vieil Horace? Le péril de ses enfants, la mort de sa fille, le déshonneur de son fils ne sont que des moyens dramatiques pour faire contempler dans toutes ses attitudes cette vieille figure romaine du père et du citoyen qui, dominant tous les personnages et concentrant tous les faits, produit au moins l'unité d'intérêt."

58 This is one of the ideas expressed in the excellent study of the play by Félix Hémon, a critic more plagiarised than acknowledged. The same study appears in his edition of *Horace*, Paris, 1925, and in the general book on Corneille (Librairie Delagrave, no date).

59 *Jugement sur quelques auteurs français*, 1692.

60 *Cf.* Guérin de Bouscal: *Suite de la Mort de César* (*privilège*, 1636); Scudéry: *La Mort de César* (*priv.*, 1636) and *Didon* (*priv.*, 1637); Chevreau: *Lucrèce Romaine* (*priv.*, 1637); Du Ryer: *Lucrèce* (*priv.*, 1638); Desmaretz: *Scipion* (*priv.*, 1639).

61 Guez de Balzac: *Œuvres Choisies*, vol. II, Paris, 1822, p. 263 *et seq.* This dissertation was first published in 1644, but almost certainly dates from the late 1630s; it was probably well known via the *salon* of Madame de Rambouillet, before appearing in print. The italics are mine.

62 *Essais*, Book I, chapter 14.

63 *Cf.* the definition of *générosité* given by Père Le Moyne in his *Galerie des Femmes Fortes*, 1660, p. 236: "Une Grandeur de Courage ou une Hauteur d'Esprit, par laquelle une Âme élevée dessus de l'Intérêt et de l'Utile, se porte inviolablement et sans détour au Devoir qui est laborieux et à l'Honnête qui coûte et qui paraît difficile."

64 P. Bénichou: *Morales du Grand Siècle*, 1948; O. Nadal: *Le Sentiment de l'Amour dans l'Œuvre de P. Corneille*, 1948.

65 *Op. cit.*, p. 32, note 2.

66 Du Vair: *La Philosophie Morale des Stoïques*, first published between 1592 and 1603. My quotations are from the best modern edition, by G. Michaut, Paris, 1946, p. 64.

67 Du Vair, *op. cit.*, pp. 80–1. It is important to bear in mind, in this context, that by "reason" the rationalist does not necessarily mean deductive logic, but equally the intuitive perception of truth; thus Descartes gives the following definition: "Par intuition, j'entends...la conception ferme d'un esprit pur et attentif, qui naît de la seule lumière de la raison, et qui, étant pur et simple, est par suite plus sûre que la déduction même." For the Cornelian hero, such as Rodrigue or Horace, the perception of duty comes as a spontaneous illumination rather than as the result of a series of logical deductions.

It was partly because of his misinterpretation of this concept of reason that Gustave Lanson falsified the picture of Cornelian heroism in his celebrated article: "Le Héros cornélien et le « généreux » selon Descartes," *Revue d'Histoire Littéraire de la France*, 1894. A sound criticism of Lanson's thesis is provided by P. Bénichou, *op. cit.*, pp. 25–7. The views of both these critics are discussed in

my article: "A propos de l'héroïsme cornélien," *Revue des Sciences Humaines*, 1962, pp. 169–73.
68 *Op. cit.*, pp. 81–2.
69 *Traité de la Comédie*, in the *Essais de Morale*; quoted from the 1733 edition, Paris, vol. III, p. 251. This passage is accompanied by detailed examples from *Le Cid* and *Horace*, including the following attack on the presentation of Camille's "horrible imprécation contre sa patrie": "Si l'on dépouille l'image de cette passion de tout le fard dont le Poète l'a déguisée, et qu'on la considère par la raison, on ne saurait s'imaginer rien de plus détestable que la furie de cette fille insensée, à qui une folle passion fait violer toutes les lois de la nature. Cependant cette même disposition d'esprit si criminelle en soi n'a rien d'horrible, lorsqu'elle est revêtue de ces ornements: et les spectateurs sont plus portés à aimer cette furieuse, qu'à la haïr" (p. 261).
70 It is interesting to recall that the frontispiece to the first authentic edition of the *Maximes* betrays the specifically anti-Stoic intentions of the author: it portrays Truth, in the form of a child, tearing off the mask hiding the true face of Seneca, the great Roman exponent of Stoicism.
71 The *Dialogue de la Gloire* is published by Fidao-Justiniani in *L'Esprit Classique et la Préciosité au XVIIe Siècle*, Paris, 1914, pp. 147–90.
72 *Discours du Poème Dramatique*.
73 In the article "A propos de l'héroïsme cornélien," Campion's text is described in more detail and the date of composition established. The book was not published till 1704, in Paris. In it, Corneille is referred to as "ce Poète, notre ami."
74 *Op. cit.*, p. 464: "Il est vrai qu'il ne faut pas s'étonner de l'erreur des esprits les plus éclairés dans le jugement qu'ils font des personnes publiques. Ils raisonnent et les autres agissent: la raison cherche toujours de la règle et de la stabilité; l'action est une agitation perpétuelle, sujette à une infinité de révolutions et de changements: de sorte qu'il n'est pas impossible que celui qui a cédé beaucoup de fois aux mouvements d'une passion déréglée, ne puisse en d'autres occasions dompter les plus violents efforts de cette même passion sous laquelle il avait ci-devant succombé." One is reminded here of the dynamism of La Rochefoucauld's analysis of man in the *Maximes*, with its similar emphasis on the *génération perpétuelle de passions* in the human heart.
75 *Op. cit.*, pp. 469–72.
76 Campion comments in the *Entretiens* on Richelieu's aim in the following terms: "S'il attire les Muses en France, ce n'est que pour les y rendre esclaves: car je vous prie de me dire s'il y en a aujourd'hui quelqu'une qui ose ouvrir la bouche, à moins que ce ne soit pour publier ses louanges; et si ce n'est pas un crime, je ne dis pas seulement de parler contre lui, mais de produire aucun ouvrage d'esprit, qui ne soit fondé sur ses éloges, ou du moins entrepris sous ses auspices?" (p. 453).
77 Letter to M. de Mentin, October 14th, 1626; in the *Recueil de Lettres Nouvelles* edited by N. Faret, Paris, 1627, p. 66 *et seq.*
78 Extract from the *Archives des Affaires Étrangères*, France, 787, fol. 23. Fancan discreetly used a code to refer to certain figures: OO=the King; Herman=the King's brother, Gaston d'Orléans; H is not identified.
79 *Ibid.*
80 *Testament Politique*, ed. L. André, Paris, 1947, p. 128.
81 *Considérations sur les Causes de la Grandeur des Romains et de leur Décadence*, 1734, chapter XI.
82 *Op. cit.*, p. 190.

CHAPTER TWO

RACINE

Jean Racine (1639–1699)
Painting attributed to Mignard

Among the innumerable problems raised by the tragic drama, with its public representation of private grief and its exploration of the mystery of man's place in the universe, is that of the particular kind of pleasure derived from witnessing such a spectacle. Most of our time, in the daily routine of living and surviving, we doubtless immerse ourselves in a flurry of activity designed, if Pascal's analysis is right, to conceal our inner anxieties about the riddle of existence; and, as Shakespeare put it, "we have our philosophical persons to make modern and familiar, things supernatural and causeless. Hence it is that we make trifles of terrors, ensconcing ourselves into seeming knowledge, when we should submit ourselves to an unknown fear."[1] But when we go to witness a great tragedy, what we do is precisely to "submit ourselves to an unknown fear", and perhaps this is the secret of the pleasure provided by tragedy—that it affords a necessary confrontation with the hidden anxieties. Perhaps the burden of repression is too great and calls for a periodic cathartic release, so that we ultimately accept 'terror' through familiarity with it.

However, while I think that this question of the psychology of the tragic emotions is of fundamental importance, without which we shall never solve some of the basic aesthetic issues, my own approach must stay within the limits of my professional competence, and I would describe my aim here as rather to provide an anatomy of Racinian tragedy, beginning with the simpler elements of poetic tonality, and then proceeding to the more complex questions of structure.

It is Racine himself who, in the critical utterances of his Prefaces, seems to invite us not to complicate the issues: he often writes, with a polemical dig at his French rival in the field, Pierre Corneille, of the virtues of "simplicity". Minimising apparently the importance of plot and "incidents", he writes in the preface to *Bérénice* that it is sufficient for the dramatic action to have a certain seriousness, and for the actors to be of heroic proportions—that is, enhanced by the prestige and aura of myth, legend or history—and for them to be presented as suffering: for, as Aristotle says in chapter XI of the *Poetics*, it is the spectacle of suffering that generates tragic pathos, or what Racine calls "cette tristesse majestueuse qui fait tout le plaisir de la tragédie". In order to reinforce his argument, Racine supports it with an appeal to the authority of Sophocles and quotes the case of the tragedy *Ajax*, which is the essence of simplicity: a play, he says, "qui n'est autre chose qu'Ajax qui se tue de regret à cause de la fureur où il était tombé après le refus qu'on lui avait fait des armes d'Achille."

The central nerve of tragic emotion, Racine seems to say here, is man's lamentation for lost glory, and, provided the extent of the protagonists' loss is sufficiently great, our "tragic qualm" (as P. H. Frye called it)[2] will be aroused. It is in this respect that Erich Auerbach, in his *Mimesis*, stresses the epithet in the phrase *tristesse majestueuse*: the poetry of lamentation is indissolubly linked with exalted beings, whose supreme value lies in their pride of princely rank, their *gloire*, without which they would lack what Lessing termed *Fallhöhe*.[3] Only by entering fully through our imagination into this aristocratic mentality of *gloire* do we appreciate the resonance of Racinian pathos, and such an imaginative effort is more easily made by those who already know the background of Racine's age.

It is perhaps a critical commonplace to evoke the ethics of Descartes, with its Stoic emphasis on man's innate duty to realise his capacity for total freedom from bondage to the passions, but there is no doubt that this code of behaviour, and its ideal of *générosité*, provides a significant clue to the tonality of the dramatic literature of the seventeenth century in France. For the semi-feudal nobility of the time, the notion of *vertu* was inseparable from strength of character, and when Descartes wrote of the tensions between the will and the passions, exalting the joys of self-conquest—"la joie d'avoir vaincu"—he gave us the best insight into the world of Corneille's heroes, who sing almost lyrically of their moral triumphs. We are reminded, for example, of Corneille's portrayal of the Roman Emperor Auguste, in *Cinna*, who crowns his political career with an act of supreme *générosité*: if he forgives those who have been caught plotting against him, it is not from calculated political motives of a Machiavellian nature, but from a superior impulse; the act of mercy is an act of self-liberation from all material bondage, and Auguste proclaims himself sublimely free:

> Je suis maître de moi, comme de l'univers;
> Je le suis, je veux l'être.
>
> (1696-7)

Situations such as this explain why Corneille made much, in his critical theory, of the place of 'admiration' (astonishment) among the appropriate emotions aroused by tragedy; at the same time, they also make understandable the common viewpoint that Corneille does not truly qualify as a tragic writer: the "unknown fear" is too fully sublimated by the will. Be that as it may—and I have certainly oversimplified the point[4]—there is no doubt that, when we turn to Racine, the basic contrasts are striking. Not that Racine immediately found his true genius, for his first two plays still show him a prisoner of the predominant seventeenth-century dramatic tradition of seeking admiration for heroic figures whose superiority to the ordinary run of mortals lay in what Corneille had called "le caractère brillant et élevé d'une habitude vertueuse ou criminelle". The Cornelian fascination for the superhuman criminal protagonist is thus clearly a principal feature of *La Thébaïde* (1664), where Créon is ready to sacrifice all other human feelings to his political ambitions:

> Quand on est sur le trône on a bien d'autres soins;
> Et les remords sont ceux qui nous pèsent le moins
> ....
> Et je n'ai plus un cœur que le crime effarouche.
>
> (893-4; 900)

Similarly, when Jocaste, mother of the *frères ennemis*, goes to her self-inflicted death, her final words to her sons show despair yielding to shrill defiance:

> Je n'ai plus pour mon sang ni pitié ni tendresse—
> Votre exemple m'apprend à ne le plus chérir;
> Et moi je vais, cruels, vous apprendre à mourir.
>
> (1188–90)

In the following year, with *Alexandre*, Racine turned his hand to the *tragédie galante* made fashionable by authors such as Quinault and Thomas Corneille, but here too we are still in a world of heroes of impeccable *grandeur d'âme*. When Alexandre finally forgives his defeated enemy, Porus, it is in the accents of Corneille's Auguste, and Racine's Prefaces to the play betray the extent to which the young author was emulating the *style sublime* of *Cinna*: "Il n'y a pas un vers dans la tragédie qui ne soit à la louange d'Alexandre ... Il ne se contente pas de vaincre Porus par la force de ses armes: il triomphe de sa fierté même par la générosité qu'il fait paraître en lui rendant ses États".

It was not until *Andromaque* (1667), therefore, that Racine definitively found his real personal style: the same pride is there in the characters, but no longer as a sententious self-glorification; instead, it is, as one of the best modern writers on the French seventeenth century has said, a "yard-stick of dishonour, a measure of the derogation from the ideal". Here is the passage in which Paul Bénichou formulates the point:

> La nouveauté de Racine réside en ce que cet orgueil n'est plus exaltant. C'est une blessure du moi à laquelle on pense toujours, sans pouvoir la fermer; les pensées d'orgueil sont là pour entretenir, au moyen d'une honte cruelle et qui ne peut plus s'oublier que dans la violence, le sentiment de la déchéance. L'orgueil n'est plus l'aiguillon de l'honneur, mais la mesure du déshonneur.[5]

We find ourselves, with Racine, in a world where the dominant tone is one of anxiety, where the ego is constantly threatened and vulnerable, dependent upon the whim of others, a state of affairs which is closely linked with the change in the fortunes of the aristocracy that followed upon the defeat of the anti-absolutist forces in the civil war, the Fronde, of 1648–53. As a result of the entrenchment of royal power under Louis XIV, the nobility were deprived of their traditional feudal privileges and virtual political independence, and consequently they found their old code of honour was meaningless. This was, of course, merely the end of a process that had been steadily evolving for well over a century, and which had been particularly accelerated by Richelieu and Mazarin; already in La Rochefoucauld's *Mémoires*, the mood of the aristocracy in the early years of the century is captured in the following phrases: "Tous les grands du royaume qui se voyaient abattus croyaient avoir passé de la liberté à la servitude. J'avais été nourri dans ces sentiments". But from 1660, the situation became more acute: at Court, where they were forced to do regular homage to the Sun King, they lived through the daily humiliations of a system where *grandeur* proved to be something gratuitous, dependent upon the arbitrary dictates of the sovereign. To understand the change in tone between Corneille and Racine and to see why the elder generation of aristocrats such as La Rochefoucauld preferred the former, it helps to remember La Bruyère's description of the new atmosphere at Court—phrases such as:

> N'espérez plus de candeur, de franchise, d'équité, de bons offices, de services, de bienveillance, de générosité, de fermeté dans un homme qui s'est depuis quelque temps livré à la cour...
>
> Vous êtes un homme de bien, vous ne songez ni à plaire ni à déplaire aux favoris, uniquement attaché à votre maître et à votre devoir: vous êtes perdu.[6]

This interpretation of the impact of the social and political background upon Racine's work is consistent with what another modern critic wrote some time ago about the importance, in the tragedies, of the constant allusions to the expressions on the characters' faces, all betraying hidden inner tensions and conflicts. It was Le Bidois who wrote:

> Les personnages de Racine ont sans cesse les yeux ouverts. Il y a toujours quelqu'un plus maître d'eux qu'eux-mêmes, et de qui dépend

> leur destinée. C'est à capter sa bienveillance, à surprendre les secrets mouvements de son cœur, à chercher par où s'insinuer, qu'ils dépensent tous leurs soins. Ainsi le visage, ce vestibule de l'âme, est sans cesse assiégé de leurs regards ardents.[7]

Innumerable passages of Saint-Simon's *Mémoires*, where he writes of Versailles and of "la promptitude des yeux à voler partout en sondant les âmes", could have been adduced by Le Bidois to show the topicality of Racine's vision.

This is particularly in evidence in a play such as *Britannicus*, set at the court of Néron, who wielded capriciously the same arbitrary powers as the French sovereign's; and the situation there, where the emperor's mother, Agrippine, senses her gradual exclusion from power and her increasing inability to control Néron's moves, is a basic pattern of all Racine's portrayal of human relationships. In this respect, it provides the characteristic *pathétique* of lamentation, that *sentiment de la déchéance* which is found in such lines as:

> Je sens que je deviens importune à mon tour.
(14)

> Depuis ce coup fatal, le pouvoir d'Agrippine
> Vers sa chute, à grands pas, chaque jour s'achemine:
> L'ombre seule m'en reste...
(111–3)

> Que je suis malheureuse! Et par quelle infortune
> Faut-il que tous mes soins me rendent importune.
(1275–6)

I well remember a lecture at Oxford by Jean Pommier, in which he singled out another line of Agrippine as profoundly 'Racinian', both for its almost prose-like simplicity and for its content:

> Ma place est occupée, et je ne suis plus rien.
(882)

In the case of Agrippine, the lament is for lost political power, but the accent of humiliation is strangely reminiscent of those more typical Racinian figures who are rejected in love. When she utters such words as

> [...] l'on m'évite et déjà délaissée...
> Ah! je ne puis, Albine, en souffrir la pensée.
>
> (891-2)

then we are irresistibly reminded of an Oreste, powerless to find a response to his love for Hermione, or of Hermione herself, abandoned by Pyrrhus in favour of the rival Andromaque and forced to contemplate her own shame:

> Mais cependant, ce jour, il épouse Andromaque;
> Dans le temple déjà le trône est élevé,
> Ma honte est confirmée...
>
> (1214-6)

It is out of the contemplation of such *honte* that springs the violence which is an integral part of Racinian *tendresse*: the wounded ego seeks to destroy the evidence of its own impotence, as when Hermione calls for the murder of Pyrrhus:

> Qu'il périsse! Aussi bien il ne vit plus pour nous.
>
> (1408)

Similarly, with Phèdre, the agony of rejection is never greater than when she learns that Hippolyte is capable of love, but that she alone has been unable to find access to his heart:

> Je suis le seul objet qu'il ne saurait souffrir.
>
> (1212)

And so, she too plots the destruction of those whose very existence is an affront to her condition:

> Non, je ne puis souffrir un bonheur qui m'outrage.
>
> (1257)

Both Hermione and Phèdre here exemplify tellingly the Pascalian analysis of the human situation:

> La nature de l'amour-propre et de ce moi humain est de n'aimer que soi et de ne considérer que soi. Mais que fera-t-il? Il ne saurait empêcher que cet objet qu'il aime ne soit plein de défauts et de misères.

Hence, says Pascal, the ego "conçoit une haine mortelle contre cette vérité qui le reprend et qui le convainc de ses défauts".[8] But it is the irony of Racinian tragedy that all such efforts and destructive measures to suppress the evidence of the *misères* merely create further and more damning evidence which proves overwhelming, so that, as is so frequently the case in Racine, the only effective remedy is ultimately that of suicide, the supreme act of despair.

So it is that Hermione and Phèdre recognise the futility of their attempts to disguise from themselves their basic *faiblesse*: in the words of Mithridate, such outbursts of destructive hatred are

>Vains efforts, qui ne font que m'instruire
>Des faiblesses d'un cœur qui cherche à se séduire.
>
>(*Mith.*, 1403-4)

This process of recognition is beautifully enacted by Racine in the climax of the monologue of Hermione at the beginning of Act V of *Andromaque*, where she reflects on her plot to kill Pyrrhus:

>Qu'il meure, puisqu'enfin il a dû le prévoir,
>Et puisqu'il m'a forcée enfin à le vouloir.
>A le vouloir? Hé quoi? c'est donc moi qui l'ordonne?
>Sa mort sera l'effet de l'amour d'Hermione?
>..
>Je n'ai donc traversé tant de mers, tant d'États,
>Que pour venir si loin préparer son trépas?
>L'assassiner, le perdre?...
>
>(1419-22; 1427-9)

Here, in its concentrated essence, is the tragic vision which sees behind the illusions of the ego in its claim to be master of its own fate: the only possible instrument of self-orientation, the will, is convicted of total irrationality where it seeks the death of the one thing that gives any meaning to life. Racine's gift for evoking poetically the enormity of the *contrariétés* of human nature—its potential for *grandeur*, its ineradicable *misère*—was never better illustrated than here, where the juxtaposed abstractions *mort* and *amour* point up the analysis, and where the majestic sweep of the alexandrine (*tant de mers, tant d'États*) heightens the sense of tragic waste.

Perhaps it is only in *Phèdre* that Racine again matched this poetry of lament for lost glory, orchestrating the theme of *les faiblesses de l'amour* in the figures of Hippolyte and Phèdre herself. Both are victims of a prohibited love, and the same guilt-ridden conscience at odds with "un fol amour" is the agent of the tragic pathos. Racine gets a remarkable effect from the structural parallelism whereby Hippolyte's repressed passion for Aricie is revealed to Théramène (Act I, scene 1) in almost identical accents to those in which Phèdre's passion for him is revealed to Œnone (Act I, scene 3), just as the declaration of Hippolyte's love to Aricie is juxtaposed in Act II with Phèdre's avowal of love to Hippolyte. In both cases, passion is sensed as a loss of moral identity:

> Par quel trouble me vois-je emporté loin de moi!
> ....
> Maintenant je me cherche et ne me trouve plus.
>
> (536; 548)

Hippolyte sees behind this passion the hidden hand of the gods—"Et les Dieux jusque-là m'auraient humilié?" (line 96)—but it is above all in the rôle of Phèdre that we have the outstanding example in Racine's work of the theme of fatality, which is an extension of the *pathétique* of rejection. When the incestuous queen sees herself as the "triste rebut de la nature entière", we enter another dimension of human suffering—a metaphysical anguish which expresses man's sense of victimisation by the gods. In what is perhaps the greatest of all tragedies, *King Lear*, Shakespeare voices this particular theme in the celebrated phrase:

> As flies to wanton boys, are we to the Gods.
> They kill us for their sport.

In the case of Racine, it is inevitably in the plays with sources in Greek mythology and legend that this idea of vengeful deities is most apparent—especially where the influence of Euripides was predominant. Aristotle called Euripides "the most tragic" of poets, because of the unhappy endings of his plays, and this fact is in turn inseparable from the further fact that it is in his work that the cruelty of the gods seems most gratuitous. One has only to compare the Sophoclean and Euripidean versions of the same subject—as in the *Electra* plays—to see this. In both of them, the gods order Orestes and his sister to kill their mother in revenge for her part in the murder of Agamemnon; but it is only in Euripides that the criminal nature of the act of vengeance, entailing matricide, is made to appear so heinous. Orestes and Electra are destroyed morally by their terrible deed, even though it was done in obedience to the gods. As such, all idea of Justice is questioned.[9]

I shall return later to this important problem of Justice, with reference to Sophocles and Aristotle; but for the moment, let me emphasise the extent to which Racine did exploit the pathetic resonance of man's victimisation by Fate. Just as Œdipus in his misery reflects that

> Perhaps the Gods were angry with my family of old,

so, too, one of Racine's earliest tragic protagonists, Jocaste, in *La Thébaïde*, denounces bitterly the ways of gods towards men:

> Voilà de ces grands Dieux la suprême justice!
> Jusques au bord du crime ils conduisent nos pas;
> Ils nous le font commettre, et ne l'excusent pas!
> Prennent-ils donc plaisir à faire des coupables,
> Afin d'en faire après d'illustres misérables?
>
> (608-12)

The tragic poetry of fatality is developed with still more power in *Andromaque*, where the injustice of destiny provokes a veritable frenzy of metaphysical despair in Oreste:

> Je ne sais de tout temps quelle injuste puissance
> Laisse le crime en paix et poursuit l'innocence.
> De quelque part sur moi que je tourne les yeux
> Je ne vois que malheurs qui condamnent les Dieux.
>
> (773-6)

And, in his final tirade, as he witnesses the consummation of his moral ruin, when Pyrrhus lies dead by his hand, he declares with bitter irony:

> Grâce aux Dieux! mon malheur passe mon espérance.
> Oui, je te loue, ô ciel, de ta persévérance.
> Appliqué sans relâche au soin de me punir
> Au comble des douleurs tu m'as fait parvenir.
> Ta haine a pris plaisir à former ma misère:
> J'étais né pour servir d'exemple à ta colère,
> Pour être du malheur un exemple accompli.
>
> (1613–9)

A similar bitterness is found in countless other contexts—in the rôle of Antiochus in *Bérénice*, in Xipharès (*Mithridate*) and in Ériphile (*Iphigénie*), who utters the following condemnation of the gods:

> Le ciel s'est fait sans doute une joie inhumaine
> A rassembler sur moi tous les traits de sa haine.
>
> (485–6)

But, as I have said, nowhere is the oppressive hand of fatality more in evidence than in *Phèdre*, and it would be superfluous to quote the references in the text to the *haine de Vénus* which has cruelly victimised all Phèdre's lineage. It is another of those commonplaces of literary criticism to stress the influence of Jansenism in this play, with its Augustinian concept of an inscrutable God, a *Dieu caché*, whose Grace is mysteriously given or withheld, without any visible human reasons to account for it; in this context, one recalls the note which Racine wrote in the margin of his copy of Plutarch: "Grâce. L'âme est conduite de Dieu partout où il veut". Yet it is important to remember that the lines most frequently quoted to illustrate this Jansenism in *Phèdre* ("On ne peut vaincre sa destinée", etc.) are generally traceable back to the antique sources of the play, either in Euripides or Seneca. In his Preface, Racine certainly insists that Phèdre is helpless to resist her god-given passion, and he speaks of the powerful poetic resonance of the Greek fables: "les ornements de la fable, qui fournit extrêmement à la poésie". The main problem for him, however, was to use this poetic resource and yet, at the same time, reconcile it with the demands of probability ("la vraisemblance de l'histoire") in a Christian era when there was a resistance to the Greek concept of the gods. For this reason, Racine suppresses the Euripidean scenes, in which the enemy goddesses Artemis and Aphrodite actually appeared, and where the human actors are shown to be but pawns in a cosmic encounter. Even in the action of the Racinian version, there is a certain ambiguity maintained in the presentation of the *merveilleux*. For instance, Jean Pommier has pointed out the skill with which Racine handled the supposed death of Thésée and his subsequent return from the underworld: "Ramener Thésée des Enfers, c'eût été sacrifier au merveilleux païen de *Psyché* et des opéras (*Alceste*, etc.). L'entreprise épirote, d'autre part, ne pouvait guère donner lieu qu'à un sec bulletin. A moins d'y ménager une *frange*, un *halo* fabuleux. C'est à quoi Racine réussit admirablement. Qu'on veuille bien relire le vers 966: 'Lieux profonds et voisins de l'empire des ombres.' *Voisins* seulement ... L'adjectif marque au passage la distance entre l'historique (le pseudo-historique) et le légendaire."[10] Another instance is the way Racine leaves it uncertain how far Neptune really appeared to spur Hippolyte's horses to bolt and drag the young hero to his death. Théramène, who describes the scene, reports that *popular rumour* has it that the god showed himself:

> *On dit* qu'on a même vu, en ce désordre affreux,
> Un dieu qui d'aiguillons pressait leur flanc poudreux.
>
> (1539–40)

And, moreover, Racine has carefully suggested, earlier in the play, that Hippolyte had begun to lose full control of his horses through his distracted state of mind, caused by the newly-awoken love for Aricie: "Mes coursiers oisifs", he tells Aricie, in Act II, scene 3, "ont oublié ma voix".

The fact remains that there is deliberate ambiguity, and when Hippolyte dies, his last words are:

> Le ciel...m'arrache une innocente vie.
>
> (1561)

This line takes on its full significance when set against the providential faith in the gods which Hippolyte had expressed during his last appearance on stage:

> Sur l'équité des Dieux osons nous confier:
> Ils ont trop d'intérêt à me justifier.
>
> (1350–1)

Here we have one of those structural conjunctions which underlie the tragic vision of a world where man is the fool of fortune and where no man gets his true deserts. It is closely paralleled by a whole series of similar conjunctions in *Lear*, with its innumerable suggestions of a malevolent divinity at work. In particular, one recalls the moment at the end of the play where Shakespeare seems to go out of his way to rebuke the optimism of Albany; it is he who, learning of the danger in which Cordelia stands because of Edmund's order that she be killed, cries out: "The gods defend her!"—a line that is immediately countered by the stage-direction announcing the entry of Lear with the dying Cordelia in his arms.

My own view is that those critics who stress the deliberate portrayal by Racine of malicious gods, in order to create a more profound tragic pity for the criminal queen, are more likely right. Racine himself, in his annotations of Euripides' text, had written in the margin: "Vénus, *pour excuser Phèdre*, dit qu'elle l'a fait devenir amoureuse". R. C. Knight, author of the authoritative work *Racine et la Grèce*, similarly affirms that Racine 'blackened' Venus, in order to enhance the tragic beauty of the queen, and subscribes to the view of Jean Dubu[11] that Racine retired from writing secular tragedy because he became aware, with *Phèdre*, of how far his dramatic vision was in conflict with his personal religious faith in a good Christian God.

* * *

So far, in this study, I have dealt only with what I have called the general tonality of Racinian tragedy, its poetry of *tristesse majestueuse*, and it might well seem that, like the school of critics prominent earlier in this century—the exponents of the *poésie pure* view—I have treated Racine less as a *dramatic* writer than as an elegiac or lyrical poet. It was largely Valéry who gave his authority to such a view and wrote of *Phèdre* in the following terms:

> Il me demeure de *Phèdre* l'idée d'une certaine femme, l'impression de la beauté du discours. La trame, l'intrigue, les faits pâlissent promptement et l'intérêt de l'appareil purement dramatique de l'affaire se dissout.[12]

Formulated in such extreme terms, Valéry's view seems to me to be quite untenable and manifestly counter to all experience and theory of tragic poetry.

In the *Poetics*, Aristotle places great emphasis upon the action of the play, to the apparent detriment of the characters. Plot, he says, is the "soul of tragedy", so much so that we can have a tragedy without character but not without a plot. This attitude might in turn seem equally extreme, but a closer reading of the *Poetics*, with reference to the *Nichomachean Ethics*, dispels any objections. What Aristotle held was that talk of character in the abstract was meaningless, and that character or moral personality is something dynamic, which is constantly shaped by action. To quote Humphry House's comment on this point:

> Character may be looked upon as the arbitrary stabilised meeting-point of two series of actions: the antecedent series, which has gone to its formation, and the consequent series in which it will be actualised in the future.[13]

And, as Humphry House himself indicates, the modern movement in Shakespearian criticism, in reaction to Bradley with his artificially rounded view of character, is essentially in line with Aristotle—hence the new emphasis on plot, dramatic design and structure. One of my own favourite quotations in this respect is from a psychologist and pragmatist, William James, who wrote: "Sow an action and you reap a habit; sow a habit and you reap a character; sow a character and you reap a destiny."[14] There is the same understanding here as in Aristotle that character is not 'real' until it is in action; and the facts and circumstances of the tragic action are the plot.

Now, in the case of Racine, we have evidence that he approached the business of writing a tragedy in much the same spirit. His son, Louis Racine, tells in his *Mémoires* how the poet worked:

> Quand il entreprenait une tragédie, il disposait chaque acte en prose. Quand il avait ainsi lié toutes les scènes entre elles, il disait: «Ma tragédie est faite», comptant tout le reste pour rien.[15]

This second-hand piece of evidence is in turn supported by a note of Racine himself in a letter dating from 1661, describing his project for a tragedy based on the figure of the poet Ovid. Admittedly the date of the evidence is very early—some six years before the first great play was performed—but it is highly suggestive of the method of composition:

> J'ai fait un beau plan de tout ce qu'il [Ovide] doit *faire*... Ses actions étant bien réglées, il lui sera aisé après cela de dire de belles choses... J'ai fait, refait et mis enfin dans sa dernière perfection tout mon dessein.[16]

What supreme self-confidence the young Racine had in his ability to fill in the necessary "beauté du discours", once the real task—the creation of the dramatic *action*—was accomplished!

Now, what are the essential features of this structure or *dessein*? First and foremost, says Aristotle—and Racine will echo him in his Prefaces—it must be a movement from good fortune to bad, preferably in an ironic perspective so that the protagonist unwittingly creates his own downfall and only subsequently recognises his personal responsibility for the misfortune that has overtaken him. Aesthetically, the irony of deeds done in ignorance is a powerful source of tragic pathos, for we, as spectators, are given a privileged knowledge which involves us deeply in the action: to see someone walking helplessly into a trap and for us not to be able to intervene and stop the catastrophe awakens in us a profound foreboding and anxiety.[17] But, at the same time, the Aristotelian aesthetic of tragedy is inseparable from certain moral factors: in the tragedies of Sophocles, with which Aristotle was primarily concerned and from which his principal examples are taken, the essence of the pattern was that man is tragically fallible in his judgement. When a man is most sure of his grounds for action, it is then that he is most likely to be prone to error.[18] The constant moral—the call to avoid excess—is based on the notion that, being human, we are subject to an imperfect vision of the total scheme of things. Œdipus, in the *Tyrannos* play, and Creon, in the *Antigone*, are both "great and glorious men", set high above the common run of mortals. Œdipus, the "greatest of men", so we are told, has won his throne by exceptional gifts, he alone having been able to solve the riddle of the Sphinx. And Creon, we also learn, "was once an enviable man; he saved his country from her enemies, assumed the sovereign power and bore it well". In the Aristotelian sense, they are "rather good than bad", but neither totally perfect nor imperfect. The point is that their misfortune will spring precisely from that inevitable fallibility which is all the more poignant in their case because of the concomitant *Fallhöhe*.

Sophocles' tragic protagonists illustrate Aristotle's argument that the hero must not be depraved, or his catastrophe would merely strike us as "deserved": he must inspire our pity through undeserved misfortune. But, at the same time, he must not be totally innocent, or we should be indignant at the spectacle of Injustice in the world-order. We are obviously here in the presence of a view which is substantially different from the Euripidean scheme of things—that scheme which we have already characterised by the *Lear* quotation, seeing men "as flies to wanton boys".

But it is equally in *Lear* that this scheme is countered by what might be seen as a more Sophoclean vision:

> The gods are just and of our pleasant vices
> Make instruments to plague us.

For this to be an accurate formulation of Aristotle's theory, it would be necessary to interpret "vice" as a human flaw rather than as a moral depravity. For, when Aristotle speaks of the *hamartia* of the tragic protagonist, it is generally held that he means "an error of judgement". That is why Humphry House defines the phrase "a good man" as meaning, for Aristotle, one whose *intentions* are morally good. Thus, Creon, in the *Antigone*, means well when he issues the order that whoever tries to bury the traitor Polynices will be put to death; and when it turns out that the offender is his own niece Antigone, he duly condemns her to death, because he believes, sincerely but mistakenly, that the welfare of the State overrides all other factors and that this welfare depends upon a rigorous enforcement of governmental authority. Polynices has betrayed the State and must be deprived of burial, to discourage any other like-minded rebel. Antigone, too, has rebelled, and her example must not be left unpunished to breed still more disobedience. The tragic action is thus the recoil upon Creon of his own error of judgement: and its result is that his own son, in love with Antigone, and his own wife, are both brought to their doom. The play ends with Creon's discovery of this error and his self-condemnation for his "stubborn will":

> I am nothing. I have no life.
> Lead me away,
> That have killed unwittingly
> My son, my wife.[19]

As H. D. F. Kitto has remarked in his analysis of Greek tragedy, it is Sophocles who dramatises the normal Greek view that there is an immanent justice in life—a pattern that rules out chaos.[20] Occasionally, as in Sophocles' *Electra*, the disturbance of the balance *is* caused by a deliberate moral iniquity, and the retribution is then visited upon the criminal figures of Clytemnestra and Aegisthus; but more often, and more effectively, Aristotle would say, the *hamartia* is rooted in human presumption, rather than in unadulterated depravity, and the characteristic 'moral' is that of the chorus in the *Antigone*:

> For what presumption of man can match thy power
> O Zeus?...

> This law is immutable:
> For mortals to live greatly, is greatly to suffer.
> Of happiness the crown
> And chiefest part
> Is wisdom—and to hold
> The gods in awe.
> This is the law
> That, seeing the stricken heart
> Of pride brought down,
> We learn when we are old.[21]

Now, when we turn back to Racine, it is clear that both in practice and in theory he is in general agreement with Aristotle: the tragedies are essentially ironic structures, incorporating *hamartia* and consequent reversal of fortune. And not only did Racine himself translate that part of the *Poetics* which deals with these elements of tragedy, but he also frequently, in his Prefaces, quoted Aristotle to justify the design of his plays. It is true that his actual statement of the Aristotelian concepts seems to introduce *nuances* which raise problems, but before tackling such problems, it is important to show first of all that in practice we do find Racine reproducing the Sophoclean pattern approved by Aristotle. An outstanding example of this is in *Phèdre*, where the rôle of Thésée is very similar in its tragic qualities to that of Creon in the *Antigone*.

First, just as Sophocles carefully establishes the heroic dimensions of his protagonists, so too Racine presents Thésée as the true successor of Hercules: "... ce héros intrépide, / Consolant les mortels de l'absence d'Alcide" (73-4). This is the necessary framework to accentuate the degree of the subsequent fall if it is to create the tragic 'shudder'. (In the *Trachiniæ*, Hercules—"the best of all men on earth", whose heroic labours have been evoked—is finally reduced to a pathetic creature, "sobbing like a girl", provoking the comment: "I hear and shudder at the King's misfortunes: so great a man, hounded by such suffering".)

And secondly, we have a protagonist who, in good faith, but in ignorance of the truth, commits an error of judgement: Thésée, believing his son to be guilty of a criminal offence (incest and attempted rape) on the evidence of a third party (Œnone), which is not contradicted by either of the two main parties (Phèdre and Hippolyte), curses the offender and calls on Neptune to avenge the crime. It is this curse, pronounced in anger, that recoils upon Thésée, who discovers too late his error. Once Thésée is, as he says (in line 1647), "de mon erreur, hélas, trop éclairci", there remains only the prospect of tragic expiation in suffering:

> Allons.../...Expier la fureur d'un vœu que je déteste.
> (1650)

When we look closer at the structure of the play with this particular tragic perspective in mind, we see more fully how Racine, like Sophocles, harnesses the concept of Nemesis: every move we make has its consequences, setting other forces into motion which can have unforeseen and deadly results. This is inseparable from Aristotle's point that every detail in the play must be justified by the overall organic unity. Here is the relevant statement in the *Poetics*:

> Since the fable is an imitation of an action, that action must be a complete unity, and the events of which it is made up must be so plotted that if any of these elements is moved or removed, the whole is altered and upset.[22]

This remark is classically illustrated in *Phèdre*, with its network of ironies that lead to the catastrophe and emphasise the extent to which Thésée, for instance, has created his own *malheur*. First, there is the fact that the tragic avowal of love by Phèdre to Hippolyte has only happened because Thésée was absent and thought to be dead. Why was Thésée absent? He was away, abetting an attempted rape by his friend Pirithoüs:

> Je n'avais qu'un ami. Son imprudente flamme
> Du tyran de l'Épire allait ravir la femme;
> Je servais à regret ses desseins amoureux.
> (957-9)

This is only the first example of the way Racine exploited the *ornements de la fable*—in this case, Thésée's reputation as a philanderer ("Volage adorateur de mille objets divers" (636))—for the creation of dramatic irony. A second and related example is found in the way Racine treats the critical episode where Hippolyte fails to reveal to his father that he is the victim of an unjust calumny and that he is innocent of dishonouring Phèdre. Seneca apparently avoids the problem, since Hippolytus does not meet Theseus and thus has no opportunity to defend himself, though his flight is explicable by motives suggested below. In Euripides, this silence, which sealed Hippolyte's fate, was motivated by the fact that he had previously been tricked into giving an oath to say nothing; and, as Pommier says,[23] this oath is respected by the youth because, so the Greek text indicates, he has been initiated into some kind of Orphic religious mysteries which would make such an oath absolutely binding. For an audience of the seventeenth century, it was difficult to accept the psychological *vraisemblance* of so esoteric a motive, and Racine has therefore replaced it by another motive, rich in irony. Hippolyte is portrayed as a puritan, who is so profoundly shocked by Phèdre's lust that he cannot bring himself so much as to speak of it. The secret is locked away in his heart as in some Pandora's box, lest it contaminate whatever it touches. The mere thought of it provokes in him a sense of defilement, as we see in his immediate reaction after Phèdre's avowal:

> Je ne puis sans horreur me regarder moi-même.
> Phèdre... Mais non, grands dieux! qu'en un profond oubli
> Cet horrible secret demeure enseveli.
>
> (718–20)

The same "horror" will again surge up in Hippolyte in the crucial scene (Act IV, scene 2), when his father accuses him:

> D'un amour criminel Phèdre accuse Hippolyte!
> Un tel excès d'horreur rend mon âme interdite.
>
> (1077–8)

Skilfully fusing the antique tradition of a chaste, misogynistic Hippolytus with the modern tradition of the hero-lover, Racine gives Hippolyte a particularly complex motivation. No doubt, part of his sense of guilt springs from the fact that the object of his love, Aricie, is a political enemy of his father, who has forbidden her to marry and have children, lest this lead to a resurgence of the Pallantidae and a renewed threat to Thésée's hold over the throne of Athens. But at the same time, Racine has exploited aspects of the way Seneca treated the character, showing not only Hippolytus's shocked indignation at Phaedra's lust, but also a profound sense of personal guilt rooted in puritanical feelings: "I am guilty. I have deserved to die: I have stirred my step-mother to love."

If we ask why this core of ascetic puritanism is so strong in Hippolyte, the answer is partly that he had grown up to watch, in shame and humiliation, his own father's licentious behaviour towards women: that is the real organic significance of the passage early on in the play, where Hippolyte described his mixed feelings for his father (lines 83–96). What might seem at first sight to have been a case of Racine's introducing the 'local colour' of the fable for its own sake, turns out to be of vital importance to the tragic action; in a word, Hippolyte's *pudeur*—for which Thésée shares the responsibility—is in turn the source of Thésée's tragic error.

When Thésée, in his final terrible recognition of error, speaks of expiating "la fureur d'un vœu que je déteste", we are reminded of a note which Racine wrote in the margin of his copy of Psalm CV: "C'est dans sa colère que Dieu accorde la plupart des choses qu'on lui demande avec passion". The reference to passion as blinding judgement is, of course, equally applicable to the Sophoclean figure of Creon, who is frequently reminded—by the prophet Tiresias, for instance—that "only a fool is governed by self-will", and who himself ends by recognising his own *hubris*:

> Oh! the curse of my stubborn will.

Nevertheless, the connection between passion and *hamartia* is much more pronounced in so many of Racine's other major tragic figures, such as Hermione, Roxane or Phèdre; and, what is more, the essence of the Racinian *schéma* might be summed up as the *crime passionnel*, executed with an element of deliberate cruelty which, in the eyes of the neo-Classical critics of Racine's age, seemed to destroy the very foundations of the tragic. The reason for their condemnation of Racine's practice—seen clearly in the case of *Andromaque*, where Pyrrhus was immediately denounced as being guilty of excessive ferocity—was that such cruelty robbed the protagonist of any claim to our pity, which was taken to be the essential tragic emotion. Corneille had equally run into similar strictures, from the *querelle du Cid* onwards: critics like Chapelain, La Mesnardière and the Abbé d'Aubignac firmly believed that pity could only be fully extended to characters who remained morally innocent and who met virtually undeserved misfortune. The essence of their view is seen in the following extract from d'Aubignac's comments on Corneille's *Œdipe*:

> Je sais bien que la compassion est le plus parfait sentiment qui règne au théâtre... En France, il n'y faut jamais joindre l'horreur des incidents, ni le crime des princes malheureux. Il y faut tant d'innocence quand on veut que nous y compâtissions, que je conseillerais toujours à nos poètes d'éviter ces sujets [i.e., horror subjects, such as incest and parricide] comme trop difficiles et presque toujours dangereux.[24]

This was the attitude which had made d'Aubignac critical of Corneille's *Horace*, where the hero kills his own sister. According to d'Aubignac, the subject was better avoided altogether, but the only alternative was to alter the historical facts and arrange them so that Camille's death was an accident, the result of her falling accidentally upon her brother's sword. The same attitude will reappear concerning the subject of Phèdre and Hippolyte, with its equally scandalous material involving incest: hence Subligny's stock neo-Classical response in his *Dissertation sur les Tragédies de Phèdre et d'Hippolyte* of 1677, where he writes: "Ce sujet n'est guère propre au théâtre français... Un pareil crime, ne donnant que de très méchantes idées, ne devait jamais remplir notre scène". Where the subject is used by Racine's fellow seventeenth-century French dramatists, it therefore had to be purged of the scandal. Thus, in

Gilbert's version of 1646, Phèdre is no longer married to Thésée, but merely affianced; moreover, this Hippolyte is actually in love with Phèdre, and while the traditional calumny and vengeance are retained, Gilbert falls back on d'Aubignac's ploy of making everything hang upon an accident: Thésée completely misunderstands Phèdre's words which were never intended to harm Hippolyte. Similar attenuations are used by Pradon and Bidar in their versions.

Few serious critics today would accept the limitations which d'Aubignac's definition places upon the domain of the tragic: to begin with, our understanding of human beings is such that we no longer believe in total 'innocence'. Not only does experience tell us that life around us is full of cruelty and horror, but also we are far too aware of the presence of similar guilty feelings and instincts in our own selves. We have not ceased to long for innocence, but the longing is the stronger for our sense of *déchéance*. What is really surprising, however, is that critics like d'Aubignac did not recognise this, since the whole Christian tradition in which they lived was penetrated with the idea of sin, and indeed it is interesting to note that the orthodox Latin translation of *hamartia* was *peccatum*. It was not necessary to be a Jansenist to have such an understanding, and we find in the very orthodox Bossuet the classical Christian viewpoint when he writes: "Il faut aller jusqu'à l'horreur quand on se connaît".[25]

The significance of this point is, first of all, that the portrayal of morally guilty protagonists, as in Racine, is not necessarily a barrier to exciting pity for them, but could well be a more effective means to that very end: identification, based on a fellow-feeling for the dramatic character, would seem to be more surely achieved if we can find there an echo of our own guilt.

What then of Aristotle's point about the aesthetic objection to portraying 'depraved' characters? Must the guilt of the protagonist have limits and be offset by a glimmer of conscience which partially redeems him in our eyes? This is the kind of problem that has equally faced Shakespearian critics in dealing with *Macbeth*, and it is instructive to glance for a moment at some of the proposed answers which might have relevance to Racine.

Most of Shakespeare's heroes are either like Lear—"more sinned against than sinning"—or like Brutus, who is involved in crime as a result of "good intentions"; but, as Quiller-Couch wrote, concerning the "capital difficulty of *Macbeth*": "Tragedy demands some sympathy with the fortunes of its hero; but where is there room for sympathy in the fortunes of a disloyal, self-seeking murderer?"[26] Quiller-Couch's suggestion is that Shakespeare's way out of the dilemma was "to make our hero—supposed great, supposed brave, supposed of certain winning natural gifts—proceed to his crime under some fatal hallucination". For this reason, Shakespeare "left vague the proportions of [the witches'] influence and Macbeth's own guilty promptings".

Another complementary suggestion is made by the American critic Wayne Booth, who stresses the way the play focuses our attention upon the humanity and conscience of Macbeth—a man "too full of the milk of human kindness", ambitious, but "without the illness should attend it". Thus Shakespeare is careful not to show us the murder of Duncan, but gives prominence rather to the terrible effect upon the murderer: "We must identify Macbeth with the murder of a blameless king, but only intellectually; emotionally we should be attending only to the effects on Macbeth", so that "we feel primarily his own suffering".[27]

It is along similar lines that Racine's solution to the problem of making tragic figures out of guilty protagonists has sometimes been explained, notably by Eugène Vinaver.[28] By studying Racine's translation of parts of the *Poetics*, as well as several other passages (such as the Prefaces to *Andromaque*) in which Racine restated the Aristotelian principles, Vinaver suggested that Racine deliberately translated *hamartia* as *faute*, rather than as *erreur*, in order to accommodate the concept of a moral flaw. Furthermore that, where Aristotle understood by 'recognition' (*anagnorisis*) the recognition of a material error (notably a failure to recognise the true identity of the victim, such as Œdipus's unwitting killing of his father, etc.), Racine understood the recognition by the protagonist of the moral horror of the deed and of the *déchéance* of the self.

The outstanding example in Racine's work which seems to confirm this interpretation is that of Phèdre, and Vinaver quotes a piece of contemporary evidence which strengthens his argument—namely, a conversation of Racine reported by Mme de Lafayette:

> Dans une conversation, Racine soutint qu'un bon poète pouvait faire excuser les plus grands crimes, et même inspirer de la compassion pour les criminels. Il ajouta qu'il ne fallait que de la fécondité, de la délicatesse, de la justesse d'esprit, pour diminuer tellement l'horreur des crimes de Médée ou de Phèdre, qu'on les rendrait aimables aux spectateurs, au point de leur inspirer de la pitié pour leurs malheurs. Comme les assistants lui nièrent que cela fût possible...le dépit qu'il en eut le fit résoudre à entreprendre la tragédie de Phèdre, où il réussit si bien à faire plaindre ses malheurs, que le spectateur a plus de pitié de la criminelle belle-mère que du vertueux Hippolyte.[29]

This evidence is backed up by Racine's Preface to the play, which explains by similar motives the changes he made in the plot as he found it in his sources. For instance, while in the Senecan and Euripidean versions, it is Phaedra herself who accuses Hippolytus of assaulting her, in the French version the accusation is made by Phèdre's nurse, Œnone, who acts from misguided loyalty to her mistress. Or again, there is the introduction by Racine of the false news of Thésée's death, in order to explain Phèdre's final yielding and confessing her love to Hippolyte. But, of course, the most 'Racinian' aspect of the play is the way the author shows the temporary, but fatal, eclipse of reason by passion; and, if this has evoked more admiration from critics than any of the other tragedies, it is because the effect of passion is studied in so much more depth than hitherto. For all her struggle to remain pure, Phèdre is defeated because, even when she acts with "good intentions" (as Aristotle demanded of the tragic hero), her subconscious will betrays her. In a word, Racine has dramatised in her the Augustinian psychology which was particularly developed by the Jansenist community in which he was brought up, and which is expressed in such *maximes* of La Rochefoucauld's as: "L'esprit est toujours la dupe du cœur".[30] Or: "L'homme croit souvent se conduire, lorsqu'il est conduit, et pendant que par son esprit il tend à un but, son cœur l'entraîne insensiblement à un autre".[31] The Jansenist writer Nicole spoke similarly, in his *Traité de la Grâce Générale*, of the dominant rôle of the subconscious, which is referred to in such terms as "les pensées imperceptibles".[32]

In some instances, it is obvious that Racine already found suggestions for this in Euripides; that is the case when Phèdre first enters and speaks the lines:

> Dieux! que ne suis-je assise à l'ombre des forêts!
> Quand pourrai-je, au travers d'une noble poussière,
> Suivre de l'œil un char fuyant dans la carrière?
>
> (176-8)

—lines which betray her repressed erotic fantasies provoked by the image of Hippolyte the huntsman. In Seneca, the sensuality is much more brazen and conscious: Phaedra actually appears dressed in full Amazonian hunting costume. In Racine and Euripides, it is an aberration, quickly checked when it becomes conscious through verbalisation:

> Insensée, où suis-je? et qu'ai-je dit?
> Où laissé-je égarer mes vœux et mon esprit?
> Je l'ai perdu: les dieux m'en ont ravi l'usage.
>
> (179-81)

Later, in the same scene, when Phèdre evokes her past struggle to rid herself of her guilty passion, she provides another striking example of how her *esprit* is the *dupe du cœur*: she tells how she had built a temple to Venus and sacrificed victims to the goddess, but, even as she spoke the goddess's name, she found that it was in fact Hippolyte she was worshipping:

> En vain sur les autels ma main brûlait l'encens:
> Quand ma bouche implorait le nom de la déesse,
> J'adorais Hippolyte; et le voyant sans cesse,
> Même au pied des autels que je faisais fumer,
> J'offrais tout à ce dieu que je n'osais nommer.
>
> (248-52)

But it is above all in the famous declaration scene of Act II, scene 5, that Racine shows his genius for suggesting the hidden subterfuges of the will, and a comparison with the Senecan version (the scene has no equivalent in Euripides, where Phaedra and Hippolytus do not confront each other on the stage) will bring out the full originality of the French poet. In Seneca, the same brazen sensuality already noted above shows itself quickly: Phaedra faints, and as she returns to consciousness, she finds Hippolytus holding her; it is then that she reveals, in an aside, her decision to confess her love to the youth:

> Fearless be thy words and firm: the chief part of my guilt is long since accomplished: too late for me is modesty: I *have* loved basely; ...Success makes sins honest![33]

She then confesses her love, thinly disguising her sentiments under a deliberate confusion of Theseus and Hippolytus.

Racine has removed from this situation any explicit suggestion of deliberation on the part of Phèdre; she has come to see Hippolyte in order to plead with him for her son's rights to the throne of Athens, but, once in his presence, her passion undermines her will: "J'oublie, en le voyant, ce que je viens lui dire" (line 582). What Racine says in his Preface of the confession to Œnone in Act I, scene 3, seems equally applicable here: "Elle en parle avec une confusion qui fait bien voir que son crime est plutôt une punition des dieux qu'un mouvement de sa volonté".[34] Still more remarkable is the following situation where Phèdre seeks to expiate her guilt by pleading with Hippolyte to kill her. No doubt her motives are 'sincere', but the inescapable suggestion is that Hippolyte's sword-thrust will in fact give her a sense of erotic consummation. The American poet Robert Lowell clearly felt this hidden undertone when he translated the line:

> Au défaut de ton bras, prête-moi ton épée
>
> (710)

by the following words:

> I want your sword's spasmodic final inch.[35]

The translation is quite unacceptable, since it makes explicit what must be at the most merely a hint of subconscious desire. But Lowell has nevertheless made my point for me. It is further borne out by the way Phèdre is presented on her next appearance, at the start of Act III. She is now fully possessed by her passion and, as a result of her last encounter with Hippolyte, she says:

> [...] l'espoir, malgré moi, s'est glissé dans mon cœur.
> (768)

Following this, there are two critical moments when the problem of the degree of Phèdre's complicity with evil is most acute: in Act III, scenes 3-4, when she accepts Œnone's plan to accuse Hippolyte of assaulting her, and in Act IV, scenes 4-5, where, on learning that "Hippolyte est sensible et ne sent rien pour moi", she stifles her impulse to tell Thésée the truth. In the first case, it is again instructive to see how radically Racine's version differs from Seneca's: in the latter, the initiative for the calumny also comes from the Nurse, but it is Phaedra herself who, when the Nurse is threatened with torture by Theseus, denounces her step-son for having violated her body. In the French version, Phèdre misinterprets the look in Hippolyte's eyes—"Dans ses yeux insolents, je vois ma perte écrite"—and her complicity is prompted by a momentary panic which robs her of all rational control, as Racine emphasises in the Preface: "Phèdre n'y donne les mains que parce qu'elle est dans une agitation d'esprit qui la met hors d'elle-même".

It is true that the following lines spoken by Phèdre in her brief encounter with Thésée are ambiguous (ll. 915-20), and could suggest a deliberate casuistry to fit Œnone's projected calumny, but this is doubtful: we have at least one witness as to the apparent import of Phèdre's words—Hippolyte, who declares:

> Où tendait ce discours qui m'a glacé d'effroi?
> Phèdre toujours en proie à sa fureur extrême

Veut-elle s'accuser et se perdre soi-même?

(988–90)

The impulse to confess the truth is already present in Phèdre at this stage, and it is surely what brings her back to confront her husband in Act IV, scene 4 ("Je cédais au remords dont j'étais tourmentée ... Peut-être à m'accuser j'aurais pu consentir"). Again, however, the impulse is lost in the *agitation d'esprit* which arises from her attack of jealousy, though this too is momentary: as Jean Pommier remarks, all the evidence suggests that Phèdre's decision to die is taken at the end of Act IV, before she has any knowledge of the catastrophe that overtakes Hippolyte—hence his verdict: "*Phèdre* ou la tragédie de l'expiation".[36]

The death of Phèdre is one more instance of Racine's original handling of his source material, notably of his skilful blending of elements taken from Euripides and Seneca. From the Greek, Racine took over the acute conscience and zeal for purity in his heroine— for the Euripidean Phaedra never yields to her guilty passion and her only motive for the posthumous calumny of her step-son is to avenge his unjust smears upon her virtue. From Seneca, he took a figure in whom the sensuality is a constant and overwhelming force, but he stopped short at the more radical abdication to passion which is seen in the Roman Phaedra, even in her death: for when Phaedra falls upon her sword, she is still dreaming of being joined in death with Hippolytus.

* * *

I would therefore agree that, at least on one level, the case of Phèdre can be seen as a striking illustration of Vinaver's interpretation of Racine's conception of the tragic action, and it may well be that it accounts for the highest achievement of the poet's tragic vision. But what does not seem legitimate to me is to give this formula absolute validity as a statement of the tragic pattern either in Racine's theatre or elsewhere. As regards Racine's work, its major drawback is that it fits so few of the plays, because the protagonists who commit a crime and subsequently recognise its morally heinous character are the exceptions. In fact, Phèdre herself is virtually a unique figure, since, as Professor Raymond Picard argues,[37] Racine has combined in her the two types that stand opposed in his previous plays: those like Hermione and Roxane, whose passionate frenzy stands in the way of any sustained self-knowledge, and those like Junie and Monime, who are pure and lucid.

Apart from Phèdre, Vinaver's formula is perhaps applicable only to Oreste in *Andromaque*—Oreste, who loses his reason as he perceives the full moral horror of his act of regicide.[38] It could be shown that Pyrrhus has momentary insights into the guilty nature of his love (lines 695-9), just as we have already indicated similar insights in Hermione (lines 1419-29); but both these characters die off-stage without any final moral 'recognition', the one assassinated, the other killing herself in a frenzy of despair, brought on by motives at which we can only guess.

On another level of interpretation, even *Phèdre* is much more than just this pattern of crime and retribution, following self-recognition. The more conventional Aristotelian pattern of Thésée's tragic experience has already been outlined; but it would be equally reasonable to see the whole play in terms of a series of miscalculations that recoil onto the different protagonists. Bénichou does just this when he writes:

> Ce n'est pas par hasard que toute la pièce est agencée comme une suite de pièges où toute volonté est déjouée, où l'action contredit ironiquement l'intention. Œnone perd Phèdre en voulant l'aider, Hippolyte en croyant se justifier devant son père lui fait une confidence qui lui coûtera la vie. Thésée se souille d'un meurtre en voulant purifier sa maison. Les intentions de Phèdre sont sans doute plus ambigues, et la fatalité qui la fait trébucher en dépit d'elle-même est d'abord celle de ses propres désirs. Mais justement Racine semble vouloir effacer ce que son cas a par là de spécial; dans le monde qu'il représente, il semble que ce soit le sort de la volonté humaine d'être tournée en dérision.[39]

If we turn to a play such as *Britannicus* (which I, for one, hold to be among the greatest of tragedies) the Vinaver formula proves even more unhelpful; for here, the strictly ethical factors are apparently quite irrelevant to the tragic action. On the one hand, there is the young hero, Britannicus, whose only 'flaw' (as Racine says in his Preface) is his very innocence—his "franchise" and his "crédulités", which lead him unsuspectingly into the trap set by Néron. On the other hand, there is Agrippine, and lest we neglect her importance, Racine reminds us in his second Preface that "C'est elle que je me suis surtout efforcé de bien exprimer, et ma tragédie n'est pas moins la disgrâce d'Agrippine que la mort de Britannicus. Cette mort fut un coup de foudre pour elle". No one could pretend that Agrippine, who boasts of the ruthlessness of her rise to power, is a "morally average" character in the Aristotelian sense. Her *hamartia* is, in the strictest sense, an "error of judgement" which is a classical example of *hubris*. Having reasserted her authority over Néron in the great scene of Act IV, she fatally misjudges her son's character, boasts of her triumph, and thereby pushes Néron into murdering Britannicus, an act which in turn seals her own downfall. As such her fate is a telling illustration of the mutability of fortune to which even the most powerful are subject through their own miscalculations, and we experience a sense of awe at the presence of doom and retribution on such a scale.

And lastly, what of Néron? No one can deny that he bestrides the play, dramatically speaking, like a colossus, one of the most exciting figures ever portrayed by Racine. Bernard Weinberg, in his *The Art of Jean Racine*, published in 1963, and whose criterion for the 'tragic' comes closest to that of seventeenth-century critics like d'Aubignac, can only conclude that Néron is "an essentially bad man"; failing to qualify for our moral approval, he cannot have our pity and is untragic. This approach seems highly questionable, but no more so than Weinberg's other statement that Néron "moves from an unsatisfactory state ... to a satisfactory state" (p. 127). What then are we to make of the final description of Néron, after his plans have gone wrong and Junie has escaped him?

> Le seul nom de Junie échappe de sa bouche.
> Il marche sans dessein; ses yeux mal assurés

> N'osent lever au ciel leurs regards égarés;
> Et l'on craint [......................
> ....]
> Que sa douleur bientôt n'attente sur ses jours.
>
> (1756–62)

Hardly the picture of a "satisfactory state" in which to leave the ruler of Rome. It suggests, rather, complete moral disintegration.

Are we then to follow Jasinski's lead and see the play as an attempt by Racine to inspire pity for Néron? In his book *Vers le vrai Racine* (1958), Jasinski argued that Néron was not depraved, but merely weak. He is, we are told, a "poignant" character: "Le fond de son cœur est resté pur".[40] To accept this would be to dismiss my own *experience* of the play. It would seem more appropriate to apply to it and its central figure what was said of *Macbeth*, namely that it is "a statement of evil". Seldom was Aristotle's point about the primacy of actions over character more relevant than here, where Racine has constructed a concatenation of moves which slowly and inevitably unleash a hidden monster.

In the sense that heredity—"Des fiers Domitius, l'humeur triste et sauvage"—is a vital element in the monster's nature, Racine can justly claim in his Preface that "[Néron] a toujours été un très méchant homme... un monstre"; but in tragic drama what counts is the existential 'process of becoming' rather than some abstract essence called 'character', and Roland Barthes sounds the proper note when he writes in his book *Sur Racine*:

> *Britannicus* est la représentation d'un acte, non d'un effet. L'accent est mis sur un *faire* véritable. *Néron se fait, Britannicus* est une naissance. Sans doute c'est la naissance d'un monstre, mais ce monstre va revivre et c'est peut-être pour vivre qu'il se fait monstre. (p. 87)

This no doubt helps to account for the complex mixture of responses provoked by the play, for, as the 'Première Préface' testifies, even in Racine's day there were those who accused the poet of having falsified history by making his emperor "trop bon", while others (such as Saint-Évremond) thought the picture altogether "trop cruel". Certainly, as we witness the spectacle of the de-humanisation of Néron, in whom the last vestige of normal human sensibility appears to be extinguished, it is difficult not to share the overwhelming sense of horror and pain expressed by Burrhus as he describes the scene of the murder:

> Son crime seul n'est pas ce qui me désespère;
> Sa jalousie a pu l'armer contre son frère.
> Mais, s'il vous faut, Madame, expliquer ma douleur,
> Néron l'a vu mourir sans changer de couleur.
>
> (1707–10)

Here, there seems no room for any talk of 'pity for Néron'; yet, to quote George Meredith's verses in *Modern Love*:

> The wrong is mixed. In tragic life, God wot,
> No villain need be! Passions spin the plot:
> We are betrayed by what is false within.

—and the fact that we have seen a fatal web of circumstances engulfing the protagonist and making a mockery of human freedom guarantees a kind of compassion that precludes either moralising outrage or the notion of 'villain', both more readily associated with the melodrama or the *drame bourgeois*.[41]

One major conclusion which I would draw from this is that we can go hopelessly wrong by seeking to imprison Racine's concept of the tragic in a narrow formula and, more especially, by building such a formula upon an aesthetic of pity. Eric Bentley, in his admirable book *The Life of the Drama*, makes a comment along these lines which is relevant to my argument:

> As far as the drama is concerned, one cannot ask to have pity excluded altogether: Aristotle was right to give it a legitimate place. Yet pity is unacceptable when it goes on too long. One can stand just so much of it: sentimental people are people who can stand more than that. They need further education. Tears, as Ovid noticed, are voluptuous, and the drama cannot afford too much voluptuousness. People have to stop crying so that the play can continue.
>
> Pity is needed in melodrama, and stays within bounds if it is properly offset by more 'manly' emotions. In Greek tragedy, there is less pity

than the famous phrase of Aristotle might suggest. How little pity goes to the victims in the *Agamemnon*! How marvellous the way Aeschylus manages to present what is in itself a most pitiful situation—that of Prometheus—and then lavish very little pity on him! Even in *Œdipus Rex*, how much stronger the fear, the awe, the sense of doom, than the pity we feel even for a man who puts his eyes out![42]

Is it not this sense of doom which envelops us as the curtain falls at the end of *Britannicus*? And this brings me to a second conclusion, namely that the total effect of the play is not to be limited in terms of our response to any specific characters, but rather to the global movement of the action. When Aristotle speaks of character being subordinate to action, he writes: "Without seeing anything, the fable ought to have been so plotted that, if one hears the bare facts, the chain of circumstances would make one shudder and pity." Appropriately, the terms relating to our emotions are left vague: the "pity" is not necessarily for one character or another; it is a reaction, inseparable from the "shudder", essentially born of an intellectual perception of the structure of events. Indeed, once we let our pity for any one character or isolated situation get out of hand, it will swamp us and our perception, thereby ceasing to contribute to that true tragic recognition which is ultimately the spectator's, *whether or not he shares it with the dramatic protagonists*. Lanson is really making the same point when, in his *Esquisse d'une histoire de la tragédie française*, he uses Aristotle's reference to the statue of Mitys to distinguish between mere pathos and the tragic: the statue falls and kills a bystander, and we have pathos; the bystander is the man who originally killed Mitys: that is the tragic, where events are purged of the alloy of "mean accident", and where emotion is rooted in the vision of some higher meaning. When Aristotle called tragedy "the imitation of an *action*" (*praxis*), he was referring precisely to such a "higher meaning" of which the plot-events were symbolic. Similarly, Racine seems to use the term "sujet" in the same way in the final phrase of the Second Preface to *Andromaque*. It is there that he quotes a Greek scholiast to the effect that we should seek to understand the underlying reason for the changes which poets make in their source material: "Il faut s'attacher à considérer l'excellent usage qu'ils ont fait de ces changements et la manière ingénieuse dont ils ont su accommoder la fable à leur sujet".[43]

For ultimately, as has already been suggested in this essay, all talk of the nature of the tragic *character* is really only a function of this search for a "higher meaning" in life. If the stress is laid on the "pleasant vices" of men, then we are led to the view that "the gods are just" and to what has been called "retributive tragedy".[44] If the stress shifts to the fact that there is no adequate equation to be found between men's moral being and their fate—to the fact that fools, knaves, and innocents all go the same way to their appointed doom—then we are more likely to conclude that "as flies to wanton boys are we to the Gods", a view closely related to the medieval mutability-ethic which Sir Philip Sidney echoed when he wrote of tragedy teaching "the uncertainty of this world". Critics have argued for both in the work of Shakespeare, more often affirming that they are not mutually exclusive, but exist simultaneously, "translucent and super-imposed", so that in seeing one we see the other.[45] The foregoing remarks on some of Racine's plays suggest that we can claim the same paradoxical ambiguity as shaping their meaning. Moreover, another variant of the tragic pattern found in Shakespeare—that of "sacrificial tragedy", in which the concept of atonement is emphasised—might equally be invoked to account for the complexity of meaning in *Phèdre*. Just as the death of the "star-crossed" lovers, Romeo and Juliet, may be interpreted as the process whereby Verona is "cleansed of senseless rage",[46] so the innocent Hippolyte's destruction seems to exhaust the malevolent forces which have created such a trail of havoc. Not merely are Thésée and Aricie reconciled, thus ending the long feud that has divided their lines, but also Phèdre herself is thereby brought to exorcise, in her self-sacrifice, the disorder which has cursed her and her family:

> Et la mort, à mes yeux dérobant la clarté,
> Rend au jour, qu'ils souillaient, toute sa pureté.
>
> (1643–4)

This ending of Racine's greatest tragedy thus adds perhaps another dimension to our concept of the author's tragic vision, but it is hardly typical; and, of the three varieties of tragic 'meaning' listed above, it is probably the second, with its emphasis upon the frail "uncertainty of this world" and of all human values, that dominates our response. Without question, Racine and Shakespeare excel in the depiction of titanic passions; their protagonists illustrate above all the line of Sophocles' chorus in the *Antigone*: "For mortals to live greatly, is greatly to suffer", and their greatness comes through to us in the greatness of their passion. But both writers at the same time force us unceasingly to question the real quality of such greatness. A. P. Rossiter draws attention, in this respect, to the way Shakespeare insists on the pettier and less dignified aspects of his heroes and heroines—Hamlet mad "in his shirt"; Ophelia mad and bawdy; Cleopatra mocking Antony till he looks ridiculous; Macbeth glimpsed as in "a giant's robe upon a dwarfish thief"—and concludes:

> The final alarmingness is not loss of life (with no promise of any afterlife), nor the injustice of excessive or too widespread retribution, but the threat of indignity, of the loss of heroic existence, by the mocking devaluation of those very qualities by which the hero commands our admiration. Here it is that the commonplace about tragedy and comedy conjoining at their limits is demonstrable.[47]

Mr Rossiter rightly sees here a typically English element in Shakespeare, with no Aristotelian or Classical precedent, made possible by the absence of any orthodox principle of 'strict segregation' of the *genres*. Yet, in spite of the principle, it is curious to see how often Racine came close to creating similar effects. One of the most notorious instances is, of course, in *Britannicus*, where Néron shocked the neo-Classical critics by his undignified eavesdropping during the first encounter on the stage of Britannicus and Junie (Act II, scene 6). Thus Voltaire writes: "C'est une puérilité de se cacher derrière une tapisserie pour écouter l'entretien de Britannicus et de Junie." But the very words used by Voltaire here recall what G. Wilson Knight wrote of *Lear* in an essay that argues the effectiveness of introducing certain comic elements to heighten the tragic vision, namely that the whole play's basis is the theme of "greatness linked to puerility".[48]

A much more sustained and refined illustration of the same process is in *Andromaque*, where the ironic structure of the play is constantly exploited by Racine to demolish the heroic façade adopted by his characters. For example, when Pyrrhus and Oreste debate the fate of Astyanax in Act I, scene 2, their arguments might seem at first to be based on objective political considerations, and Pyrrhus's defence of the child on humanitarian grounds has a noble ring. But the total reversal of attitudes in the two men in Act II, after Andromaque has resisted Pyrrhus's blackmailing threats, reveals fully the truth of Andromaque's own ironic analysis of her captor's motives:

> Voulez-vous qu'un dessein si beau, si généreux,
> Passe pour le transport d'un esprit amoureux?
>
> (299–300)

Paul Bénichou is not alone in sensing the 'comic' element in the ironic situations of *Andromaque*. Writing of the false use to which Racinian characters put their reason and which leads us to see in them almost a caricature of heroism, he quotes in particular the situation in Act II, scene 2, where Hermione invokes her *gloire* and her *devoir* as pretexts for not leaving Epirus, in spite of her humiliating rejection by Pyrrhus:

> ... Songez quelle honte pour nous
> Si d'une Phrygienne il devenait l'époux!
>
> (571–2)

And Bénichou comments: "L'inconscience touche ici au comique, par le contraste des motifs invoqués et des mobiles réels".[49]

We are far removed here from that limiting concept of 'tragic pity', and at the centre of our attention is the fact that the very *gloire*, or dignity, which ranked so high in the values of this aristocratic civilisation of the French seventeenth century, is seen in all its precariousness. It therefore seems appropriate to apply, once more, to the Racinian theatre what Rossiter wrote of Shakespearian tragedy:

> The full tragic qualm, the image of the terrifying uncertainty of human fate, could *only* be rendered through the illusions of the theatre by the hint that all the heroic gestures, all human distinction and greatness, might be played by strutting, fretting humans against a vast cosmic background which made them small, "full of sound and fury,/ Signifying nothing." [50]

NOTES

1 *All's Well that Ends Well*, Act II, scene 3.

2 "The tragic qualm is perhaps nothing more or less than a sudden and appalling recognition of our desperate plight in a universe apparently indiscriminate of good and evil, as of happiness and misery," *Romance and Tragedy*, 1922 (1961).

3 *Cf.* Thésée in *Phèdre*:

> L'éclat de mon nom augmente mon supplice.
> Moins connu des mortels, je me cacherais mieux.
>
> (1610–11)

4 For instance, I think that a good case could be made for the argument that the 'tragic' in *Cinna* has nothing to do with whether or not the *dénouement* is happy (hence Corneille's use of the term: *tragédie heureuse*). Far more significant is the point that, through the protagonists, we become aware of the fact that ultimately man is alone and must shoulder complete responsibility for his actions in a universe which (to quote P. H. Frye again) is "apparently indiscriminate of good and evil, as of happiness and misery". This is certainly the recognition which implicitly comes to Auguste and which is the springboard for his final act of will: it is only when his reliance upon a providential order is shattered by the revelation that Maxime has also betrayed him (thus undermining the belief expressed in lines 1663–5:

> Mais enfin le Ciel m'aime, et ses bienfaits nouveaux
> Ont enlevé Maxime à la fureur des eaux.
> Approche, seul ami que j'éprouve fidèle.)

that Auguste assumes full moral responsibility for himself and, with it, finds the serenity that issues in his act of clemency.

This does not rule out a providential view (it is explicitly voiced by both Émilie and Livie), but it underlines that man must, through free will, cooperate with grace and prove himself worthy of it. *Cf. Polyeucte*, lines 29 sq.:

> [Dieu] est toujours tout juste et tout bon; mais sa grâce
> Ne descend pas toujours avec même efficace;
> Après certains moments que perdent nos longueurs
> Elle quitte ces traits qui pénètrent les cœurs.

5 *Morales du Grand Siècle*, Paris, 1948, p. 143.
6 *Les Caractères*, Ch. VIII: "De la Cour."

7 Georges Le Bidois: *La Vie dans la Tragédie de Racine*, Paris, 1929, pp. 78–9.
8 *Pensées*, ed. Lafuma, Paris, 1952, n°. 99.
9 A comparison of Sophocles' *Trachiniæ* and Euripides' *Heracles*, both dealing with the death of Hercules, suggests the same conclusions. Sophocles' play ends with an ambiguity; though we are told that by human standards the catastrophe *seems* "shameful for the Gods", nevertheless there *is* a hidden Justice at work: "There is nothing here which is not Zeus".
No such ambiguity is possible in Euripides' version: the villain of the piece is the goddess Hera, who maliciously goads Hercules to the crime which ultimately ruins him.
10 *Aspects de Racine*, 1954, p. 191.
11 *Bulletin du XVIIe Siècle*, 1953, quoted by R. C. Knight in "Les Dieux païens dans la tragédie française", *Revue d'Histoire littéraire de la France*, 1964, pp. 414 sq. M. Dubu writes of Racine's retirement from the theatre as "la conséquence de la clairvoyance et de l'inquiétude d'un artiste devant l'incompatibilité de deux domaines métaphysiques".
One of the earliest critics to emphasise the aesthetic purpose behind the presentation of Phèdre as victim of the gods was the Abbé Du Bos in his *Réflexions critiques sur la Poésie et sur la Peinture*, of 1719: "Phèdre ne commet pas volontairement les crimes dont elle est punie: c'est un pouvoir divin auquel une mortelle ne saurait résister dans le système du paganisme, qui la force d'être incestueuse et perfide... La haine en tombe sur Vénus. Phèdre, plus malheureuse qu'elle ne devait l'être, est un véritable personnage de tragédie".
12 "Sur Phèdre femme", *Variété V*, Gallimard, Paris, 1945, pp. 78–79.
13 *Aristotle's Poetics*, London, 1956, p. 71.
14 Epigraph to his book: *Psychology*, New York, 1915.
15 *Œuvres de Racine*, ed. Grands Écrivains, 1885, I, p. 268.
16 Quoted by Pommier, *op. cit.*, p. 184.
17 This anxiety is what Corneille, in his *Discours de la Tragédie* of 1660, calls "un certain mouvement de trépidation intérieure". In the same context, he argues characteristically against the Aristotelian formula of deeds done in ignorance of their real meaning, for he sees this as failing to create a sustained sense of tragic pity—the pity being limited, in his view, to the moment of the recognition of the error. Hence Corneille's preference for situations in which "on agit à visage découvert" and where "on sait à qui on en veut". His approach is based on the view that the spectator essentially identifies with the protagonist (easiest when the main emotion is *admiration*) and sees things through his eyes.
18 *Cf.* the speech of Isabella in *Measure for Measure*:

> But man, proud man,
> Dress'd in a little brief authority,
> Most ignorant of what he's most assur'd,
> His glassy essence, like an angry ape,
> Plays such fantastic tricks before high heaven
> As makes the angels weep.

19 Sophocles: *The Theban Plays*, trans. E. F. Watling, Penguin Classics, 1966, pp. 161–2.
20 *Cf.* H. D. F. Kitto: *Greek Tragedy*, 3rd ed., London, 1961, p. 140 sq.
21 *Op. cit.*, pp. 142–3; 162.
22 *Poetics*, trans. and ed. L. J. Potts, Cambridge, 1953, chapter 8.
23 *Op. cit.*, p. 323 sq.
24 *Remarques sur Œdipe*, Paris, 1663, p. 54.

25 Quoted by François Mauriac, in *La Vie de Jean Racine*, Paris, 1928, p. 136.
26 In *Shakespeare's Tragedies*, ed. L. Lerner, Penguin Books, 1963, pp. 174-9.
27 "Shakespeare's Tragic Villain", in the Lerner anthology, pp. 180-90.
28 See *Principes de la Tragédie*, ed. E. Vinaver, Manchester University Press, 1944, pp. 39-55.
29 Abbé de la Porte: *Anecdotes dramatiques*, Paris, 1775, II, p. 57.
30 *Œuvres*, ed. Grands Écrivains, maxime 102.
31 *Ibid.*, maxime 43.
32 *Cf.* F. J. Tanquerey: "Le Jansénisme et les Tragédies de Racine", in *Revue des Cours et Conférences*, 1936-7, p. 457.
33 *Roman Drama*, trans. S. Lieberman and F. Miller, Bantam Classics, 1964, p. 305.
34 *Cf.* Martin Turnell: *The Classical Moment*, London, 1947, where the author writes of *Phèdre*, Act II, scene 5: "Phèdre's tactics are far from being carefully rehearsed and deliberately calculated. In reality, the confession is torn from her in spite of herself and it is this which gives it its peculiar intensity. The more we study the passage, the more conscious we become that Phèdre is speaking in a trance in which she betrays her innermost feelings" (p. 204). Mr Turnell interprets the reference to the Labyrinth as a Freudian symbol: "The whole passage is an allegory of the sexual act".

The same opinion is expressed by J. D. Hubert: *Essai d'exégèse racinienne*, Paris, 1956, p. 208: "La descente au labyrinthe est d'ailleurs un symbole érotique des plus clairs: le souhait d'enseigner au jeune homme les détours de ce labyrinthe équivaut en somme à lui apprendre les secrets de l'amour".

M. Bénichou (*L'Écrivain et ses Travaux*, Paris, 1967) offers an interpretation similar to my own: Phèdre is "à demi hallucinée", a phrase which recalls Quiller-Couch's description of Macbeth as "proceeding to his crime under some fatal hallucination".

35 *Phaedra*, trans. Robert Lowell, New York, 1961. Lowell borrowed from Swinburne this phrase: "spasmodic final inch".
36 *Op. cit.*, p. 220.
37 *Œuvres complètes de Racine*, Bibl. de la Pléiade, 1952, ed. R. Picard, pp. 737-8.
38 *Cf.* especially lines 1565-82 of *Andromaque*; even here, I think it arguable that what matters is less the sense of self-horror than the realisation of the futility of all he has done, through the ironic reversal—hence his final mockery of the gods for the tricks they play on us (line 1617).
39 *L'Écrivain et ses Travaux*, p. 320.
40 p. 314.
41 See also Jules Brody: "Les Yeux de César: The language of Vision in *Britannicus*", in *Studies in Seventeenth-Century French Literature*, ed. J. J. Demorest, Doubleday Anchor Books, 1966, pp. 185-200. Mr Brody studies the gradual dehumanisation of Néron, culminating in the lines 1711-2:

> Ses yeux indifférents ont déjà la constance
> D'un tyran dans le crime endurci dès l'enfance.

The view of *Macbeth* as "a statement of evil" is taken from L. C. Knight's "How many children had Lady Macbeth?", reprinted in *Explorations*, Peregrine Books, 1964, pp. 13-50. The importance of this essay is that it specifically sets out to argue against those critics like Wayne Booth who have wrongly "sentimentalised Macbeth" and who, by overstressing "conventional sympathy for the hero", have distorted the total pattern of the drama—thereby "ignoring the completeness with which Shakespeare shows Macbeth's final identification with evil". Equally relevant to Racinian studies is De Quincey's fine essay of 1823: "On the knocking on the gate in *Macbeth*", where he parallels my argument about Néron, suggesting that we are meant to feel sympathy *with* (not *for*) Macbeth—"I mean a sympathy of comprehension not a sympathy of pity or approbation". This sympathy will not soften our horror, for "we were to be made to feel that the human nature, i.e. the divine nature of love and mercy was gone, vanished, extinct; and that the fiendish nature had taken its place... The retiring of the human heart was to be expressed and made sensible. Another world has stept in; and the murderers are taken out of the region of human things... They are transfigured: Lady Macbeth is 'unsexed'; Macbeth has forgot he was born of woman; both are conformed to the image of devils". Such are Racine's *monstres*.

42 *The Life of the Drama*, New York, 1964, p. 284.

43 *Cf.* R. Wellek and A. Warren: *Theory of Literature*, Peregrine Books, 1963, p. 218: "*Sujet* is plot mediated through 'point of view', 'focus of narration' ... The *sujet* is an abstraction from the *fable*; or, better, a sharper focusing of narrative vision".

44 The term "punitive tragedy" is often used, and is applied by Wayne Booth (*loc. cit.*) to *Richard III*, where "we desire the downfall of the protagonist". I am not at all sure that this *is* my response to *Richard III*, and if it were, I would not want to call it a tragic response. I think that Eric Bentley is right in saying that at the heart of the tragic response must lie "an experience of chaos".

45 See Alfred Harbage's introduction to *Shakespeare: The Tragedies: A Collection of Critical Essays*, Prentice-Hall, 1964, p. 9.

46 *Ibid.*, p. 8.

47 "Shakespearian Tragedy", an essay reproduced in: *Tragedy: Modern Essays in Criticism*, ed. L. Michel and R. B. Sewell, Prentice-Hall, 1963, pp. 196–7.

It is worth recalling here one of Racine's marginal annotations to Plato: "Comédie et tragédie est du même genre" (*Œuvres*, ed. Picard, II, p. 896).

48 "*King Lear* and the Comedy of the Grotesque", in the Lerner anthology, pp. 130–46.

49 *Morales du Grand Siècle*, p. 140. See also the same author's *L'Écrivain et ses Travaux*, p. 235: "La tragédie fait normalement sa place à l'ironie ... et il est difficile de dire quand cette ironie cesse d'être terrible pour devenir comique ... On a l'impression quelquefois dans *Andromaque* d'une véritable parodie du théâtre héroïque, qui en maintient les dehors en vue d'un effet, recherché plus ou moins clairement, de dérision... Le contraste de l'apparence et de la vérité a été utilisé ici, non plus pour l'éblouissement du spectateur, mais comme l'arme d'un auteur cruel qui bafoue ses propres personnages".

This last sentence recalls the reactions of Shakespearian critics to the way the Trojan War theme is handled in *Troilus and Cressida*. *Cf*. the essays that accompany the Signet Classic edition of the play (1963), where Boas describes it as offering "the materials for a merciless satire of the high-flown ideals of love", while R. A. Foakes classifies it as a "heroic farce".

50 *Op. cit.*, p. 197. This chapter is an extended version of my article: "Towards a definition of *le tragique racinien*", *Symposium*, 1967.

CHAPTER THREE

MOLIÈRE

Jean-Baptiste Poquelin de Molière (1622–1673)
Painting by Le Brun

Like all other literary *genres* in Europe, comedy was profoundly influenced by the revival of interest in the cultures of ancient Greece and Rome which gave its name to the Renaissance. In sixteenth-century France, when the movement was at its height, humanists such as Du Bellay dismissed with contempt most of the literary tradition of medieval times and called for the re-creation of their national culture by the study and imitation of antiquity, thereby following the example of the Italians, in whose country the Classical revival had begun a century earlier.

As applied to comedy, this method meant the rejection of the indigenous farce—which Du Bellay no doubt included among those "épiceries qui corrompent le goût de notre langue"—and the conscious reproduction of the pattern first exemplified in Athenian 'New Comedy', represented in the work of Menander, and continued in ancient Rome by Plautus and Terence. With its skilfully constructed intrigues and gallery of conventional comic types—avaricious fathers, old men in love, braggart soldiers and cunning servant-slaves—it served as a model for the Italian writers of the Renaissance, such as Ariosto, Bibbiena, Barbieri and Della Porta, and in due course it reached France, where its main disseminator was Pierre de Larivey. Adopting the principle laid down by Du Bellay, Larivey translated a whole series of Italian comedies, and his most famous play, *Les Esprits*, is a typical example of the heredity of the *genre*. It is a free translation of Lorenzino de Medici's *Aridioso*, itself a combination of several antique comedies, including Terence's *Adelphi*, as well as Plautus's *Mostellaria* and *Aulularia*.

The main claim to fame of *Les Esprits* is that it produced the admirable comic character of Séverin, the miser, which supplied Molière with many details for his portrait of Harpagon. Yet such really comic characters are rare, and are the exceptions which prove the rule: namely, that the essential comic effects here are those provided, not by character, but by the surprise impact of continually changing situations, brought about by a web of errors, fortuitous meetings, and so on—all controlled by the arbitrary dictates of the author's exuberant fantasy. As in Shakespeare's *Comedy of Errors*—a title that would fit innumerable plays written in France in the seventeenth century—the intrigue is everything, with its stock *romanesque* elements based on tales of shipwrecks, pirates and kidnappings, ransomed slaves and changelings.[1] While writers such as Rotrou, Tristan and Quinault looked mainly to Italy for their comic material, others, including Scarron, Boisrobert and Thomas Corneille, found similar inspiration in Spanish sources.[2] Here again, it is the complications of the plot, often highly melodramatic and violent in its incidents, that strike the reader most forcibly, although in some cases there is a greater concentration upon character-comedy, particularly where the author is writing specifically for the celebrated *farceur* Jodelet; the latter was one of the star performers at the Théâtre du Marais until Molière returned to Paris in 1658 and engaged his services, notably for *Les Précieuses ridicules*.[3]

The most famous of these plays drawn from the Spanish tradition is undoubtedly Pierre Corneille's *Le Menteur*,[4] but in spite of its title, it would be wrong to see in this an anticipation of Molière's essential preoccupation with character-comedy. Perhaps the earliest and best statement of Molière's originality in this respect came from Corneille's own nephew, Fontenelle:

> Quoique *Le Menteur* soit très agréable et qu'on l'applaudisse encore aujourd'hui sur le théâtre, j'avoue que la comédie n'était point encore arrivée à sa perfection. Ce qui dominait dans les pièces, c'était l'intrigue et les incidents, erreurs de nom, lettres interceptées, aventures nocturnes; et c'est pourquoi on prenait presque tous les sujets chez les Espagnols, qui triomphent sur ces matières... Mais enfin la plus grande beauté de la comédie était inconnue: on ne songeait point aux mœurs et aux caractères, on allait chercher bien loin les sujets de rire dans des événements imaginés avec beaucoup de peine, et on ne s'avisait point

de l'aller prendre dans le cœur humain, qui en fourmille. Molière est le premier qui l'ait été chercher là et celui qui l'a le mieux mis en œuvre. Homme inimitable et à qui la comédie doit autant que la tragédie à M. Corneille.[5]

Molière's early exercises in full-scale literary comedy before he re-established himself in Paris—*L'Étourdi* (1655) and *Le Dépit amoureux* (1656)—were both closely built upon Italian sources,[6] and there is a corresponding emphasis upon the intrigue. But with the first major comedy of the Parisian period—*L'École des Femmes* of 1662, in which the five-act structure and use of alexandrine verse unmistakably underlined its claim to be treated as literary *haute comédie*, as opposed to popular farce—it was precisely the absence of a conventional intrigue which aroused the critics. The real novelty of the play is admirably reflected in the carping comments of one of these critics, figured in Robinet's *Panégyrique de l'École des Femmes* (1664). Accusing Molière of having destroyed "la belle comédie", as exemplified by *Le Menteur* or Thomas Corneille's *Don Bertrand de Cigarral*, he says:

> Je remarquerais avec beaucoup de justice qu'il n'y a presque point du tout d'action, qui est le caractère de la comédie, et qui la discerne d'avec les poèmes de récit, et que Zoïle [Molière] renouvelle la coutume des anciens comédiens, dont les représentations ne consistaient qu'en perspectives, en grimaces et en gestes.[7]

As some modern critics have since indicated, this verdict contained much more "justice" than its author realised. With Molière, the structure of classical comedy is modified in a way that, to a certain extent, parallels the evolution of tragedy, as found in the work of Racine: the action is simplified and subordinated to the presentation of character, its whole purpose being to supply us with a series of *perspectives* of the central figures.[8]

Moreover, the suggestion by Robinet's spokesman that *L'École des Femmes* was, in fact, a return to the methods of the "anciens comédiens" is equally revealing of the heredity of Molière's comic style. The immediate reference is to the old farce tradition of which the most recent indigenous representatives were the celebrated trio of *farceurs* who acted at the Hôtel de Bourgogne in the early decades of the century.[9] But it applies equally to their Italian counterparts of the *commedia dell'arte*, who shared Molière's theatres with him in Paris. Both groups illustrate the tendency of popular comedy to build its material upon the comic personality of the actor, rather than upon more literary effects, such as an elaborate, carefully integrated intrigue. In the case of the Italian players, for instance, the action was outlined in a scenario, which often juxtaposed fairly loosely a series of *tableaux* that enabled stock comic figures, or 'masks', to perform impromptu their own typical comic responses, relying heavily upon mime and slapstick—those "grimaces et gestes" of which Robinet's text speaks.[10]

The fact that Molière was at the same time author and actor, himself taking the central comic rôles of his plays, does much to explain the essentially popular roots of his comic genius and style. No one knew better than he that "les comédies ne sont faites que pour être jouées"; and he adds to this phrase from the Preface to *L'Amour médecin* the warning: "Je ne conseille de lire celle-ci qu'aux personnes qui ont des yeux pour découvrir dans la lecture tout le jeu du théâtre". Molière was, by common consent, a superb mime, and, like the famous leader of the Italian troupe in Paris, Scaramouche—whom he was also frequently accused of aping—he used every kind of facial expression and gesture to evoke character.[11]

It is in the two short plays written by Molière in 1663, during the polemical aftermath of *L'École des Femmes* — *La Critique de l'École des Femmes* and *L'Impromptu de Versailles*—that one finds the fullest expression of his theoretical views on comedy. Here, he sees it as essentially concerned with the satirical exposure of human faults as manifested in the society of his time: the claim of comedy to be treated as a serious art-form, worthy to rank with tragedy, is justified, he says, so long as it deals primarily with the realities of human nature in the context of important issues. In his own words, it is the business of the comic playwright to "entrer comme il faut dans le ridicule des hommes", since "l'affaire de la comédie est de représenter en général tous les défauts des hommes, et principalement des hommes de notre siècle."

When he turns to the nature of *le ridicule*, he gives considerable prominence, as one would expect from an actor-author-producer, to the physical behaviour of his characters: to the actor Brécourt, whose rôle in *L'Impromptu de Versailles* is not meant to be comic, since he represents the ideal "honnête homme de cour", he says: "Vous devez prendre un air posé, un ton de voix naturel, et gesticuler le moins qu'il vous sera possible". But to those whose rôles are satirically conceived, he spells out the appropriate *grimaces et gestes*. The most striking example is that of the *précieuse ridicule* who is told: "Prenez bien garde à vous déhancher comme il faut, et à faire bien des façons", and this image of physical dislocation and obtrusive mannerisms is taken up again more fully in another context where the *précieuse* is pictured as

> [...] la plus grande façonnière du monde; il semble que tout son corps soit démonté et que les mouvements de ses hanches, de ses épaules et de sa tête, n'aillent que par ressorts; elle affecte un ton de voix languissant et niais, fait la moue pour montrer une petite bouche, et roule les yeux pour les faire paraître grands.[12]

What this description evokes is a kind of marionette figure, lacking any real co-ordination of self, moving with the jerkiness of someone who is suffering from alienation; such behaviour indicates a form of dehumanisation, that robs the victim of his dignity; as such, it has traditionally been one of the stock devices of the satirist's aggressive wit. It is, as a modern writer on satire has indicated, akin to the belittling process exploited by the mimic:

> The mimic's power—and it can be a malicious, even deadly, power—comes from his ability to spot the compulsive unconscious gestures in his victim, and then reproduce them. He thus reduces his victim to a lower order of being, by insisting on his repeatability. Mimicry is an invasion of privacy, in that it destroys every man's private conviction that he is unique and inimitable: even though it may be affectionate in its malice, it is another weapon against human pride.[13]

This reference to human pride as the ultimate target of the satirist takes us to the heart of Molière's comic world and to the principle by which he selected his gallery of figures suitable for ridicule. In every case, the physical grotesqueness which his characters share with clowns and other stock farce types is not an end in itself, but rather the symptom of some basic moral disturbances associated with an inflated self-importance. The word Molière himself frequently uses to link the moral and physical aspects of such characters is *affectation*—his *précieuse* is convicted of "une affectation de délicatesse ridicule"—and it is here that one sees how fully his comic vision is grounded in the notion of *bienséance* as expounded by the moralists of the *salons*. Men like La Rochefoucauld and the Chevalier de Méré, both celebrated for their analyses of *honnêteté*, were in full agreement when they characterised this quality as the product of a totally integrated personality, so that an outward grace is the most tangible manifestation of an inner moral balance. Méré illustrates the point by comparing the *art de vivre* with architecture, where symmetry and proportion are sovereign features: "Tout ce qu'on fait et tout ce qu'on dit est une espèce d'architecture: il y faut de la symétrie";[14] and La Rochefoucauld follows this up in his *Réflexions*, developing the notion already formulated in one of the *maximes*, where the condemnation of affectation is reflected in the definition of the *honnête homme* as "celui qui ne se pique de rien":

Il y a un air qui convient à la figure et aux talents de chaque personne: on perd toujours quand on le quitte pour en prendre un autre. Il faut essayer de connaître celui qui nous est naturel, n'en point sortir, et le perfectionner autant qu'il nous est possible.

Ce qui fait que la plupart des petits enfants plaisent, c'est qu'ils sont encore renfermés dans cet air et dans ces manières que la nature leur a donnés, et qu'ils n'en connaissent point d'autres. Ils les changent et les corrompent quand ils sortent de l'enfance: ils croient qu'il faut imiter ce qu'ils voient faire aux autres, et ils ne le peuvent parfaitement imiter; il y a toujours quelque chose de faux et d'incertain dans cette imitation. Ils n'ont rien de fixe dans leurs manières ni dans leurs sentiments; au lieu d'être en effet ce qu'ils veulent paraître, ils cherchent à paraître ce qu'ils ne sont pas. Chacun veut être un autre, et n'être plus ce qu'il est: ils cherchent une contenance hors d'eux-mêmes, et un autre esprit que le leur; ils prennent des tons et des manières au hasard; ils en font l'expérience sur eux, sans considérer que ce qui convient à quelques-uns ne convient pas à tout le monde, qu'il n'y a point de règle générale pour les tons et les manières, et qu'il n'y a point de bonnes copies.[15]

The concept of *bienséance* has rarely been better defined, and it is in terms of this definition that the principle of character comedy in Molière's theatre is set out in the *Lettre sur la comédie de l'Imposteur*, an anonymous pamphlet published in 1667, in defence of *Tartuffe*, its particular interest being that many critics believe it to be inspired by Molière.[16]

The *Lettre* bases its theory on the notion that laughter is primarily provoked by the intellectual perception of what is irrational or false. Our sense of the ridiculous is aroused by subjects which visibly offend against the laws of their own being and thereby take on an element of incongruity—"une espèce de disconvenance." It is our simultaneous double vision of what is proper to a given being and the self-willed breach of that propriety that produces what the philosopher Hobbes picturesquely described as "sudden glory" and what the author of the *Lettre* calls "une joie mêlée de mépris", both writers basing their observation on the view that human pride instinctively enjoys a sense of superiority at the spectacle of error in others. It is thus the business of the comic author to construct situations that demonstrate tangibly the presence of falsity and artifice in his characters, so that the spectator 'sees through' their excessive pretensions and enjoys the deflation of their counterfeited dignity. In the words of the *Lettre*:

> Si le ridicule consiste dans quelque disconvenance, il s'ensuit que tout mensonge, déguisement, fourberie, dissimulation, toute apparence différente du fond, enfin toute contrariété entre actions qui procèdent d'un même principe, est essentiellement ridicule.[17]

An excellent illustration of this definition is contained in *La Critique de l'École des Femmes*, where one of Molière's obviously 'sympathetic' figures is talking about the nature of true *honnêteté* in women:

> L'honnêteté d'une femme n'est pas dans les grimaces. Il sied mal de vouloir être plus sage que celles qui sont sages. L'affectation en cette

> matière est pire qu'en toute autre, et je ne vois rien de si ridicule que cette délicatesse d'honneur qui prend tout en mauvaise part, donne un sens criminel aux plus innocentes paroles, et s'offense de l'ombre des choses. Croyez-moi, celles qui font tant de façons n'en sont pas estimées plus femmes de bien. Au contraire, leur sévérité mystérieuse, et leurs grimaces affectées, irritent la censure de tout le monde contre les actions de leur vie. On est ravi de découvrir ce qu'il peut y avoir à redire...[18]

The phrase used here—"il sied mal de vouloir être plus sage que celles qui sont sages"—serves as a reminder of how far La Rochefoucauld's concept of *bienséance* was in the Montaigne tradition of a moral balance that respects the limitations of the human condition: "La sagesse ne force pas nos conditions naturelles".[19] As such it points directly to the criterion of *le ridicule* in Molière's great comic protagonists, notably those he himself acted—the Sganarelles, Arnolphe, Orgon, Alceste, Harpagon, and Argan, for instance. All of them arrogantly proclaim their own exclusive possession of the key to true *sagesse* and blindly reject the warnings of their fellow-men concerning the inherent limitations of humanity. It is this excessive arrogance that leads to their errors and consequent self-inflicted downfall, which the audience greets with the appropriate "joie mêlée de mépris". They take their place in that category of people referred to in *L'Avare*—"des tempéraments rétifs, que la vérité fait cabrer, qui toujours se roidissent contre le droit chemin de la raison".[20]

All of them illustrate the instinctive tendency in the human ego to bolster itself with a fictitious self-esteem and sense of authority in the face of unpalatable evidence of its own inadequacy. They are *imaginaires* who create a false image of their own self so as to conceal their basic insecurity, bearing out the validity of Béralde's argument, in *Le Malade Imaginaire*, when he speaks of those "pures idées dont nous aimons à nous repaître, et de tout temps il s'est glissé parmi les hommes de belles imaginations que nous venons à croire, parce qu'elles nous flattent, et qu'il serait souhaitable qu'elles fussent véritables."[21]

It is this aspect of Molière's comedy which perhaps more than any other reveals his enormous debt to the tradition of the popular farce and its central preoccupation with the *cocu* whose marital misfortunes stem from his own tyrannical behaviour in the home; for, if the theme of *cocuage* looms so large in popular literature, it is largely because marriage and family life constitute the most immediate social group in which a man lives, and which therefore offer the greatest challenge to the egoist. Sganarelle, in *L'École des Maris*, and Arnolphe, in *L'École des Femmes*, are the direct descendants of the butts of innumerable medieval farces and *contes*, whose obsessions with women's 'fickleness' were rooted in their own weakness. For love is a passion that robs a man of self-possession: it demands the sacrifice of the self and leaves the ego exposed; the lover craves affection, but often cannot give it, since it means unbending and making himself emotionally vulnerable. Hence the resort to authoritarianism in the comic lover or husband, who tries to command affection and force subservience upon the object of his passion. The theme of the *cocu imaginaire* is thus, as it were, an archetypal form of the basic human predicament, and it is worth examining in detail the way Molière exploits it in his first full-scale masterpiece, *L'École des Femmes*.

* * *

Perhaps the most striking feature of this play is the total dominance of the rôle of Arnolphe, who appears in 31 of the 32 scenes; as Jacques Schérer remarks in his study of French Classical dramaturgy,[22] there had been nothing comparable in dramatic structure before Molière, and it confirms what has already been said about his tendency to build his action round a particular comic personality in a series of *tableaux* that are often quite loosely juxtaposed. The most notorious instance of this in *L'École des Femmes* is the scene with the Notaire (Act IV, scene 2), who is another *masque* type (a monomaniac like Arnolphe) and whose introduction must be judged on grounds different from the normal neo-Classical conception of dramatic action, where, as Voltaire put it, "every scene should serve to tie and untie the intrigue, every speech should be preparation or obstacle". It was on the same inadequate view of dramatic unity that the critics of 1663 based their condemnation of Chrysalde as a 'protatic' character: certainly, on the most superficial level of plot, the play could do without him, as it could do without the Notaire. (Molière's interest lies elsewhere—in the quirks of human nature, such as the way men become so wrapped in their private, self-centred imaginations that all real communication is impossible.) The clue to the organic connection between Act I, scene 1, and Act IV, scene 2 lies in the similarity of their endings: in both cases, the interlocutors depart, each convinced that the other is raving mad. In this respect, modern writers like Ionesco and Pinter offer nothing that is not already supremely well done in Molière.

The stage-directions in the scene with the Notaire repeatedly characterise Arnolphe as "se croyant seul", and the phrase does duty as a general commentary on all Molière's monomaniacs, in whom an obsessive *idée fixe* insulates them against awareness of the independent existence of others. They might be described as *solipsists* who, having found reality unacceptable, withdraw into a make-believe world where their private fantasies shape the laws. Symbolic of this is the way Arnolphe has created a new identity for himself as M. de la Souche—just as the two girls in *Les Précieuses ridicules* of 1659 rejected their undistinguished names of Cathos and Madelon in favour of the more glamorous names of Aminte and Polixène, drawn from the fashionable heroic romances of the day. On the face of it, Arnolphe and these two *précieuses* are poles apart, representing the extremes of seventeenth-century French society, and thereby illustrating the way Molière has successfully fused *comédie de caractère* and *comédie de mœurs*. The phenomenon known as *préciosité* which flourished in the *salons* was not merely a literary fashion, but was also a manifestation of the Humanist pressures for greater freedom of the individual, so that one of its forms was a vocal feminist movement.[23] It was precisely because the old social order of male supremacy was being so effectively challenged that the predicament of Arnolphe took on a new urgency, with the *précieuses* representing the basic threat to the male ego.

Yet, when one looks closer, it is clear that Arnolphe and the *précieuses ridicules* are fundamentally alike in Molière's eyes: both are essentially haunted by anxieties about the opposite sex and both betray a highly ambiguous sexual behaviour. The girls automatically recoil at the thought of any physical contact with men: "Comment est-ce qu'on peut souffrir la pensée de coucher contre un homme vraiment nu!"—"et j'ai mal au cœur de la seule vision que cela me fait"; yet, as their suitors remark, this prudishness is at odds with their persistent coquetry: "C'est un ambigu de coquette et de précieuse que leur personne".

The same ambiguity is present in Arnolphe, with his mixture of lechery and puritanism. To all appearances, in his initial encounter with Chrysalde as the play opens, Arnolphe is anything but unsure of himself, and, indeed, such is his comic *hubris* that he refers to himself as a mere *spectateur* (l. 44), able to stand aside and laugh at other men's sexual misfortunes, as though he were not part of the picture of human vulnerability. Significantly, Molière depicts him as a satirist, gleefully collecting stories of marital disaster, but not for the last time in Molière's theatre we have here the theme of the 'satirist satirised'; for, as Freud pointed out in his study of *Wit and its Relation to the Unconscious,* men who joke obsessively about sexual capriciousness in others merely reveal their own neurotic complexes. Freud himself would almost certainly have seen in Arnolphe's fear of cuckoldry all the classical symptoms of the male castration complex.

The name of Monsieur de la Souche, leaving aside its obvious comic etymology, is no doubt evocative for Arnolphe of some feudal lord who reigns absolutely over his fief, and to this end he has surrounded himself with puppets devoid of any will of their own: hence his choice of two doltish peasants, Alain and Georgette, to be his servants. And the scenes in which they figure are not merely an opportunity for some excellent slapstick: their function is also to illustrate in counterpoint the main themes of the play. Alain's views on the nature of the husband-wife relationship reflect those of his master—"la femme est en effet le potage de l'homme"—but, more significantly, Molière provides here the first concrete demonstration of the validity of Chrysalde's arguments against the methods which Arnolphe is applying to Agnès: no scheme is safe that relies for its execution upon mindless imbeciles (cf. ll. 107–16).

To ensure that his wife-to-be will present no challenge to his authority, Arnolphe has chosen a girl who apparently starts with the disadvantage of having neither money nor social status that could be used as weapons in the tug-of-war of marriage (cf. ll. 122–4). In this respect he foreshadows Alceste who, in *Le Misanthrope*, struggling with a sense of impotence in the face of Célimène's independence (social and moral), declares:

> Ah! rien n'est comparable à mon amour extrême;
> Et, dans l'ardeur qu'il a de se montrer à tous,
> Il va jusqu'à former des souhaits contre vous.
> Oui, je voudrais qu'aucun ne vous trouvât aimable,
> Que vous fussiez réduite en un sort misérable,
> Que le ciel, en naissant, ne vous eût donné rien;
> Que vous n'eussiez ni rang, ni naissance, ni bien
> Afin que de mon cœur l'éclatant sacrifice
> Vous pût d'un pareil sort réparer l'injustice;
> Et que j'eusse la joie et la gloire en ce jour
> De vous voir tenir tout des mains de mon amour.
>
> (1422–32)

It is a splendid example of the very dubious motives behind the male Galahad fantasy, as the quick-witted Célimène immediately points out. Unlike Alceste, however, Arnolphe at least begins with all the trumps in his own hand and dwells with satisfaction on his Pygmalion-project:

> Ainsi que je voudrai, je tournerai cette âme.
> Comme un morceau de cire entre mes mains elle est,
> Et je lui puis donner la forme qui me plaît.
>
> (809–11)

Provided he gets the docility he requires, he will purr with specious benevolence, as in the scene where he misinterprets Agnès's enthusiasm for marriage as enthusiasm for his own charms:

> Vous voir bien contente est ce que je désire.
>
> (624)

But once the misunderstanding is revealed, the mask of kindliness is quickly dropped and the real face of the bully appears:

> C'est assez.
> Je suis maître, je parle; allez, obéissez.
>
> (641-2)

The special significance of these lines is that they are taken direct by Molière from Corneille's tragedy *Sertorius*, which had been first performed in Paris at the start of 1662, and they indicate the degree to which Molière's comedy draws upon the burlesquing of the heroic style. Arnolphe is for ever dramatising himself: in imagination, he assumes the *persona* of a Cornelian hero such as the Emperor Auguste whose self-mastery has a hypnotic quality that reduces those around him to a state of respectful obedience. Just as M. Jourdain, in *Le Bourgeois Gentilhomme*, has his "visions de noblesse",[24] so Arnolphe has his "visions de grandeur"; but one can say of these comic *imaginaires* what La Bruyère writes of a similar figure, Ménippe, in *Les Caractères*: "Lui seul ignore combien il est au-dessous du sublime et de l'héroïque".

Molière's method is constantly to juxtapose the heroic posture with the crude, unsublime realities of human nature, illustrating the comic 'law' formulated by the philosopher Bergson in his analysis of laughter—namely that "any incident is comic that calls our attention to the physical in a person, when it is the moral side that is concerned."[25] In Bergson's words, Arnolphe is "embarrassed by his body"; and while he presents himself as a "sage philosophe" (l. 1188), he is at the same time the helpless victim of a panic that makes him roll his eyes, groan, grimace and break out in a sweat. It is this physical ludicrousness that must be kept in mind if one is to avoid misjudging the tone of many speeches where the diction is apparently that of serious drama. The neo-Classical critics of the seventeenth century made this very error when they accused Molière of having failed to observe the rule of the separation of the *genres*, and the outstanding instance of this in the play which is always quoted is Arnolphe's speech in Act V, scene 5 (ll. 1586 sq.). Here is how the point was made by one of the contemporary critics:

> Cette *École* est contre toutes les règles du comique: le héros y montrant presque toujours un amour qui va jusqu'à la fureur et le porte à demander à Agnès si elle veut qu'il se tue, ce qui n'est propre que dans la tragédie, à laquelle on réserve les plaintes, les gémissements et les pleurs ... de sorte qu'on ne sait si l'on doit rire ou pleurer dans une pièce où il semble qu'on veuille aussitôt exciter la pitié que le plaisir.[26]

A similar attitude still lingers on in some more modern interpretations, as when Jacques Arnavon writes of the same scene in the following terms:

> Le ton de la comédie est largement dépassé. On est en pleine crise humaine et celle-ci ne gagnerait rien à être soit atténuée par la recherche du comique, soit aggravée par des effets forcés de pathétique... Ce qui compte, c'est le trouble de cette âme ravagée, dévastée, scalpée pour ainsi dire...[27]

The proper corrective to this point of view is supplied by Molière's own reference to the scene in the *Critique*, emphasising the satirical perspective and the deliberately deflating effects of Arnolphe's behaviour "lorsqu'il explique à Agnès la violence de son amour avec ces roulements d'yeux extravagants, ces soupirs ridicules, et ces larmes niaises qui font rire tout le monde". To the charge that he is guilty of "quelque chose de trop comique et de trop outré", Molière replies that if you observe men closely, you will see that even the most balanced of them are given to extraordinarily grotesque aberrations when possessed by passion.[28]

The text of *L'École des Femmes* is scattered with similar situations. Thus, when Arnolphe has first learned of the meeting of Horace and Agnès during his absence, and comes, in Act II, scene 2, to question the servants, his physical antics are obviously so wild that Alain concludes his master must have been bitten by a mad dog. Arnolphe's speech in this context contains plenty of indications how the rôle should be played:

> Ouf! je ne puis parler, tant je suis prévenu;
> Je suffoque, et voudrais me pouvoir mettre nu.
> ....
> ... Je suis en eau: prenons un peu d'haleine.
> Il faut que je m'évente et que je me promène.
>
> (393-4; 403-4)

In the monologue of Act II, scene 4, Arnolphe tries to replace the philosophical mask of *sagesse* before confronting Agnès again to sound her out on her encounter with Horace. The interrogation begins with an attempt at casual small-talk which ill-disguises Arnolphe's fears—and when these fears seem finally to be confirmed, the dialogue once more moves into a more sonorous register reminiscent of tragic rhetoric:

> O fâcheux examen d'un mystère fatal,
> Où l'examinateur souffre seul tout le mal.
>
> (565-6)

This is the mock-heroic at its most effective, where the "mystère fatal" refers to nothing less than the question of whether or not Agnès has lost her virginity; and it is this kind of inflation of language which naturally goes with Arnolphe's persistent tendency to over-dramatise his predicament, picturing himself as some star-crossed victim of fatality—so much so that one critic, J. D. Hubert, sees the play essentially as a *tragédie burlesque*.[29] The value of this perspective is that it illustrates one more aspect of the comic protagonist's habitual refusal of self-knowledge: the more his personal inadequacy becomes apparent in the failure to command the kind of affection he wants, the more he seeks to shift the responsibility by claiming that his defeat is the work of some supernatural agency. Hence, just as Racine's tragic heroes are so often presented as victims of a metaphysical conspiracy—"Tout m'afflige et me nuit, et conspire à me nuire"—so Arnolphe takes refuge in an alibi which enables him to blame "ce bourreau de destin" and "l'astre qui s'obstine à me désespérer".

Molière shows himself here to be an expert in the subterfuges of *mauvaise foi* and it was inevitable that his satire should move to deal in depth with the subject of religious hypocrisy. Arnolphe is thus the first major example of those *faux monnayeurs de la dévotion* denounced in the Preface to *Tartuffe*. The mark of the *faux dévot* is that he shelters behind the authority of a highly puritanical moral code to compensate for his thwarted natural instincts: lacking the personal attraction which would naturally inspire love, he therefore condemns the pleasure-principle as sinful and behaves like the *prude* in *La Critique de l'École des Femmes*:

> Bien qu'elle ait de l'esprit, elle a suivi le mauvais exemple de celles qui, étant sur le retour de l'âge, veulent remplacer de quelque chose ce qu'elles voient qu'elles perdent, et prétendent que les grimaces d'une pruderie scrupuleuse leur tiendront lieu de jeunesse et de beauté.[30]

In such instances, an ethic of self-mortification is at once a means of self-inflation and a weapon for coercing others; thus, when Arnolphe lectures Agnès on the *austères devoirs* of a married woman, and tries to terrify her with tales of the boiling cauldrons of Hell which await the unfaithful spouse, he is clearly *using* religious sanctions to bolster his own tyrannical hold over her and to enforce his basically lecherous designs. Similarly, when Agnès expresses naïve surprise that a mere marriage ceremony automatically makes legitimate those sensual pleasures which, according to Arnolphe, would be sinful outside the marriage bond, Molière is employing one of the stock devices of the satirist, namely the use, as a mouthpiece, "of a child or savage who does not understand the rules of adult and civilised society, and who refuses to see the symbolic values which such a society attaches to apparently trivial objects or actions; thus the absurdity of social institutions is exposed when they are reduced to childish or primitive terms".[31] In *L'École des Femmes*, the very structure of the play underlines the double-dealing of Arnolphe, since, once he finds in Act V that neither bullying nor any other form of coercion can make Agnès submit to his whims, he readily adopts a craven permissiveness that is totally at variance with the rigorous principles he had earlier declared to be binding on all Christian consciences. With the phrase:

> Tout comme tu voudras tu pourras te conduire
>
> (1596)

—thrown out as a last desperate gesture to win the girl's allegiance —we are given the full measure of the play's irony: in the true comic manner we, as spectators, see through the sham moral façades, and the satire deflates both the character and his specious moralising.

Though the incongruities of Arnolphe's behaviour are so glaring, it would be a mistake to conclude that his hypocrisy is fully conscious: Molière, like La Rochefoucauld, knows that men's capacity for self-deception is infinite, and there is every reason to think that, in his twisted way, Arnolphe really believes in his "chaudières bouillantes" and in his ideas of demonic possession, through the "assauts du malin" (l. 721). The notion that the Devil is in league against him, like the belief in the "astre qui s'obstine à me désespérer", is one of those "belles imaginations que nous venons à croire parce qu'elles nous flattent et qu'il serait souhaitable qu'elles fussent véritables".

If women prefer young *blondins* like Horace to superior men like himself, it can only be because of the intervention of some diabolical agency:

> O que les femmes sont du diable bien tentées
> Lorsqu'elles vont choisir ces têtes éventées!
>
> (840–1)

Hence his face-saving conclusion about Agnès's "great betrayal":

> Quoi! pour une innocente un esprit si présent!
> Elle a feint d'être telle à mes yeux, la traîtresse,
> Ou le diable à son âme a soufflé cette adresse.
> ....
> Je vois qu'il a, le traître, empaumé son esprit,
> Qu'à ma suppression il s'est ancré chez elle.
>
> (979–84)

* * *

In *Tartuffe*, Molière will deal in even greater depth with the way *mauvaise foi* affects religious attitudes, but before we examine that play it is well to make a final observation on an aspect of *L'École des Femmes* which also foreshadows the later work, namely the theme of love. In many respects, Arnolphe is just an extended version of the comic protagonist of *L'École des Maris*[32]—but with one major difference. Sganarelle, the jealous guardian and suitor of the earlier play, only discovers at the very last moment that Isabelle is unfaithful to him, and the curtain comes down as he rails with self-righteous indignation at women's fickleness. There is no indication that his feelings for the girl were ever deeply involved, and his last words express a firm resolve to have no more dealings with the female of the species:

> C'est un sexe engendré pour damner tout le monde.
> J'y renonce à jamais, à ce sexe trompeur,
> Et je le donne tout au diable de bon cœur.
>
> (1108–10)

Arnolphe, however, is a far richer and more complex figure, who finally finds himself totally overcome by Agnès's attractions, so that he is quite helpless to resist her. The "Ouf!" with which he departs from the stage is the only appropriate, speechless, reaction for a man who is irrevocably enslaved by his natural instincts. Molière has here incorporated one of the central tenets of the *précieux* world, the sovereignty of love, from which there is no escape either for mortals or—as *Amphitryon* will show—for gods:

> Il le faut avouer, l'amour est un grand maître:
> Ce qu'on ne fut jamais, il nous enseigne à l'être;
> Et souvent de nos mœurs l'absolu changement
> Devient par ses leçons l'ouvrage d'un moment.
> De la nature en nous il force les obstacles,
> Et ses effets soudains ont de l'air des miracles.
> D'un avare à l'instant il fait un libéral,
> Un vaillant d'un poltron, un civil d'un brutal;
> Il rend agile à tout l'âme la plus pesante,
> Et donne de l'esprit à la plus innocente.
>
> (900–9)

These words are spoken in *L'École des Femmes* by Horace, who is commenting on the miraculous change in Agnès, transformed from a mindless puppet into a real person, through the awakening of love. (Anyone who has seen, or heard the recording of, the great Jouvet production of the play will know how effectively the transformation is rendered—Agnès at first behaving and talking like an automaton, in dehumanised, mechanical tones, until love does its work, softening her voice and quickening her whole being with tenderness.)

But the commentary on Agnès is equally applicable to Arnolphe—just as it will prove applicable to Tartuffe and others whose comic *hubris* is to think they can manipulate instinct to suit themselves. Already in this early masterpiece of 1662, therefore, the focal moral idea underlying the comic structure of Molière's work is fully present: it is the great Humanist theme which the Renaissance had taken over from antiquity and which is echoed in the Montaigne-derived phrase of Pascal: "Qui veut faire l'ange, fait la bête".[33] The key to all true *sagesse* lies in the recognition of human limitations and *folie*—with all the range of associations which Erasmus gave the word in his *Praise of Folly*.[34] To attempt to stifle the irrational, instinctive elements in our nature is to deny its most vital component, and any such attempt merely builds up a tension that will eventually explode, thus defeating itself. In this sense, the comic mechanism is admirably summed up in a line of one of Boileau's *Satires*:

> Chassez le naturel: il revient au galop.

In his translation of Plutarch, Amyot gives the following gloss on the great Delphic maxim, "Know Thyself": "Connais toi-même est un avertissement et un recors (=rappel) à l'homme mortel de l'imbécillité et débilité de sa nature". This was to become the *leitmotif* of Amyot's contemporary, Montaigne, whose *Essais* unceasingly call for the realistic acceptance of the fact that

> ...notre être est cimenté de qualités maladives: l'ambition, la jalousie, l'envie, la vengeance, la superstition, le désespoir logent en nous d'une

si naturelle possession que l'image s'en reconnaît aux bêtes... Desquelles qualités qui ôterait les semences en l'homme, détruirait les fondamentales conditions de notre vie.

(III, 1)

In writing the *Essais*, Montaigne had no thought of campaigning against the follies of men, for "les hommes vont ainsi.... Il n'y a remède". (III, 9; III, 13). His design was rather to create within himself a fuller understanding of his place in the natural scheme of things so that he could live "à propos", with the minimum friction and the greatest possible harmony, whence his supreme tolerance. It seems fitting to apply to Montaigne what D. H. Lawrence said of his own enterprise: that his motto was "Art for My Sake", and that "The business of art is to reveal the relation between man and his circumambient universe at the living moment ... the Now".

Is this not also the clue to the vexed question of the moral basis of Molière's comedy? All talk of Molière's *intentions* must be largely hypothetical, and today's exponents of the 'intentional fallacy' would in any case query the value of the artist's theoretical pronouncements. The principal instance of Molière's referring to the corrective value of his work is in the Preface to *Tartuffe*, and it is common now to find this discounted as special pleading, designed to get round the initial ban on the play because of its 'subversive' character. Yet when René Bray concludes that "le comique ne peut comporter ni moralité, ni immoralité",[35] he surely oversimplifies the issue, and, incidentally, overlooks the fact that a similar 'corrective' view is contained in *La Critique*, where the eminently sensible character Uranie says in defence of *L'École des Femmes*: "Je trouve, pour moi, que cette comédie serait plutôt capable de guérir les gens que de les rendre malades." (scene 3)

Everything hangs on what one means by 'correction'. It almost certainly does not mean that Molière, any more than Montaigne, saw his work in any real sense as an agent of social reform; but, like any serious art, its entertainment value is inseparable from its concern to present a valid statement about "the relation between man and his circumambient universe". Being a work cast in the dramatic mould, it objectifies in its various characters the opposing poles of our experience—in Arnolphe, all the 'old Adam' that kicks against the painful limitations with which reality confronts our ego; in Chrysalde, the voice which is for ever reminding us of those limitations and warning us of the folly of fighting them. This explains why virtually all Chrysalde's arguments are traceable back to Montaigne, including Montaigne's declaration that "ne pouvant régler les événements, je me règle moi-même, et m'applique à eux, s'ils ne s'appliquent à moi".[36] The same contrasting tensions will re-appear in *Le Misanthrope* with the juxtaposition of Alceste and Philinte: again, we can recognise in them the two polar tendencies of our own being—provided we are ready and mature enough to respond in the right way. For, as Eric Bentley remarks in *The Life of the Drama*:

> Art is a matter...not of cognition, but of re-cognition: it does not tell you anything you didn't know... It tells you something you 'know' and makes you realise.[37]

It is in the process of realising just how much of ourselves bears the stamp of an Arnolphe or an Alceste that we may come closer to that Delphic wisdom which sees in self-knowledge the beginning of moral serenity, leading to forbearance and moderation. Baudelaire's celebrated line: "Hypocrite lecteur, mon semblable, mon frère" does equal duty as an *avis au lecteur* for every reader-spectator of Molière's theatre.[38]

* * *

If the foregoing analysis is correct, it suggests at least a provisional answer to the controversial question whether Molière's work is essentially an expression of the satiric spirit or of the comic spirit; in other words, what is the real 'quality' of his laughter? Again, everything is a matter of definitions. If one accepts George Meredith's view that the crucial feature of the satiric spirit is that it provokes a laughter full of contempt and indignation—"If you detect the ridicule and your kindliness is chilled by it, you are slipping into the grasp of Satire.... The laughter of satire is a blow in the back or face"[39]—then it is difficult, on the evidence so far adduced, to place Molière in this category. At the same time, it is apparently out of the question to distinguish his comic effects from a carefully controlled moral perspective and to classify them as 'pure comedy' in the sense that Lamb gave the term when he wrote of English Restoration comedy:

> I could never connect those sports of a witty fancy in any shape with any result to be drawn from them to imitation in real life. They are a world of themselves, almost as much as fairy-land... The Fainalls and the Mirabells, the Dorimants and the Lady Touchwoods, in their own sphere, do not offend my moral sense... It is altogether a speculative scene of things which has no reference whatever to the world that is...[40]

Meredith himself perhaps finds the proper key to Molière when he defines the Comic Spirit as "the genius of thoughtful laughter" and when he sees its products as shaped by a critical intelligence that elicits a moral judgement, while never losing the serenity that is grounded in mature humanity:

> To love comedy, you must know the real world, and know men and women well enough not to expect too much of them, though you may still hope for good... You may estimate your capacity for comic perception by being able to detect the ridicule of them you love without loving them the less; and more, by being able to see yourself somewhat ridiculous in dear eyes, and accepting the correction their image of you proposes... The laughter of comedy is impersonal and of unrivalled politeness, nearer a smile—often no more than a smile. It laughs through the mind, for the mind directs it; and it might be called the humour of the mind... And the test of true comedy is that it shall awaken thoughtful laughter.[41]

These, then, are the definitions which it is useful to keep in mind when approaching the study of *Tartuffe*, for no play of Molière focuses more acutely the questions just raised concerning the nature of Molière's comic genius. How far does the play remain "altogether in a speculative scene of things" and how far does it plunge us into the realities of "the world that is"? How far does the author preserve the equilibrium of the Comic Spirit, and how far is he caught up in the drama of the contemporary struggle between the reactionary, repressive forces of the Counter-Reformation and the opposing currents of liberal Humanism?

The question is bedevilled by the historical circumstances surrounding its first performances in the years 1664–9, when public reactions were preconditioned by deep religious passions and prejudices. In a society where a strong puritan element was hostile to any kind of theatre—where the old arguments of Plato's *Republic*, warning against the poetic representation of love, anger, etc., on the grounds that it "watered the growth of the passions", were being repeated by austere Christians like Nicole and Pascal—there was a predisposition to condemn Molière, all the more so when it was learned that his *Tartuffe* was apparently to follow up the themes of *L'École des Femmes*, already denounced as dangerously libertine in its permissive attitudes.

The fact, then, that *Tartuffe* was quickly banned as subversive by the civil and ecclesiastical authorities perhaps tells us more about the climate of seventeenth-century opinion than about the play itself, and those who find it more profitable to dwell on the poetic and comic aspects of the work could point to a quite different, but perhaps equally relevant, feature of the historical context surrounding its creation. It was first acted in May 1664, as part of the royal festivities that lasted for several days in the gardens of the château of Versailles and that were known as *Les Plaisirs de l'Ile enchantée*. The principal *motif* of this entertainment was taken from Ariosto's epic romance of magic and heroic deeds, the *Orlando Furioso*, with the King and courtiers dressing up as Ariosto's characters. The King masqueraded as the heroic knight Roger, and on one of the days, the revellers enacted the episode where the sorceress Alcine keeps the hero a prisoner on her island, and, by magic spells, makes him believe he is in love with her (the Homeric echoes of the *Odyssey* are obvious here). The whole atmosphere was one of enchantment and illusion, with the King in the rôle of the *amoureux imaginaire*.

The significance of this context is, of course, that it reproduces a central feature of Molière's dramatic offering: namely, what M. Schérer calls the "indistinction de la réalité et de l'illusion".[42] Sainte-Beuve had already emphasised this feature in *Tartuffe* when he said that it gives us "la poésie de l'imposture"—and everything in the play hangs upon the success with which Molière conjures up in our imagination a convincing picture of Orgon's total mesmerisation by Tartuffe. It is made clear from the start that the impostor has fooled nobody except Orgon and his mother, Mme Pernelle, and it is arguable that the sceptical attitude of most of the others is of little concern to him. Admittedly he goes through the motions of piety in front of Dorine and Cléante, but in a very offhand manner, for all that ultimately matters to him is that the head of the house should believe in him. Provided Orgon is mesmerised, Tartuffe knows that he holds the whip hand. We have in fact a situation very similar to that already tried out in *Les Précieuses ridicules* of 1659, where Mascarille's performance as a *marquis* was both crude and effective: crude, because it only reproduced the outward trappings of sophistication; effective, because it appealed primarily to the profound vanity of the victims, whose only concern with such sophistication was that it increased their self-importance and chances of social success. This is also the situation in *Tartuffe*, where we are told that the impostor "connaît sa dupe"— so much so that he can boast: "Et je l'ai mis au point de voir tout, sans rien croire" (l. 1526)—and where all the terms used to describe Orgon's state stress the idea of an infatuation which suspends any kind of normal working of the faculties of perception. He is, says Dorine, "un homme hébété / Depuis que de Tartuffe on le voit entêté" (l. 184). Cléante likewise refers to the *charme* (with its implications of a magic spell) which Tartuffe exercises over Orgon, while Elmire speaks of her husband's *aveuglement*, adding:

> C'est être bien coiffé, bien prévenu de lui.
>
> (l. 1315)

This is what George Meredith, in his *Essay on Comedy*, refers to picturesquely as Orgon's "roseate prepossession" with the hypocrite, showing how Molière's "idealistic conception of comedy" provides a livelier view of humanity than any realistic work could achieve:

> How (he writes) shall an audience be assured that an evident and monstrous dupe is actually deceived without being an absolute fool? In *Le Tartuffe*, the note of high comedy strikes when Orgon, on his return home, hears of his idol's excellent appetite. "Le pauvre homme!", he exclaims. He is told that the wife of his bosom has been unwell. "Et Tartuffe?" he asks, impatient to hear him spoken of, his mind suffused with the thought of Tartuffe, crazy with tenderness; and again he croons: "Le pauvre homme!" It is the mother's cry of pitying delight at a nurse's recital of the feats of young animal gluttony of her cherished infant. After this master-stroke of the comic, you not only put faith in Orgon's roseate prepossession, you share it with him by comic sympathy . . .[43]

To explain the dupe's "crazy tenderness", at least one well-known producer of the play has thought it necessary to hint at a homosexual attraction, but this is simply to miss the main point. The most succinct explanation is given by Erich Auerbach in his book, *Mimesis*:

> Orgon's most deeply instinctive and secret craving, which he can indulge precisely by selling himself and his soul to Tartuffe, is the sadism of the family tyrant. What he would never dare to do without piety making it legitimate, for he is as sentimental and uncertain of himself as he is choleric, he can now give himself up to with a clear conscience: *faire enrager le monde est ma plus grande joie*. (Act III, scene 7; cf. also Act IV, scene 3: *je porte en ce contrat de quoi vous faire rire*.) He loves Tartuffe and lets himself be duped by him because Tartuffe makes it possible for him to satisfy his instinctive urge to tyrannise over and torment his family.[44]

In a word, Orgon is of the same family as Arnolphe: religious sanctions serve as an alibi for bullying, though the subterfuges of the ego are such that the duplicity involved remains quite unconscious. Like Arnolphe, Orgon has heroic fantasies, the inauthenticity of which is underlined by the fact that the very language in which they are expressed is full of secondhand echoes of Cornelian prototypes. Arnolphe assumes the mask of the heroic Pompée in *Sertorius*; Alceste will borrow the rhetoric of Corneille's Curiace, in *Horace*; Orgon appropriately seems to look to the Christian martyrs of *Polyeucte* for his gestures and rhetoric, when he proclaims lyrically his debt to Tartuffe:

> Qui suit bien ses leçons goûte une paix profonde
> Et comme du fumier regarde tout le monde.
> Oui, je deviens tout autre avec son entretien,
> Il m'enseigne à n'avoir affection pour rien,
> De toutes amitiés il détache mon âme;
> Et je verrais mourir frère, enfants, mère et femme,
> Que je m'en soucierais autant que de cela.
>
> (273-9)

The heroic fantasies of the character are admirably illustrated again in Act IV, scene 3, where Orgon is listening to the pleas of his daughter Mariane that she be released from the odious match with the hypocrite. Momentarily his purpose falters as the natural sentiments of fatherly affection are stirred by the sight of the girl's distress, but quickly he checks the instinct and re-asserts the mask of the *dévot*. Here is how the *Lettre sur la comédie de l'Imposteur* describes and evaluates the episode as it was played by Molière in 1667:

> D'abord Mariane se jette à ses genoux et le harangue si bien qu'elle le touche. On voit cela dans la mine du pauvre homme; et c'est cela qui est un trait admirable de l'entêtement ordinaire aux bigots, pour montrer comme ils se défont de toutes les inclinations naturelles et raisonnables. Car celui-ci, se sentant attendrir, se ravise tout d'un coup, et se dit à soi-même, croyant faire une chose fort héroïque: "Ferme, ferme, mon cœur, point de faiblesse humaine".[45]

Molière's method with Orgon is the same as with all those characters who profess a self-mastery that can hold in check the rebellious natural instincts. Just as the *maître de philosophie* in *Le Bourgeois Gentilhomme* preaches a lesson in stoic apathy and then immediately loses his temper, so Orgon constantly gives way to childish petulance whenever his will is challenged. The process is well demonstrated in Act II, scene 2, where Orgon first announces to Mariane his intention to marry her to Tartuffe and where he repeatedly flies into a rage each time he is interrupted by the servant Dorine. It is she who, following one such outburst, points up the comic incongruity with the remark:

> Ah! vous êtes dévot, et vous vous emportez?
> (552)

Caught out, Orgon swiftly seeks to re-adjust the mask of *sagesse* and turns back to his daughter with the words:

> ...Comme sage,
> J'ai pesé mûrement toutes choses...
> (557–8)

Once again, therefore, *Tartuffe* points to the way Molière's comic vision has its roots in the Sceptic tradition handed down by Montaigne, with its emphasis on the necessary imperfections that go to make up human nature. Strong confirmation for this comes from the Preface of 1669, where Molière, arguing for the legitimacy of the theatre against those who proclaim its dangers, writes:

> Je ne vois pas quel grand crime c'est que de s'attendrir à la vue d'une passion honnête; et c'est un haut étage de vertu que cette pleine insensibilité où ils veulent faire monter notre âme. *Je doute qu'une si grande perfection soit dans les forces de la nature humaine...*

Given such a moral standpoint, *insensibilité* is automatically suspect, and the likelihood is that the instincts that are repressed will inevitably find their outlet in some other sublimated form.

Wherever Molière introduces religious attitudes in the characters that are ridiculed—in Arnolphe, in Orgon, in the Sganarelle of *Dom Juan*, for instance—these attitudes are always of the same stamp: they are narrowly dogmatic, puritanical and intolerant, and represent a religion based not on love, but on fear and repressiveness. But the real point, in keeping with the satirical perspective of the author and its Sceptic assumptions, is that in each case the religious attitude is essentially contingent upon the moral character of the one who expounds it (this reflecting the Sceptic idea of the universal relativity of all phenomena): Arnolphe's domestic authoritarianism, his conception of husband-wife relations as based on force and blind obedience to force, is reproduced in his image of the relationship between man and God. The same is true of Orgon, with Tartuffe (as we have suggested) providing exactly the brand of religious rigorism which he knows will appeal to Orgon, and a close examination of *Dom Juan* will show a similar pattern in the portrayal of Sganarelle: while attacking his master's *libertinage*, he secretly admires and hankers after the latter's apparently god-like strength of personality that seems to enable him to defy every moral and religious law. Sganarelle's religion is above all compounded of terror of the supernatural, whether it be a vengeful deity or such products of popular superstition as the dreaded *moine bourru* or the *loup-garou*. It would be true to say that he serves God as he serves Dom Juan, more from fear than from zeal: "La crainte fait en moi l'office du zèle".

The idea that shapes this satire in the matter of religion—the idea that a man makes God in his own image—has been expressed by countless thinkers, such as Goethe: "Wie einer ist, so ist sein Gott"; or, in a more ironic formula, by Voltaire: "Dieu a fait l'homme à son image; l'homme le lui a bien rendu!" But lest this pedigree seem suspicious, it can be shown that the idea can also be traced back to highly respectable Christian traditions, especially to those of a neo-Platonic origin. From among the many pieces of documentary evidence available, one text should be quoted which seems to provide the perfect commentary on characters like Arnolphe and Orgon. It is the work of John Smith, one of Molière's contemporaries and a member of the seventeenth-century school of Cambridge Platonists. Here is one of the relevant passages from his treatise, *The Excellency and Nobleness of True Religion*:

> That which many men . . . call their Religion is indeed nothing else but a fear of demons . . . such an apprehension of God as renders him

grievous to men, and so destroys all free and cheerful converse with him, and begets instead thereof a forc'd and dry devotion, void of inward life and Love. Those Servile spirits, which are not acquainted with God and his Goodness, may be so haunted by the frightful thoughts of a Deity, as to scare and terrifie them into some worship and observance of him. They are apt to look upon him as ... an hard master; and therefore they think something must be done to please him and to mitigate his severity towards them ... and purchase his favour with some cheap services ...

Because they are not acquainted with God ... they are ready to paint him forth to themselves in their own shape: and because they themselves are full of Peevishness and Self-will and are easily entic'd by Flatteries, they are apt to represent the Divinity also to themselves in the same form ...

The spirit of true Religion is of a more free, noble, ingenuous and generous nature ... It [Divine Love] thaws all those frozen affections which a Slavish fear had congealed and lock'd up, and makes the Soul most cheerful, free, and nobly resolved in all its motions after God.[46]

Not only does this passage give us an accurate insight into Molière's comic protagonists—those "Servile spirits, easily entic'd by Flatteries"—but it also points to the positive moral and religious criteria which underlie and justify the satire. True religion is for Smith a living principle of holiness within man, inseparable from love and generosity, and this squares exactly with the words that Molière placed in the mouth of the wise character Cléante in *Tartuffe*, the character that the play's Preface designates as "le véritable homme de bien" placed in deliberate contrast to Orgon. For Cléante, the truly devout practise a religion that is "humaine et traitable"; they avoid censoriousness and instruct only by good example; they avoid intrigues and over-zealousness; they think evil of no man and concentrate solely on leading a good life.

Molière is here in the direct line of Christian Humanism as it was first shaped by Erasmus. He is also immediately in step with his fellow satirist, Boileau, whose *Satire XI* attacks the *faux chrétiens* who have never understood the spirit of the Gospels:

> L'Évangile au chrétien ne dit en aucun lieu:
> « Soit dévot »; elle dit: « Sois doux, simple, équitable. »

In the 1669 Preface, Molière, defending *Tartuffe*'s value as a salutary satire, wrote: "Les plus beaux traits d'une sérieuse morale sont moins puissants, le plus souvent, que ceux de la satire" and it must be admitted that the play itself, as we now have it, confirms this judgement—for there is little doubt that on the few occasions when Cléante does moralise, as in Act I, scene 5, there is a great threat of tedium. Judging by the account of the 1667 version, Cléante was originally a more dramatic figure, using a certain amount of satirical wit to make his point; but part of the price Molière had to pay for getting the ban on the play lifted was a toning down of elements that might have been construed as unduly provocative or which blurred the positive 'message'. As a result, his "véritable homme de bien" can appear something of a bore on the stage. This is always a problem with the *raisonneurs*, and some producers try to get round it by exploiting the comic potential of such rôles, stressing their pomposity (Jouvet, for instance, made Chrysalde gabble his speeches as though he were parroting an *idée fixe*). While this is understandable in a modern context, it probably betrays the original intentions of the author in the extremely delicate social situation of the 1660s.

* * *

If our judgement of the comic tone of *Tartuffe* depended only on the way Orgon is portrayed, there would be few problems, and it would be easy to see the play as the perfect embodiment of Meredith's Comic Spirit. As Antoine Adam says, Orgon is consistently "lunaire et guignolesque", and he has only to show his face on stage for everything else to be forgotten: "Tant de sottise et d'assurance, ce prodigieux et gai entêtement ne laissent plus le temps de penser au drame qui se noue".[47]

But, as this phrase indicates, one novel feature of this play in the development of Molière's work is that there is indeed "un drame qui se noue". We have now moved from the semi-abstract décor of *L'École des Femmes* (with its 'Place de Ville', very much in the farce tradition) into a much more realistic milieu—the interior of a bourgeois household, what M. Adam calls a "décor du drame réaliste de la fin du XIXe siècle"; and with this goes a genuinely dramatic situation which jeopardises the comic atmosphere. The *Lettre sur la comédie de l'Imposteur* makes it quite clear that this was so in Molière's production in 1667, when it refers to the state of affairs in Act V, following the apparent triumph of Tartuffe:

> Permettez-moi de vous faire remarquer que l'esprit de tout cet acte, et son seul effet et but jusqu'ici n'a été que de représenter les affaires de cette pauvre famille dans la dernière désolation par la violence et l'impudence de l'imposteur, jusque-là qu'il paraît que c'est une affaire sans ressources dans les formes, de sorte qu'à moins de quelque dieu qui y mette la main, c'est-à-dire de la machine,...tout est déploré.

The real point, then, is that Tartuffe himself, in the rôle of the villain, is at least potentially a sinister figure who cannot be viewed with the kind of comic detachment that was normally possible with the previous central figures of Molière's theatre. With them, we could remain detached as spectators, because we saw their faults as self-defeating and their air of superiority as illusory. But with Tartuffe, we can never feel entirely at ease. Certainly, on his first entry, we are tempted to treat him as a figure of ridicule because of his ludicrous appearance. Even allowing for a degree of exaggeration in what his enemies say about him, it is obvious enough that he is uncouth, with a heartiness that clashes with the gestures of self-mortification. Dorine's description of him as "gros et gras", "l'oreille rouge et le teint bien fleuri", goes hand in hand with Damis's reference to a *pied-plat*, a term which the seventeenth-century *Dictionnaire de l'Académie* defines as "un paysan, un lourdaud, un campagnard grossier". All of this provides the same elements of incongruity as the satirist Boileau seized on when ridiculing the *directeur de conscience* in his *Satire X*:

> Bon! vers nous à propos je le vois qui s'avance.
> Qu'il paraît bien nourri! Quel vermillon! Quel teint!
> Le printemps dans sa fleur sur son visage est peint.
> Cependant, à l'entendre, il se soutient à peine...
>
> (558–61)

Yet, notwithstanding this surface absurdity, there is a constant hint of something disturbing in Tartuffe, a hint of concealed strength and cunning, so that we are disposed to take seriously the warning given by Dorine when she says: "Son esprit est rusé, / Et peut-être à surprendre il sera malaisé." Hence the feeling of many critics that the character remains highly ambiguous, perhaps even incoherent. M. Adam puts the point well:

> On hésite à définir Tartuffe. Faut-il voir en lui un calculateur profond qui mène son jeu avec une froide lucidité? Est-il au contraire un rustre dont toute la force est d'instinct, une sorte de bête de proie, un gros animal qui finira par tomber lourdement dans le piège? Machiavel ou Raspoutine? Ou bien, Machiavel et Raspoutine, figure mal cohérente où Molière a mêlé des traits incompatibles?[48]

Jules Lemaître had written in a similar vein of the two contradictory aspects of Tartuffe and had concluded that "Jamais acteur n'a réussi à les fondre en un seul personnage".[49]

One solution to this difficulty has already been suggested: Tartuffe's hypocrisy *is* crude, but deliberately so; he can afford to indulge his real appetites precisely because the one person that needs to be duped, Orgon, is completely in his power. Tartuffe seems to know just how far he can go, and, as the *Lettre* of 1667 says, he is "l'âme de toutes la plus concertée"—a fact that will be borne out in the skilful way he handles Orgon at the end of Act III, after being denounced by Damis. There is an undeniable brilliance shown by Tartuffe as he frames his confession of guilt in terms calculated to appeal to Orgon with his predisposition to see in his idol a sublime Christian martyr-penitent, taking upon himself all the sins of humanity (cf. ll. 1074 sq.).

At the same time, it equally remains a fact that in at least two crucial moments of the play, Tartuffe is responsible for his own discomfiture, including the final break with Orgon, and it is here that Molière restores substantially the comic perspective on the impostor—following the pattern already outlined in our study of *L'École des Femmes*, where the eruption of instinct finally throws off balance Arnolphe's self-satisfied act as the manipulator of others.

The two crucial moments are the interviews with Elmire in Acts III and IV, and while theoretically there is something profoundly repugnant about the idea of a *dévot* attempting to seduce his benefactor's wife, the scenes remain essentially comic for the standard reason that in both cases we have the situation of the 'trompeur qui se trompe'. It is not merely that on each occasion we, the spectators, know that there is a hidden witness to the action, unknown to the impostor: Damis in Act III; Orgon himself, under the table, in Act IV. What is much more important is that Tartuffe ceases to be the "calculateur profond qui mène son jeu avec une froide lucidité", and loses his head as his passion for Elmire takes control. That, at all events, is how Molière apparently intended the rôle to be acted, and all the evidence of the 1667 *Lettre* points that way. The first major instance is found in the commentary on Act III, scene 2, where Dorine accosts Tartuffe (or, rather, Panulphe, as he was re-named in 1667) and tells him that Elmire is asking to see him:

> Enfin elle fait son message, et il le reçoit avec une joie qui le décontenance et le jette un peu hors de son rôle: et c'est ici que l'on voit représentée, mieux que nulle part ailleurs, la force de l'amour, et les grands et beaux jeux que cette passion peut faire, par les effets involontaires qu'il produit dans l'âme de toutes la plus concertée.[50]

The terms used here—*décontenancer, jeter hors de son rôle, effets involontaires*—all emphasise the notion of a mask that slips, of a self-control that is ruined by instinct. And the same kind of point is made about the following scene where Tartuffe finally comes face to face with the object of his passion:

> A peine la dame paraît que notre cagot la reçoit avec un empressement qui, bien qu'il ne soit pas fort grand, paraît extraordinaire dans un homme de sa figure...
> Les choses étant dans cet état, et, pendant ce dévotieux entretien, notre cagot s'approchant toujours de la dame, même sans y penser, à ce qu'il semble, à mesure qu'elle s'éloigne; enfin, il lui prend la main, comme par manière de geste, et pour lui faire quelque protestation qui exige d'elle une attention particulière; et, tenant cette main, il la presse

> si fort entre les siennes qu'elle est contrainte de lui dire: « Que vous me serrez fort », à quoi il répond soudain, à propos de ce qu'il disait, se recueillant et s'apercevant de son transport: « C'est par excès de zèle ». Un moment après, il s'oublie de nouveau, et promenant sa main sur le genou de la dame, elle lui dit, confuse de cette liberté, « ce que fait là sa main ? » Il répond, aussi surpris que la première fois, qu'« il trouve son étoffe moelleuse », et pour rendre plus vraisemblable cette défaite, par un artifice fort naturel, il continue de considérer son ajustement... Enfin, enflammé par tous ces petits commencements, par la présence d'une femme bien faite qu'il adore, et qui le traite avec beaucoup de civilité, et par les douceurs attachées à la première découverte d'une passion amoureuse, il lui fait sa déclaration... Il s'étend admirablement là-dessus, et lui fait sentir si bien son humanité et sa faiblesse pour elle qu'il ferait presque pitié, s'il n'était interrompu par Damis...

The same tell-tale pointers to the comic process of self-betrayal run through this passage: *sans y penser*; *se recueillant*; *il s'oublie*; *enflammé*, etc., including the final reminder of the basic "humanité" and "faiblesse" of a nature which had thought to set itself above the common level.

The second interview, in Act IV, scene 5, gives us a Tartuffe who is doubly on his guard, but who will again succumb to the same fatal flaws. What heightens the comic perspective in this encounter is that it enacts another stock comic process: "A trompeur, trompeur et demi", for he is beaten at his own game by an Elmire who adopts an equivocal language akin to his own, exploiting the ambiguities of the *langage précieux*, and reproducing therefore many features of Tartuffe's own verbal irony. His earlier declaration that "Pour être dévot, je n'en suis pas moins homme" (l. 966) is thus paralleled in lines 1411 sq. with what is tantamount to the declaration by Elmire: "Pour être pleine de pudeur, je n'en suis pas moins femme". Here is the 1667 commentary:

> Panulphe témoigne d'abord quelque doute... Enfin, insensiblement ému par la présence d'une belle personne qu'il adore, qui effectivement avait reçu avec beaucoup de modération, de retenue et de bonté, la déclaration de son amour, qui le cajole à présent, et qui le paye de raisons assez plausibles, il commence à s'aveugler, à se rendre, et à croire qu'il se peut faire que c'est tout de bon qu'elle parle, et qu'elle ressent ce qu'elle dit.

Once again, it is a splendid illustration of the characteristic Molière theme of the profound gullibility of men once their vanity is involved, for it is above all then that they become *visionnaires* who, as the *Lettre* says, "jugent des choses plus par les yeux que par la raison", so that "on ne saurait dire combien les paroles peuvent sur les esprits des hommes".[51] In this respect, therefore, Tartuffe is to a large extent brought within the realm of the Comic Spirit, exemplifying the remarks of Ernst Cassirer when he wrote that it was the great glory of the Renaissance to have endowed the comic with a new force. What he says, with Rabelais and Cervantes largely in mind, takes up the essence of Meredith's views on Molière's achievement:

> Yet if the comic thus became the strongest aggressive weapon of modern times, its effect was, on the other hand, to take away the violence and bitterness of that struggle out of which the modern era arose. For the comic spirit contains also an element of balance and reconciliation. It does not entertain feelings of hatred towards the world which its free play is destroying.[52]

This is capped with a reference to Shakespeare's handling of the puritanical Malvolio in *Twelfth Night*, with a phrase that might well be applied to Molière: "Arrogant seriousness, when seen through the spectacle of Shakespeare's humour, becomes mere pomposity."

It is nevertheless the case, as we have indicated above, that Molière apparently felt it insufficient to leave the matter there in *Tartuffe*: the impostor has a last trump card—the *donation*—and Act V does produce a renewal and intensification of the *drame*, where the *dénouement* is impossible without the intervention of the King's justice. It is as though Molière wants to reinforce the urgency of the situation created by the *faux dévots*, to stress that this is not just a laughing-matter in the context of 1664–9. True, there is a last resurgence of the comic—it is Tartuffe himself who has brought down this Justice on himself: "Venant vous accuser, il s'est trahi lui-même", says the Exempt—but the one major reflection voiced by Tartuffe's enemies is that their mistake lay in not taking him seriously enough. They, too, were the dupes of his apparent crudeness (cf. Cléante, in ll. 1703 sq.; and Elmire, in lines 1713-4). Once again, then, this underlines the argument we have advanced about the psychological coherence of the impostor's rôle, where the combination of wiliness and clumsiness is achieved with great subtlety.[53]

* * *

The only other play of Molière's which really poses the same kind of problem as *Tartuffe* is *Dom Juan*, which was first acted in early 1665 with enormous success, but which disappeared abruptly from the repertoire after only fifteen performances, in such a way as to suggest an official ban. It is Ramón Fernandez who, in his *Vie de Molière*, states most satisfactorily the nature of the problem, at the same time indicating the connection with *Tartuffe*:

> Le thème favori de Molière, qui convenait d'ailleurs à l'agencement comique, c'est l'impunité punie: l'homme qui se croit hors d'atteinte et tout puissant et contre lequel se retournent, pour l'écraser, les forces qu'il a déchaînées. Afin que la leçon de la comédie — qui ne fait qu'un avec le mécanisme du comique — puisse jouer, il faut que l'impunité soit l'illusion du personnage ridicule, qui prépare lui-même sa punition sans le savoir... Dans *Tartuffe* et dans *Dom Juan*, ce n'est pas le personnage ridicule qui jouit de l'impunité et la leçon de la comédie n'y peut plus être tirée nécessairement des lois du comique... Le fait que Tartuffe, et surtout Dom Juan, échappent aux moyens de correction dont dispose la comédie signifie seulement ceci, que les spectateurs ne possédaient pas une idée de la vérité et de l'erreur qui leur permissent de dominer tout de suite ces personnages... Ils reconnaissaient ce qu'avait d'inquiétant la toute-puissance et le cynisme de Dom Juan, mais devant cet homme plus intelligent que tous les gens de bien qu'on lui opposait, ils ne savaient plus si c'était eux ou lui qui détenaient la vérité.[54]

It was precisely because, in the view of the *dévots* of 1665, Molière depicted his *grand seigneur, méchant homme* in an uncritical light—stressing his superiority in intelligence over his victims, and reserving his more obvious effects of ridicule for Sganarelle, the self-styled religious apologist—that the play provoked such intense hostility. Even today, a critic as penetrating as Paul Bénichou concedes that Molière's attitude to his 'hero' remains essentially ambiguous:

> Molière, tenté avant tout de reproduire fidèlement un état de choses, ne semble pas avoir beaucoup pensé à prendre position lui-même dans le débat: le prestige qu'il a donné à son héros était conforme au sentiment, secret tout au moins, du public; mais ce prestige est fortement compensé par une adhésion, non moins évidente, à la réprobation qui entourait le personnage... D'où l'impression énigmatique que laisse la pièce à un spectateur qui ne peut ni admirer sans danger le demidieu, ni le réprouver sans regret, ni l'absoudre sans inconséquence.[55]

We shall return to this problem in due course, but first it is necessary to consider the structure of the play, which is episodic in the extreme. Apart from the M. Dimanche episode, all the basic elements of Molière's intrigue already figured in earlier dramatic versions of the legend, and, like his French predecessors, Dorimond and Villiers (both of whose versions were called *Le Festin de Pierre* and had been published in 1659 and 1660 respectively), Molière could very well have given his material the kind of integration that was expected in the literary tradition of the *commedia sostenuta*. Dorimond's *tragi-comédie* is thus primarily built round the story of Dom Juan's flight after he has attempted to seduce a girl and killed her father while making his escape; when Dom Juan is later about to be caught by his pursuers, he meets a pilgrim whom he forces to change clothes with him so as not to be recognised, and the *dénouement* comes when Dom Juan comes face to face with the agent of retribution, which is appropriately the Statue of the wronged girl's father, whom he had murdered.

These few details of Dorimond's version serve to illustrate by contrast two significant aspects of Molière's play: first, he turns his back on purely *romanesque* action, such as the attempted seduction and the killing of the father, both of which incidents are enacted in Dorimond; and secondly, he does not bother with interlinking the different strands of the action: his Commandeur is unconnected with the other figures (that is, he is not Elvire's father), just as the scene with the Pauper (Act III, scene 2) is more or less gratuitously introduced, there being no question of using him as a way for Dom Juan to escape from the pursuers.

To explain this lack of integration by the fact that Molière had to write *Dom Juan* in great haste following the ban on *Tartuffe* in 1664 is really not good enough: there was nothing to stop Molière following the plot-line of the printed sources, and the evidence suggests simply that he was not interested in the *romanesque* story. What mattered was the possibilities it offered for dramatising a series of confrontations to illustrate certain moral attitudes— attitudes which gain an added dimension by always being further contrasted in the figures of the Don and his valet, who, with the exception of the first scene of the play, never appear one without the other. After Sganarelle has sketched a picture of his master to Gusman in Act I, scene 1, all the following scenes constitute a succession of juxtaposed *tableaux*, providing those additional "coups de pinceau" which Sganarelle says are necessary "pour en achever le portrait". They start with the *apologie* of Dom Juan himself in Act I, scene 2 (the term: 'profession de foi' would perhaps be inappropriate), and continue by showing him in various relationships all orchestrating a main theme: the rejection of any kind of disinterested obligations by a man who, like so many other Molière protagonists, makes arrogant claims to a monopoly of truth. Hence, once again, the heroic echoes in his pose, his belief that he belongs to an *élite* to which the laws governing ordinary humanity do not apply ("la constance n'est bonne que pour des ridicules"), and his characteristic comparison of himself to Alexander the Great and other such heroic conquerors:

> J'ai sur ce sujet l'ambition des conquérants, qui volent perpétuellement de victoire en victoire, et ne peuvent se résoudre à borner leurs souhaits. Il n'est rien qui puisse arrêter l'impétuosité de mes désirs.

At the heart of this character is the pursuit of pleasure: "songeons seulement à ce qui peut nous donner du plaisir...", which entails a corresponding refusal to recognise any kind of obligation towards others, whether man or God. The ego is treated as self-sufficing, and its only law is self-interest. In this respect, the Don would claim to be totally logical and consistent, a claim that is reflected in the mathematical formula that he uses: "je crois que deux et deux sont quatre, Sganarelle, et que quatre et quatre sont huit" (Act III, scene 1).

But this notion of 'pleasure' needs amplification, and this is easiest done by considering Dom Juan as a seducer. He clearly does not correspond to the more traditional image of the seducer who aims above all at the physical satisfaction of erotic needs. For our figure, "tout le plaisir est dans le changement", rather than in savouring the delights of love-play. Pleasure, for him, is the business of reducing other egos to his own whims, proving their inferiority, playing with them as the cat plays with the mouse. All the metaphors he uses when describing his love-strategy are of a military character, evoking love as conquest: "*combattre* par des transports ... l'innocente pudeur d'une âme qui a peine à *rendre les armes* ... *forcer pied à pied* toutes les petites résistances qu'elle nous oppose ... *vaincre* les scrupules dont elle se fait un honneur ..."

This desire to reduce others to objects, in a world where his own ego is the one self-sufficient principle, explains his outburst of hostility at the thought of the two young fiancés whom he has seen and whose mutual devotion he interprets as an act of defiance, a *défi* levelled at himself, whence his jealousy and impulse to destroy:

> Je ne pus souffrir d'abord de les voir si bien ensemble; le dépit alluma mes désirs, et je me figurai un *plaisir* extrême à pouvoir troubler leur intelligence et rompre cet attachement, dont la délicatesse de mon cœur se tenait offensée.
>
> (Act I, scene 2)

This gives us the key to the different *tableaux*, in most of which Dom Juan is in the rôle of 'seducer', out to destroy other egos who function according to a code that conflicts with his own cult of uninhibited self-seeking. He is the universal scoffer: scornful of the notion of a son's duties towards his father (an echo here of

Cyrano's *libertin* society in the *États et Empires de la Lune* where it is the parents who have to defer to the children); scornful at the notion that the aristocrat should have to honour his debts to tradesmen like M. Dimanche; equally scornful at any idea of a moral debt to the peasant, Pierrot, who had saved his life after the shipwreck (it is Molière, significantly, who invented this detail, not found in the sources).

The key-terms that recur throughout the play are *obligations* and *engagements*: they form the centre of the debate between Dom Carlos and Dom Alonse in Act III, scene 4, where Dom Carlos's attitude to the man who has saved his life is deliberately contrasted with Dom Juan's earlier attitude to Pierrot: "Je lui ai une obligation dont il faut que je m'acquitte avant toute chose", while Dom Alonse sees here only an "obligation chimérique". And the whole burden of Dom Louis's speech in Act IV, scene 4, is 'Noblesse oblige':

> Non, non, la naissance n'est rien où la vertu n'est pas. Aussi nous n'avons part à la gloire de nos ancêtres qu'autant que nous nous efforçons de leur ressembler; et cet éclat de leurs actions, qu'ils répandent sur nous, nous impose un engagement de leur faire le même honneur...

It should be noticed that this scene is quickly followed by the reappearance of Done Elvire, whose love is now transfigured, and who exemplifies total disinterestedness. She is filled, she says, by a "tendresse toute sainte, un amour détaché de tout, qui n'agit point pour soi, et ne se met en peine que de votre intérêt".

It is this "parfait et pur amour" professed by Elvire which explains why religious faith is the extreme symbol of all that Dom Juan loathes, because, more than anything else, it represents something bigger than the individual self: it stands for the suppression of self in the name of Charity. That accounts for another significant alteration made by Molière to the source material: it is he who introduces the fact that Elvire was in a convent, having taken her vows, when Dom Juan seduced her; her seduction was all the more meaningful for him in that he made her break her *engagements*, thus proving his own superiority to Christ as her 'spouse' (cf. his subsequent remark: "J'ai cru que notre mariage n'était qu'un adultère déguisé", Act I, scene 3).

And, finally, we have in the foregoing remarks the *raison d'être* for the 'scène du Pauvre' in Act III, scene 2. The essential point here is that the *pauvre* is unmistakably a religious hermit—one who has voluntarily withdrawn from the world into the *désert*, embracing poverty as a deliberate way of life, for he speaks of himself as "retiré tout seul dans ce bois depuis plus de dix ans"; this fact alone is enough to provoke Dom Juan's hostility. (Whether or not he is intended to be seen as a mendicant of the Franciscan order— the 1682 list of *dramatis personæ* calls him "Francisque, pauvre"— it is difficult to say).[56] Yet again, therefore, Dom Juan is presented in this episode as trying to humiliate and seduce by bribery another being whose way of life is a challenge to his own anti-values. That is why Dom Juan seizes with triumph upon the apparent 'contradiction' of this religious figure: the fact that, by asking for money, the hermit revealed a self-interested motive behind his ostensibly charitable act of warning the travellers of the presence of robbers in the forest ("Ah! ah! ton avis est intéressé, à ce que je vois.").

Only once in the play does Dom Juan make a concession to any kind of obligation: that is in the scene which immediately follows the encounter with the pauper, where he sees a single man, Dom Carlos, attacked by three others, and rushes to his defence with the words: "La partie est trop inégale, et je ne dois pas souffrir cette lâcheté." The physical courage is undeniable, but it is noteworthy that Dom Juan's first reaction is to deny any inconsistency in his code of behaviour: when Dom Carlos thanks him for his "action si généreuse", he swiftly retorts that "notre propre honneur est intéressé dans de pareilles aventures"; the only obligation is to oneself, which reminds us of what a Corneille character calls "la gloire de répondre à ce que je me dois".

This analysis of the structure of the play thus points to a thematic unity behind the apparently disjointed action, but it still does not suggest any solution to whether or not Molière "[a] pensé à prendre position lui-même dans le débat"; that is, whether he solicits our admiration or our condemnation regarding Dom Juan. If M. Bénichou is right in stressing the final "impression énigmatique que laisse la pièce" in this respect, then the full comic weight of the play falls upon the rôle of Sganarelle, played by the author himself. From the very first scene, the valet is presented to us as a creature of superb comic richness through his relationship to his master: principally because it is Sganarelle's constant ambition to achieve the same kind of superiority which he sees in Dom Juan, while lacking any of the required qualities. The servant, Leporello, in Mozart's *Don Giovanni*, says explicitly what is implicit in Sganarelle's behaviour: "Voglio far il gentiluomo", and the opening lines of Sganarelle's exchanges with Gusman amply illustrate this. As he praises the virtues of snuff in inspiring "des sentiments d'honneur" and making a man into an 'honnête homme', he takes on a swagger and a patronising tone that prepare us for his later, equally suspect, praise of medicine or orthodox religion. "Cet habit me met déjà en considération", says Sganarelle, as he dons the doctor's outfit, thereby underlining that all such postures are assumed solely for their prestige value, for the opportunities they offer for striking expansive, grandiloquent attitudes, exactly in the way Orgon enjoyed the prestige of his rôle as a *dévot*. For this reason, Sganarelle's denunciation of Dom Juan in Act I, scene 1, rings false; while his cowardly instincts make him a natural conformist, scandalised by so much of his master's behaviour, he nevertheless secretly hankers after what he denounces and obviously savours to the full the scandal he arouses in Gusman—a point well made by Antoine Adam:

> Lorsque Sganarelle fait le portrait de son maître, n'imaginons point qu'il parle d'un ton convaincu. Sa tirade a une allure désinvolte et détachée. Ce valet éprouve une sorte de délectation à décrire les vices de son maître. Sa diatribe est violente, mais d'une violence amusée. Ses yeux pétillent, la langue déguste les belles impiétés qu'il rapporte, il éprouve de la fierté à servir un si beau monstre.[57]

Molière's contemporaries seem to have sensed this basic *mauvaise foi* in Sganarelle, and the author of the *Observations sur ... le « Festin de Pierre »* of 1665 denounced him as a thinly-disguised *libertin*—"un valet infâme, fait au badinage de son maître, complice de ses crimes".[58] The comedy lies in this essential contradiction, in the incongruity between his conflicting impulses, and above all in the contrast between his shallow intellect, the crudeness of his instincts (cowardly and gluttonous) and his efforts to take on something of his master's lordly self-assurance and *finesse*. The scene with M. Dimanche is the most pointed illustration of this, while the scene with the pauper unmasks the "faiseur de remontrances" in all his bogusness. Having just argued with the Don in the preceding scene that "il y a quelque chose d'admirable dans l'homme... que tous les savants ne sauraient expliquer" (falling flat on his face in the process!), he still cannot resist competing with Dom Juan in trying to get the hermit to betray his faith. The one clear conclusion to be drawn from that episode is that for Sganarelle there is no problem in choosing between getting a *louis d'or* and committing apostasy: "Va, va, jure un peu, il n'y a pas de mal." Such 'religion' as he does cling to—the notion of divine retribution, and the superstitious fear of the *loup-garou* or the *moine bourru*— is merely another facet of his craven *poltronnerie*. Molière captures the full measure of his cupidity in the cry he utters as Dom Juan is swallowed up by the flames: "Mes gages, mes gages, mes gages."

Clearly, there is much to be said for the verdict of M. Schérer: "Sganarelle fournit l'élément humain jusqu'au burlesque, qui est indispensable pour faire accepter la dureté du héros et de la pièce."[59] But at the same time, it is possible to contend that Molière does ultimately do more than just give a purely detached portrait of his *grand seigneur*. For instance, W. D. Howarth admits, like Fernandez, that "Dom Juan is a strong character, immune to the normal corrective processes of comedy", but sees Molière as resorting to dramatic means of shaping our reactions—arousing our indignation through scenes such as the encounters with Elvire and Dom Louis, or the second interview with Dom Carlos, where "our moral sense enters into play and prevents us from siding with the *fourbe*."[60] He points out that "the final portrait of Dom Juan is an unfavourable one: it is no accident that the scenes which arouse our moral indignation come at the end of the play", so that, when the punishment does come, we can share the satisfaction of which Sganarelle speaks: "Voilà par sa mort un chacun satisfait... tout le monde est content."

While this point of view is valuable, it is not the whole truth, and —as in the portrayal of Tartuffe—there are aspects of Dom Juan which suggest the basic pattern of the 'trompeur trompé', a figure who will finally overreach himself.[61] As we have seen, for this corrupt *seigneur* what counts most is the immediate satisfaction of desire and the uninhibited assertion of his ego: "j'ai une pente naturelle à me laisser aller à tout ce qui m'attire." It is to give free rein to this *humeur* that he blithely dismisses all warnings of danger, whether from natural or supernatural retribution:

> Ah! n'allons point songer au mal qui nous peut arriver, et songeons seulement à ce qui nous peut donner du plaisir.

Jouvet saw the play as "une série d'avertissements providentiels donnés à Dom Juan",[62] and it is a fact that the Don is warned no less than twelve times of the inevitability of divine wrath if he persists in flouting "ce que tous les hommes révèrent"; yet such is his obsession with the idea of gratifying every instinct that he is blinded to the danger that threatens. Some critics have spoken of the "courage" with which he faces the Statue, but it seems more appropriate to designate his attitude as foolhardy obstinacy in denying tangible proofs of the supernatural, dictated solely by that "envie de se faire valoir" which La Rochefoucauld condemned as false pride.

One of the most striking elements in the way Dom Juan is portrayed is the contrast between his assumed self-possession, his claim to be free of the *faiblesses* of the common man, and his virtual slavery to the senses. The constant shift in the action from one episode to another reflects his own inner restlessness, for he is a man possessed, driven on by a series of sudden whims.[63] Thus, no sooner has he seen the young couple happy in each other's company than he is driven to intervene by an ungovernable sense of *dépit*. Similarly, in Act II, as soon as he catches sight of the peasant girl, Charlotte, he is overcome by the urgent desire to seduce her:

> Il ne faut pas que ce cœur m'échappe, et j'y ai déjà jeté des dispositions à ne pas me souffrir longtemps de pousser des soupirs.

The *délicatesse de cœur* on which he normally prides himself and which made him sneer at Elvire's bad taste in dress ("Est-elle folle, de n'avoir pas changé d'habit...?", Act I, scene 3) is quickly forgotten as he kisses the girl's filthy hands; and at the slightest sign of resistance from her fiancé, Pierrot, he becomes vicious, all his strutting self-assurance immediately evaporating.

There is also the series of occasions when Molière enables us to glimpse the falsity of Dom Juan's philosophical self-assurance. Just as hypocrisy is for him merely a means to "faire impunément tout ce que je voudrai", so his atheism is a convenient way round facing any inhibitions of conscience that might interfere with his pursuit of pleasure. There is nothing doctrinaire about his philosophy and it is ludicrous to see in his attitude any coherent statement of materialism, as did Théodore de Banville and others. On the contrary, the evidence suggests that Molière invites us to interpret the denial of the supernatural as one more of those false poses which radically conflict with the innate "limites de la condition mortelle". Dom Juan gladly taunts Sganarelle for his subservience to traditional religious sanctions and takes pleasure in provoking the hopeless muddle which his servant gets into every time he attempts to expound doctrine. And yet, each time this happens, it is invariably Dom Juan who is finally *déconcerté*. Sganarelle always resorts to what is for him the unanswerable argument: "les libertins ne font jamais une bonne fin... une méchante vie amène une méchante mort", and at such moments we get a clear instance of the comic process of providing the spectator with a double vision of the character: Dom Juan can only sustain his apology for uninhibited pleasure-seeking as long as he refuses to face up to the idea of retribution. Once Sganarelle touches on the subject, his master loses all his *sang-froid*; again, the vicious reaction betrays the human weakness behind the mask of indifference:

> Holà! maître sot, vous savez que je vous ai dit que je n'aime pas les faiseurs de remontrances.
> (Act I, scene 2)

The most telling example of all is at the end of Act III, where the Statue first gives a sign of life in response to Dom Juan's provocative invitation to dinner—a gesture which, like so much else in his behaviour, seems largely dictated by the desire to scandalise and terrify the valet, who is ordered to convey the message. As Sganarelle indicates the Statue's reaction, Dom Juan's self-assurance disappears in a flash, and with a curt: "Allons, sortons d'ici", he leads the servant away. As the following Act opens, Sganarelle is still insisting that his master should not try to "démentir ce que nous avons vu des yeux que voilà" and repeating that this is a sure sign that Heaven has produced the miracle as a final warning to the *libertin*. Dom Juan then replies with a hitherto unparalleled ferocity which leaves us in no doubt how fully he is, like Tartuffe, "décontenancé... jeté hors de son rôle":

> Écoute, si tu m'importunes davantage de tes sottes moralités, si tu me dis encore le moindre mot là-dessus, je vais appeler quelqu'un, demander un nerf de bœuf, te faire tenir par trois ou quatre, et te rouer de mille coups. M'entends-tu bien?

The great Shakespearian critic Bradley described the major impression left by tragedy as being that of 'waste': the defeat of the hero is the defeat of something noble and precious, without which mankind will be the poorer. But the typical response in comedy is the celebrated phrase of *George Dandin*: "Vous l'avez voulu!... Vous avez justement ce que vous méritez", which is the substance of Sganarelle's final comment as the flames of retribution engulf Dom Juan: "tout le monde est content".

* * *

Le Misanthrope, first performed in June, 1666, is commonly bracketed with *Tartuffe* and *Dom Juan* as forming a trilogy of Molière's great 'problem-plays', for, like them, it has given rise to continual critical controversy and has often been interpreted as hovering uneasily on the frontier that separates comedy from serious drama. The more overtly farcical and burlesque features of plays such as *L'École des Femmes* are here much less in evidence, confined principally to the short scene that ends Act IV, with the intrusion of the clownish figure of Monsieur Dubois—"plaisamment figuré" —and perhaps the portrayal of the two marquis, Acaste and Clitandre, where the puppet analogy is often marked. Antoine Adam therefore voices the general view when he writes: "Plus que *Tartuffe*..., cette comédie tend vers le drame, offre un visage ambigu, impose au spectateur cette gêne de ne pas savoir exactement s'il doit rire ou s'émouvoir, et la crainte de commettre un contresens."[64]

More than in any other play of Molière, this ambiguity arises from the fact that there is here no clear grouping of 'sympathetic' and 'unsympathetic' characters, with the comic protagonist firmly and obviously placed in the latter category, as was the case in *Tartuffe*. To quote the *Lettre écrite sur la comédie du Misanthrope*, which was published together with the original edition of the play in 1667, and which is generally attributed to Donneau de Visé:

> Le Misanthrope, malgré sa folie, si l'on peut ainsi appeler son humeur, a le caractère d'un honnête homme... Bien qu'il paraisse en quelque façon ridicule, il dit des choses fort justes.[65]

Indeed, many of the things which provoke the misanthrope's indignation are presented to us as objectively reprehensible; so much so, that many a spectator has been tempted to share Alceste's responses and to conclude that Molière was seizing the opportunity to vent his own feelings, at the same time inviting our approval of them. Some have therefore gone to the extreme point of labelling *Le Misanthrope* a piece of autobiographical 'confession', where Alceste's sense of injustice at the duplicity of Célimène is a thinly veiled transposition of Molière's suffering through the infidelity of his actress wife, Armande, and where the sordid machinations of Alceste's rivals—descending at one point to the infamous accusation that he was responsible for publishing a dangerously subversive political tract (the "livre abominable" referred to in l. 1501)—reproduce the unscrupulous tactics of the *cabale* that had mounted the onslaught on *L'École des Femmes* and succeeded in bringing about the ban on *Tartuffe* and *Dom Juan*. Even Antoine Adam, who rejects as "indecent" the idea that Molière should ever have publicly evoked his domestic troubles, is ready to affirm that Alceste is the author's spokesman in attacking such aspects of contemporary usage and taste as the "effusion de politesse" with which Philinte has embraced a stranger in the street, or "la mode des poésies galantes", exemplified by Oronte's sonnet.⁶⁶

Significant evidence in favour of seeing *Le Misanthrope* primarily as a *comédie de mœurs*, in which the satirical indictment of contemporary society is made possible by using the protagonist as spokesman, is contained in the *Lettre* where de Visé speaks of Molière's intention in writing the play:

> Il n'a point voulu faire une comédie pleine d'incidents, mais une pièce seulement où il pût parler contre les mœurs du siècle. C'est ce qui lui a fait prendre pour son héros un misanthrope, et comme misanthrope veut dire ennemi des hommes, on doit demeurer d'accord qu'il ne pouvait choisir un personnage qui vraisemblablement pût mieux parler contre les hommes que leur ennemi.

De Visé goes on to explain the rôle of Célimène as essentially performing the same function, for the "humeur satirique" of this witty *médisante* is equally well chosen to serve the author's purpose:

> L'on doit admirer que, dans une pièce où Molière veut parler contre les mœurs du siècle et n'épargner personne, il nous fait voir une médisante avec un ennemi des hommes. Je vous laisse à penser si ces deux personnes ne peuvent pas naturellement parler contre toute la terre, puisque l'un hait les hommes, et que l'autre se plaît à en dire tout le mal qu'elle en sait.

It is true that de Visé speaks of Alceste as being "en quelque façon ridicule", contrasting him unfavourably with the wise Philinte ("si raisonnable, que tout le monde devrait l'imiter"), but the inescapable suggestion is that Molière nevertheless identifies himself with the substance of Alceste's moral crusade, his determination to "n'épargner personne" coinciding with Alceste's "Et je vais n'épargner personne" (l. 88). For de Visé, Alceste's only real fault, it would seem, lies in the *manner* rather than *matter* of his diatribes:

> Il est vrai qu'il semble trop exiger, mais il faut demander beaucoup pour obtenir quelque chose; et pour obliger les hommes à se corriger un peu de leurs défauts, il est nécessaire de les leur faire paraître bien grands.

Alceste's case is that the society in which he lives is no better than a human jungle, where every sort of corruption reigns:

> Je ne trouve partout que lâche flatterie,
> Qu'injustice, intérêt, trahison, fourberie.
>
> (93–4)

Even Philinte accepts that this verdict is substantially correct; less systematic than his friend—for he is ready to concede that there are exceptions to the general rule (ll. 115–7)—he will nonetheless support Alceste's principal contention:

> Tout marche par cabale et par pur intérêt;
> Ce n'est plus que la ruse aujourd'hui qui l'emporte,
> Et les hommes devraient être faits d'autre sorte.
>
> (1556–8)

It is this analysis which the incidents of the text illustrate and confirm; insincerity and double-dealing are rife: people praise you to your face, but denigrate you once your back is turned; to win your law-suits you need influence with the judges; and to achieve any kind of advancement you must wear a mask and pander to those cliques who control the corridors of power. These aspects of social corruption, focused in the theme of hypocrisy and already closely examined in *Tartuffe* and *Dom Juan* (notably in the great speech by the Don in Act V, scene 2: "L'hypocrisie est un vice à la mode, et tous les vices à la mode passent pour des vertus...") are frequently evoked in such episodes as the one where Arsinoé —whom Michelet called a female counterpart to Tartuffe—tries to buy Alceste's favours with the promise of a post at Court:

> On peut, pour vous servir, remuer des machines,
> Et j'ai des gens en main, que j'emploierai pour vous,
> Qui vous feront à tout un chemin assez doux.
>
> (1078–80)

What is at issue in the play, therefore, is not so much the substance of Alceste's view of the human scene—even in *L'École des Femmes* there was never any suggestion that Arnolphe was wrong when he saw *cocuage* as the normal fate of man in society—but rather the validity of his particular reaction to it. In other words, does Alceste's own record of behaviour sustain his right to sit in judgement on his fellow men and justify his Juvenalian *sæva indignatio*—"ces haines vigoureuses, / Que doit donner le vice aux âmes vertueuses" (ll. 121–2)? And, as a corollary of this question, is the 'sincerity' of plain speaking quite as unambiguously objective a virtue as Alceste would claim?

To frame the question in these terms is, moreover, to place *Le Misanthrope* in the perspective adopted by the Humanists in the sixteenth and seventeenth centuries. Whether in the work of the moralists such as Montaigne and Saint-Évremond, or in that of many authors of aulic treatises dealing with manners at Court, such as Bourdonné's *Le Courtisan désabusé* of 1658, or in fiction, such as *L'Astrée* or *La Princesse de Clèves*, there is a consensus of opinion that human nature is basically flawed and that this is particularly apparent in highly organised society, as is the case at Court, where the vices are concentrated.

The rational solution therefore seemed to many that men with uncompromising moral ideals should shun society and choose to live in *le désert*—whether that be the pastoral life portrayed in *L'Astrée*, or simply the solitude of a country-house as in Mme de

Lafayette's novel. Montaigne puts the point with his customary firmness in his essay *De la Vanité*:

> Qui a ses mœurs établies en règlement au-dessus de son siècle, ou qu'il torde et émousse ses règles, ou, ce que je lui conseille plutôt, qu'il se retire à quartier et ne se mêle point de nous.[67]

Saint-Évremond, in turn, expresses the same argument in his essay of 1668, *Les Sentiments d'un honnête et habile Courtisan*, where he addresses the *vertueux* who demands a rigorous moral idealism:

> Je sais que l'ingratitude et l'avarice sont de très vilaines qualités; mais puisqu'elles sont si communes dans le monde, ou résolvez-vous de les souffrir, ou sauvez-vous dans la solitude, et portez dans une retraite cette vertu qui aura fait haïr votre personne dans une Cour.[68]

There is clearly a side to Alceste's nature which is aware of the wisdom of this counsel: Molière thus shows him repeatedly attempting to withdraw—either literally, into the *désert*, or symbolically, into himself, as is the case when Oronte arrives at the start of Act I, scene 2; or during the *scène des portraits* (Act II, scene 4); or, again, at the end of Act V, scene 1, where he retreats into his "petit coin sombre". It is as though Alceste recognises that withdrawal from involvement with those of whom he disapproves is the logical counterpart to the kind of detachment of the will from material interests which is the normal guarantee of the critic's objective rational judgement. It is precisely because, in practice, Alceste is constantly drawn back into heated involvement with the *fâcheux* who compose society that his motives are suspect and his 'sincerity' questionable.

No one has made this point more clearly than Rousseau. In the *Lettre à M. d'Alembert* of 1758, he argues that the only acceptable moral basis for a misanthrope's denunciation of vice is that he should be radically immune from that self-interest which is the root of vice in others:

> Cette contemplation continuelle des désordres de la société le détache de lui-même pour fixer toute son attention sur le genre humain. Cette

> habitude élève, agrandit ses idées, détruit en lui les inclinations basses qui nourrissent et concentrent l'amour-propre.[69]

The mark of a genuinely idealistic indignation is therefore that it detaches the misanthrope from

> tout chagrin puéril qui n'a nul fondement raisonnable et de tout intérêt personnel trop vif, dont il ne doit nullement être susceptible. Qu'il s'emporte sur tous les désordres dont il n'est que le témoin, ce sont toujours de nouveaux traits au tableau; mais qu'il soit froid sur celui qui s'adresse directement à lui: car, ayant déclaré la guerre aux méchants, il s'attend bien qu'ils la lui feront à leur tour. S'il n'avait pas prévu le mal que lui fera sa franchise, elle serait étourderie et non pas vertu... Il fallait que le misanthrope fût toujours furieux contre les vices publics et toujours tranquille sur les méchancetés personnelles dont il était la victime.[70]

What Molière has done, however, is to undermine right from the start the validity of Alceste's doctrinaire stance by showing it to be the product of a naturally choléric temperament, which feeds always on strictly personal grievances. If Philinte's *complaisance* is attacked in the opening scene, it is because Alceste sees this as implying a slight upon himself—a failure to discriminate between his own intrinsic merit and that of a mere stranger. His declared hatred of his fellow men is the angry reaction of an ego which can only compensate for its wounded pride by proclaiming universal corruption.[71] Rousseau recognises that such a reaction is irrational and comments:

> Il est naturel que cette colère dégénère en emportement et lui fasse dire alors plus qu'il ne pense de sang-froid.

But the real significance of the episode is that the 'sincerity' of plain-speaking about others is already branded as no more than a rationalisation of self-centred passion. The fact that behaviour of this kind is "natural" only strengthens the case for a philosophical distrust of the notion of sincerity: Alceste *is* sincere in the sense that his hatred *is* real at that juncture, but its irrationality is further demonstrated by the fundamental inconsistency which springs from it:

while demanding 'discrimination' for himself ("Je veux qu'on me distingue"), he nevertheless denies it to others, since he is ready to condemn "tous les pauvres mortels, sans nulle exception".

Similarly, it is because of people's *complaisance* towards *his* personal legal adversary—"le franc scélérat avec qui j'ai procès"—that they are pronounced guilty. For Alceste, all issues are ultimately judged in terms of a conflict of interests, and characteristic of this is his reply to Célimène when she explains that she cultivates Clitandre to secure his influence in the matter of her own law-suit:

> Perdez votre procès, madame, avec constance,
> Et ne ménagez point un rival qui m'offense.
>
> (493-4)

If the foregoing view of the opening encounter between Philinte and Alceste is correct, it suggests a different conclusion from that of M. Adam when he spoke of Molière's having used Alceste to express his own scorn for the "effusions de politesse" that characterised seventeenth-century polite society: for what was really at issue was not the wrongs and rights of Philinte's behaviour, but rather the degree to which any moral attitude is purely relative to a given temperament, whether it be the *phlegme* of Philinte or the *bile* of Alceste.

There are similar reasons for disagreeing with M. Adam's view that the 'scène du sonnet', in Act I, scene 2, is intended as a vehicle for Molière's own impatience with the trivialities of *précieux* poetry. Once again, it would seem that it is not the evaluation of the intrinsic merit of the folk-song as against the sonnet that matters, but the demonstration of the subjective nature of taste.

De Visé, in his *Lettre*, was the first to argue that Oronte's sonnet "n'est point méchant selon la manière d'écrire d'aujourd'hui"; it is no better nor worse than innumerable other light-hearted products of *salon* wit, but the real focus of our attention is the fatuous vanity of its author who obviously sees in it a work of genius. When Oronte boasts that "je n'ai demeuré qu'un quart d'heure à le faire", we are inevitably reminded of Mascarille in *Les Précieuses ridicules* and his claim that "les gens de qualité savent tout sans avoir rien appris".

But while Oronte's estimate of his poem is grossly inflated, Alceste's reaction is no less exaggerated. He too treats his relatively simple folk-song as a masterpiece and dwells on it with humourless over-emphasis; and when he proclaims Oronte to be *pendable* for writing such verse (l. 772, recalling his use of the same term to describe Philinte's flattery of a stranger, in lines 28–9), it becomes manifest that his judgement is prompted by very dubious motives. It is significant, of course, that Oronte is a rival of Alceste for Célimène's favours, and there is more than a suggestion that what irritates the misanthrope most of all in the sonnet is the fact that its theme reflects his own frustrations: like the lover in the sonnet, Alceste suffers from his lady's *complaisance*; he, too, is irked by "une attente éternelle [qui] pousse à bout l'ardeur de [son] zèle"; and, finally, the conclusion of the verse closely matches his relationship with Célimène: "On désespère,/ Alors qu'on espère toujours".

Similar factors underlie the passionate intensity that Alceste feels for his folk-song, for it gives expression to what we have already called his 'Galahad fantasy': the desire to possess the beloved, but this desire 'sublimated' by his declared readiness to make heroic sacrifices on her behalf. All this fits perfectly his view of himself as one whose love has never been equalled (l. 524) and whose sole aim is to prove it by an *éclatant sacrifice* (l. 1429).

Once this aspect of Alceste's motivation is made clear, it is possible to see the scene in a new light and to re-assess the nature of his *franchise*. As has often been remarked, Alceste's initial reaction to Oronte is completely at odds with the principles he had so dogmatically stated in the first scene: as part of his more rational instinct to withdraw from entanglement with a *fâcheux*, he makes use of all those polite untruths which Philinte had declared necessary for survival in society, coming out with such phrases as "C'est trop d'honneur que vous me voulez faire" (l. 277), or "J'ai le *défaut*/D'être un peu plus sincère en cela qu'il ne faut" (ll. 299–300). And when he does eventually proffer criticism, it is at first hidden behind the fiction that he is reporting what he had said to some other versifier (ll. 343 sq.)—a device that is in all essentials the same as that used by Arsinoé and Célimène when they criticise each other in Act III, scene 4. The inescapable conclusion is that it is when Alceste is most rational and self-possessed that he disguises his thoughts in the interest of self-protection, and that it is only when his *sang-froid* is destroyed and his bile aroused that he yields to a slanging match which is dressed up in the guise of objective 'sincerity'.

* * *

Many critics of *Le Misanthrope*, while readily granting that Alceste is a figure of comic contradictions in his relationship with society as a whole, have nevertheless found it impossible to accept a comic interpretation of his relationship with Célimène.[72] They admit that Alceste is guilty of inconsistency in loving a woman who so manifestly stands for all that runs counter to his ideals, but they point to the fact that Alceste himself is aware of the inconsistency, and that the consequent self-recognition, with its accompanying sense of shame, is frequently a source of tragic emotion, closely related to the Racinian pattern.

It is true that Alceste has such moments of lucidity concerning the irrationality of his love for Célimène: when first called to account for it by Philinte in Act I, scene 1, he confesses his "faible" and concedes that "la raison n'est pas ce qui règle l'amour" (l. 248). Again, in the first encounter with Célimène, he speaks of his unavailing efforts to master his passion:

> Je ne le cèle pas, je fais tout mon possible
> A rompre de ce cœur l'attachement terrible;
> Mais mes plus grands efforts n'ont rien fait jusqu'ici...
>
> (517–9)

But it is above all in the dramatic climax of Act IV, scene 3, that the echoes of tragic style are the most pronounced: having received tangible evidence of Célimène's duplicity, he nevertheless experiences the complete breakdown of his rational will and acknowledges his radical impotence:

> Ciel! rien de plus cruel peut-il être inventé?
> Et jamais cœur fut-il de la sorte traité?
> Quoi! d'un juste courroux je suis ému contre elle,
> C'est moi qui me viens plaindre, et c'est moi qu'on querelle!
> On pousse ma douleur et mes soupçons à bout,
> On me laisse tout croire, on fait gloire de tout;
> Et cependant mon cœur est encore assez lâche
> Pour ne pouvoir briser la chaîne qui l'attache
> Et pour ne pas s'armer d'un généreux mépris
> Contre l'ingrat objet dont il est épris!
> Ah! que vous savez bien ici contre moi-même,
> Perfide, vous servir de ma faiblesse extrême,
> Et ménager pour vous l'excès prodigieux
> De ce fatal amour né de vos traîtres yeux!
>
> (1371-84)

Here, certainly, is an outstanding example of the *victime pathétique*, and if Alceste is in many respects so sympathetic a character it is because, to quote René Jasinski, "sa grandeur réside surtout dans son humanité, le drame intérieur qui le déchire."[73]

Yet the real mistake of those who dwell on the tragic implications of such moments in the play is that they isolate them from their context in the overall dramatic structure. From the start, Alceste has played the part of an uncompromising critic of others: true to his name (Alceste is derived from the Greek *alkestés*, signifying 'strong man'), he has denied any possibility of mitigating circumstances for human shortcomings and proclaimed himself the sole arbiter of moral truth. It is always in close juxtaposition with such grossly inflated attitudes—with all their doubtful authenticity—that the very infrequent and fleeting moments of self-depreciation have to be judged. For instance, the passage where Alceste speaks of his helpless efforts to "rompre de ce cœur l'attachement terrible" follows hard upon the overbearing censoriousness of his first words of greeting to Célimène, when he threatens to break with her unless she mends her ways:

> Madame, voulez-vous que je vous parle net?
> De vos façons d'agir je suis mal satisfait;

> Contre elles dans mon cœur trop de bile s'assemble,
> Et je sens qu'il faudra que nous rompions ensemble.
> Oui, je vous tromperais de parler autrement:
> Tôt ou tard nous romprons indubitablement,
> Et je vous promettrais mille fois le contraire
> Que je ne serais pas en pouvoir de le faire.
>
> (447-54)

It is only when Célimène calls his bluff, threatening in turn to retract what she has said about favouring him above all other suitors, that his 'strong-man' pose collapses. Significantly, it is precisely the same pattern that is re-enacted in the big scene of Act IV. The culminating admission of his "faiblesse extrême" has to be set against the ostentatious self-complacence with which he announces to Éliante his intention to confound the coquette and sever all connection with her:

> Non, non, Madame, non, l'offense est trop mortelle,
> Il n'est point de retour, et je romps avec elle;
> Rien ne saurait changer le dessein que j'en fais,
> Et je me punirais de l'estimer jamais.
> La voici. Mon courroux redouble à cette approche;
> Je vais de sa noirceur lui faire un vif reproche,
> Pleinement la confondre, et vous porter après
> Un cœur tout dégagé de ses trompeurs attraits.
>
> (1269-76)

In the ensuing scene there are many other factors which prevent the action from ever really escaping from a comic framework—and all of them are a reminder of the kinship of Alceste with Arnolphe. First of all, the reference in lines 1279-80 to Alceste's *soupirs* and *sombres regards* recalls those deflating physical antics of Arnolphe "lorsqu'il explique à Agnès la violence de son amour avec ces roulements d'yeux extravagants, ces soupirs ridicules, et ces larmes niaises qui font rire tout le monde". (Molière himself acted both rôles and De Visé's *Lettre* suggests the continuity of the same *pantomime*: "Cette ingénieuse et admirable comédie commence par le Misanthrope, qui, par son action, fait connaître à tout le monde que c'est lui, avant même d'ouvrir la bouche".)

Secondly, Molière uses here another device which was effective in *L'École des Femmes*: as several editors have indicated, some of the phrases spoken by Alceste are uncannily reminiscent of famous speeches in Corneille's *Le Cid* and *Horace*, giving a certain air of mock-heroic parody to the alexandrines.[74]

Most significant of all, however, is the fact that this scene shows Alceste making the same kind of moral turn-about as characterised the protagonist of *L'École des Femmes*. Just as Arnolphe's authoritarian stance collapsed in the face of Agnès's resistance and led to the reversal implied in the line:

> Tout comme tu voudras tu pourras te conduire

so, too, Alceste ends by jettisoning his own high-flown moral scruples as soon as it suits him. The man who had demanded of others an uncompromising sincerity in all their relationships now pleads with his coquette that, if she cannot bring herself to be entirely faithful to him, she should at least simulate such fidelity:

> Efforcez-vous ici de paraître fidèle
> Et je m'efforcerai, moi, de vous croire telle.
>
> (1389-90)

In other words, Alceste, like those he had previously condemned with such dogmatic arrogance, illustrates the fact that there are times when every man needs to compromise with his own inner weakness and to disguise reality with a veil of insincerity.

It is this above all which demonstrates the inauthenticity of Alceste's whole code of sincerity: the real basis of the demand that others should speak the unvarnished truth of their feelings was the need to have an explicit confirmation of his own superiority, whether as a friend (vis-à-vis Philinte) or as a lover (vis-à-vis Célimène). In spite of his hostility to those whose relationships are determined by self-interest—"On devrait châtier sans pitié/ Ce commerce honteux de semblants d'amitié" (ll. 67-8)—Alceste's love for Célimène presupposes a similar *commerce*: "Je ne l'aimerais pas si je ne croyais l'être" (l. 237). But, like Arnolphe, he always speaks in terms of fashioning Célimène to fit his own requirements and it is she who must sacrifice her own identity by following him into *le désert*—"pour trouver tout en moi".

It is essentially because Célimène senses the threat which male possessiveness presents to her independent identity that she has certain affinities with other *précieuses* in Molière's theatre. The reason why she deliberately cultivates the ambiguities of the language of *préciosité*[75] is that it offers a form of protection from complete assimilation by any one of her admirers. Moreover, these ambiguities explain why critics have been divided as to her real character. Jules Brody describes her as a "chronic liar",[76] while Jacques Guicharnaud goes to the opposite extreme, writing of her total lack of hypocrisy: "Célimène est un personnage sans équivoque... Elle coïncide avec son comportement... elle ignore tout machiavélisme".[77] This judgement is based on the view that she uses the nuances of *précieux* terminology with utmost precision and that she tells only Alceste, quite unambiguously, that he enjoys "le bonheur de savoir que vous êtes aimé" (l. 503). Molière's main concern, according to Guicharnaud, is to show that it is the vanity of her suitors—all of them convinced of their innate superiority to others—which is the source of the confusion, since they all read into her words what their ego wants to believe.

However much one may sympathise with the motives that lie behind Célimène's struggle for independence in a predatory, male-dominated society, it is difficult to accept without reservation Guicharnaud's defence of her authenticity. His interpretation becomes more plausible, however, when he re-phrases it in the following terms: "Sa sincérité consiste à user de mots et de figures de style qui correspondent exactement à ce qu'elle éprouve *au moment où elle le dit*."[78] For this introduces a qualification of radical significance, and which puts the whole question of 'sincerity' back into the relativistic mode which we have seen to operate elsewhere in Molière's work. Sincerity, like all the 'virtues' questioned by La Rochefoucauld in the *Maximes*, ceases to have any absolute status, simply because the human heart is itself a constantly shifting amalgam of hidden interests and instincts: "Rien de si impétueux que ses désirs, rien de si caché que ses desseins, rien de si habile que ses conduites."

Thus, when Guicharnaud says of Célimène that she has "la sincérité de son humeur du moment", it is in the light of La Rochefoucauld's analysis of "le caprice de notre humeur" that such a verdict should be read. Whichever of her suitors she is with, or writing to, at any given moment, that is the one whose favours are most important to her; for, as Alceste reproachfully says to her: "Conserver tout le monde est votre grande étude." (l. 1641). The ambiguity of her feelings springs from within herself, and perhaps the true key to her nature is provided by Éliante when Philinte asks if Célimène really does love Alceste or not:

> C'est un point qu'il n'est pas fort aisé de savoir.
> Comment pouvoir juger s'il est vrai qu'elle l'aime?
> Son cœur de ce qu'il sent n'est pas bien sûr lui-même;
> Il aime quelquefois sans qu'il le sache bien,
> Et croit aimer aussi parfois qu'il n'en est rien.
>
> (1180–4)

It is this aspect of Célimène about which Lionel Gossman has written with considerable perception:

> Célimène has no being of her own. She is a Sphinx-like creature who acquires her reality from her suitors themselves and whose entire being, like theirs, is contained in her appearance for others . . . Like her suitors, she has no autonomous desire or will, only the desire to find herself reflected as desirable in the eyes of others. Only through the sentiments and reactions toward her that she finds in others can she experience her own self. The enigmatic being that all her suitors pursue behind her masks is perfectly elusive, because it does not exist.[79]

Not the least interesting point made here is that, ultimately, Célimène and Alceste both share certain fundamental characteristics—just as it was argued earlier in this chapter that, for all their apparent dissimilarity, there was a common psychological denominator linking Arnolphe and his declared enemies, the *précieuses*. For them both, love is at once a threat to the self and a weapon for the defence of the self, and when Célimène plays off one suitor against another, speaking each time with "la sincérité de son humeur du moment", she is only reproducing the "sincere" reaction of Alceste when, recoiling from Célimène's 'betrayal', he rushes to offer his heart to Éliante:

> Acceptez-le, madame, au lieu de l'infidèle;
> C'est par là que je puis prendre vengeance d'elle,
> Et je la veux punir par les sincères vœux,
> Par le profond amour, les soins respectueux,
> Les devoirs empressés et l'assidu service
> Dont ce cœur va vous faire un ardent sacrifice.
>
> (1253-8)

* * *

In his fable *La Besace*,[80] La Fontaine takes the Aesop story of Jupiter inviting each member of the animal kingdom to voice its grievances about its physical appearance, and promising to grant any demands for improvement. But what happens is that every animal sees itself as a paragon, and spends all its time finding fault with the other species. The fabulist then draws the following moral conclusion:

> Jupin les renvoya s'étant censurés tous,
> Du reste, contents d'eux. Mais parmi les plus fous,
> Notre espèce excella; car tout ce que nous sommes,
> Lynx envers nos pareils et taupes envers nous,
> Nous nous pardonnons tout, et rien aux autres hommes;
> On se voit d'un autre œil qu'on ne voit son prochain.

It is essentially this same vision of men that is dramatised by Molière in *Le Misanthrope*, and it is perfectly summed up by Célimène when she speaks, in line 968, of

> Ce grand aveuglement où chacun est pour soi.

Prisoners of self-love, we each claim a monopoly of truth, but all we really do is rationalise our own strictly limited and constantly changing personal viewpoint:

> Madame, on peut, je crois, louer et blâmer tout,
> Et chacun a raison, suivant l'âge ou le goût.[81]

This explains why so much of modern criticism denies or minimises the significance of the question of 'la morale de Molière' and prefers to emphasise a purely aesthetic contrasting of moral attitudes. Here is how M. Guicharnaud expresses the idea with respect to *Le Misanthrope*:

> Chacun de nous n'a pour critère du Bien et du Mal que son propre désir ou sa propre souffrance. Nous ne pouvons pas, en toute bonne foi, « juger et condamner ». Nous ne pouvons que constater, rire du dilemme, c'est-à-dire écrire des comédies. Tout le reste est présomption ou usurpation... Il ne s'agit pas dans *Le Misanthrope* d'un exposé moral, d'un débat philosophique sur le Bien et le Mal, mais d'un conflit d'attitudes qui sont *toutes* suspectes: l'objectivité elle-même n'est qu'un masque ou une arme de l'amour-propre.[82]

In the preceding pages, while discussing *L'École des Femmes*, I have already outlined my views on this question. For Molière, as for the spectator, the play offers the opportunity to experience dramatically certain basic and incompatible aspects of our nature, for in each of us there is an Alceste and a Philinte—an instinct that kicks against the limitations of life and another instinct that counsels resignation (something akin to the Freudian opposition of the 'pleasure-principle' and the 'reality-principle'). And Ramon Fernandez was almost certainly right when he spoke of the cathartic release which Molière derived through characters such as Sganarelle, Arnolphe or Alceste:

> Si la raison de Molière contredit son tempérament, c'est ce tempérament qui fait la vie de son œuvre, et il semble qu'à la faveur d'une intrigue qui condamnait d'avance la raideur et l'absolu de ce tempérament, l'acteur Molière se déchargeait, se purgeait si l'on veut, mais se satisfaisait tout de même par l'expression outrée de ses tendances profondes.[83]

But while, through art, the author and his public enjoy what Edwin Muir called an "*irresponsible* delight in vigorous events", there is always present in Molière's laughter that ironic element which ultimately deflates the self-centred ego and reconciles us with our true human condition. It is in this respect that his work fits so fully into the philosophical tradition of Scepticism, with its main Renaissance sources in Erasmus and Montaigne, that pervades seventeenth-century French thought. Erasmus's *Praise of Folly* is perhaps the seminal text for it.[84] Based upon the Pauline paradox that the wisdom of the world is nought but foolishness, it argues that real wisdom must take into account and accept the irrationalities of human nature. Hence the real fools are the dogmatists and rigid pontificators deprecated by Philinte and illustrated by those like Alceste. When Pascal wrote that "les choses du monde les plus déraisonnables deviennent les plus raisonnables à cause du dérèglement des hommes"[85] and pleaded for an ironic "pensée de derrière" in our judgement of life, he was essentially expressing the same Sceptic paradox as is contained in the celebrated lines of Philinte reminding Alceste that "A force de sagesse, on peut être blâmable" (ll. 145 sq.).

It is in this sense that one might apply Fernandez's phrase: "La vision comique souligne le désaccord entre la raison et la vie". Reason, here, is an abstraction which seeks to substitute for the dynamic complexities of existence an artificial and dogmatic simplification. But 'life' constantly resists such artificial pressures and triumphantly re-asserts its natural resilience, producing in the process those explosions whereby the natural order is restored to an equilibrium. Bergson compared the process to a jack-in-the-box which is always springing back into position whenever someone tries to force it down, providing a new metaphor for the old idea in Boileau's phrase: "Chassez le naturel: il revient au galop".

The same point is made innumerable times in Molière's work, both theoretically and in dramatic terms. And since the 'wisdom' involved is so much a matter of concrete down-to-earth experience, undistorted by the over-rationalising intellect,[86] it is appropriate that it should be so often voiced by the 'popular' mind—by those dynamically exuberant servant figures of Molière's theatre, of whom Sosie, in *Amphitryon*, is an outstanding example. Sosie may grumble, for instance, at the way there is one law for the rich and another for the poor, one set of rules for the great, and another for the humble members of society like himself. But he philosophically accepts this as one of those irrational facts of life with which we all have, in the long run, to come to terms. Life, he says, is full of apparent inconsistencies: "Cela choque le sens commun", adding however: "Mais cela ne laisse pas d'être".[87]

When his wife, Cléanthis, incensed at not receiving from her husband the amorous attentions that her ego demands, reflects that all men are more trouble than they are worth and that women would be better off without them ("Si toutes nous faisions bien,/ Nous donnerions tous les hommes au diable!"), Sosie retorts:

> Cela se dit dans le courroux.
> Mais aux hommes par trop vous êtes accrochées:
> Et vous seriez, ma foi! toutes bien empêchées
> Si le diable les prenait tous.
>
> (1215-8)

Cléanthis's "Si nous faisions bien" is the logic of 'reason'—the same reason which makes George Dandin end by declaring: "Le meilleur parti qu'on puisse prendre, c'est de s'aller jeter dans l'eau la tête la première." But that again is one of those statements of which Sosie says: "Cela se dit dans le courroux", and, as such, its truth is as partial and unrepresentative as that of any statement that rationalises the mood of a given moment. For man, as Pascal says, is a paradox, a mixture of body and mind, and neither component of his being can grasp, in isolation, the complexity of human truth. Sosie gets nearer to the heart of things than any of his superiors (those who make his life so difficult) when he declares:

> Cependant notre âme insensée
> S'acharne au vain honneur de demeurer près d'eux
> Et s'y veut contenter de la fausse pensée
> Qu'ont tous les autres gens que nous sommes heureux.
> Vers la retraite en vain la raison nous appelle;
> En vain notre dépit quelquefois y consent.
>   Leur vue a sur notre zèle
>   Un ascendant trop puissant,
> Et la moindre faveur d'un coup d'œil caressant
>   Nous rengage de plus belle.
>
> (177-86)

Reason says: "opt out", just as reason told Cléanthis she would be better without men and Dandin that he'd be better dead; but such reasoning only wins a hold over us because of our ego's momentary *dépit* at not finding the world just as we want it to be, and it is this hidden duplicity of motivation which robs such dramatic gestures (such as Alceste's departure to his *désert*) of any really serious content.

All Molière's great comic characters are of choleric disposition, always boiling over with self-righteous indignation at the illogical injustices of life; but, as Jupiter remarks in *Amphitryon*:

> ...lorsque de la sorte on se met en colère
> On fait croire qu'on a de mauvaises raisons.
> (1634-5)

Like his divine double, Mercure, Sosie is a true Sceptic, for they both reiterate the central Sceptic thesis that, in human affairs, there can be no absolutes, but only relative truths. Nature, in forming us, has shown her capriciousness:

> En nous formant, Nature a ses caprices.
> Divers penchants en nous elle a fait observer.
> (726-7)

—and it is this contingency of our personal temperament or status that dictates our view of things:

> Et suivant ce qu'on peut être
> Les choses changent de nom.[88]
> (130-1)

It is not, I think, an exaggeration to say that Molière's comic work is inconceivable without such a foundation of Scepticism. It was this philosophical attitude which revealed to him the basic incongruities of human nature—its extravagant pretensions to dignity and importance, together with its innate *faiblesse*—as well as the essentially comic perspective: man is 'absurd', because everything in him reflects the contingency of all phenomena. And what contributes above all else to this sense of universal contingency in human activity is the stress which Molière places upon the self-interest that lies hidden behind man's every action. The poet's fellow-actor, Brécourt, helps to illustrate this point when he says, in the assessment of Molière's achievement shortly after the latter's death:

> Il attaqua les mœurs et se mit inconsidérément à blâmer toutes les sottises du monde... Il dévoila les mystères de chaque chose: fit connaître publiquement quel intérêt faisait agir les hommes et fit si bien enfin que, par les lumières qu'il en donnait, on commençait de bonne foi à trouver presque toutes les choses de la vie un peu ridicules.[89]

The final impression that emerges from Molière's work, therefore, is one which was formulated by the Sceptic Montaigne:

> Je ne pense point qu'il y ait tant de malheur en nous comme il y a de vanité, ni tant de malice comme de sottise.

According to the testimony of those who knew him personally, Molière was not a naturally gay person; rather, there was a deeply serious streak in his nature that made him easily prone to melancholy. If that is the case, his work seems to have exercised for him a therapeutic function—"Art for *my* sake"— acting as a means of his coming to terms philosophically with life's disorders. Whether or not Molière wrote or inspired the *Lettre sur la comédie de l'Imposteur*, there is little doubt that he subscribed to the sentiments expressed in one of its pages:

> N'étant pas assez fort pour résister aux mauvais exemples du siècle, je m'accoutume insensiblement, Dieu merci, à rire de tout comme les autres, et à ne regarder toutes les choses qui se passent dans le monde que comme les diverses scènes de la grande comédie qui se joue sur la terre entre les hommes.[90]

NOTES

1 Hence the verdict expressed in the *Segraisiana*, which points out the enormous influence on early seventeenth-century drama of Honoré d'Urfé's *romanesque* novel, *L'Astrée*:

Pendant près de 40 ans, on a tiré tous les sujets des pièces de l'*Astrée*, et les poètes se contentaient ordinairement de mettre en vers ce que M. d'Urfé y fait dire en prose aux personnages de son roman. Ces pièces-là s'appelaient des *Pastorales*, auxquelles les Comédies succédèrent. (Quoted by E. Lintilhac: *Histoire générale du Théâtre en France*, t. III, p. 29).

2 *Cf.* Rotrou's *Clarice* (1642), based on a play by Sforza d'Oddi of 1572, and his *La Sœur* (1647), taken from *La Sorella* of Della Porta (1589). The most popular Spanish models are Calderon, Lope de Vega and Francisco de Rojas.

3 An article by R. Garapon: "Sur les dernières comédies de Molière", in *L'Information littéraire*, 1958, pp. 1–7, stresses the degree to which Molière's later work is indebted to the burlesque comedies of Scarron and Thomas Corneille.

4 *Le Menteur* was first performed in the 1643–4 season in Paris. Its source is Alarcon's *La Verdad Sospechosa*.

5 *La Vie de Corneille* in *Œuvres*, Paris, 1742, t. III, p. 104. P. Kohler, in his book: *L'Esprit classique et la Comédie*, 1925, p. 177, writes justly of Corneille's comedy: "Dorante est menteur, mais à sa manière. Le mensonge en lui n'est pas un vice, à peine un travers; c'est une inclination, un talent. Il invente à plaisir, et pour plaire... Il est vraiment difficile de voir là une comédie de caractère."

6 Respectively, Barbieri's *L'Inavvertito* (1629) and Secchi's *L'Interesse* (1581).

7 *Panégyrique*, scene 5.

8 The parallelism of the two *genres* is reinforced by a remark attributed to Saint-Évremond, concerning the evolution of Classical tragedy: "Autrefois on prenait un grand sujet et on y faisait entrer un caractère; aujourd'hui, on forme sur les caractères la constitution du sujet." This view should nevertheless be modified in the light of the discussion of the relationship between Character and Action in the work of Racine, chapter 2, pp. 82–3.

9 The original trio consisted of Turlupin, Gros-Guillaume and Gaultier-Garguille, who reached the height of their fame in the years 1622–33; their most outstanding successor was Jodelet. For further details see G. Attinger: *L'Esprit de la Commedia dell'arte dans le Théâtre français*, 1950, p. 100 sq.

10 A full study of the structure of *commedia dell'arte* can be found in Attinger, *op. cit.*; in K. M. Lea: *Italian Popular Comedy*, 2 vols., 1934; and in Allardyce Nicoll: *Masks, Mimes and Miracles*, 1931. The influence of this tradition on Molière was studied in detail by G. Lanson: "Molière et la farce", *Revue de Paris*, May, 1901.

11 Just as a stage-direction in the Gherardi collection of Italian *scenarii* says of Scaramouche: "Scaramuccia non parla, e dice gran cose", so a contemporary account of Molière's performance as Sganarelle in *Le Cocu imaginaire* (1660) says: "Son visage et ses gestes expriment si bien la jalousie qu'il ne serait pas nécessaire qu'il parlât pour paraître le plus jaloux de tous les hommes... Sa pantomime excitait des éclats de rire interminables."

12 *La Critique*, scene 2.

13 M. Hodgart: *Satire*, 1969, p. 121.

14 *Œuvres complètes du Chevalier de Méré*, ed. Ch.-H. Boudhors, 1930, t. II, p. 37. The fullest study of the theory of *honnêteté* is in M. Magendie: *La Politesse mondaine et les théories de l'honnêteté en France au XVIIe siècle*, (no date), 2 vols. I have myself already discussed these points in my article: "Essai de définition du comique moliéresque", *Revue des Sciences humaines*, 1964, pp. 9–24, parts of which are reproduced in this chapter with the permission of the *Revue*.

15 *Œuvres de La Rochefoucauld*, ed. Grands Écrivains, 1868, t. I, pp. 686–7 ("De l'Air et des Manières").

16 Quotations from the *Lettre* are taken from the *Œuvres de Molière*, ed. Despois et Mesnard, t. IV, pp. 529–66. It is studied by René Robert in his article: "Des Commentaires de première main sur les chefs-d'œuvre les plus discutés

de Molière", *Revue des Sciences humaines*, 1956, pp. 19–49. M. Robert suggests that the author of the *Lettre* was Donneau de Visé, acting as spokesman for Molière. There is also a study of the *Lettre* in C. S. Gutkind: *Molière und das komische Drama*, 1928, pp. 85–111.

17 *Op. cit.*, p. 564. This definition is not entirely satisfactory insofar as it suggests that any form of incongruity is ridiculous, whereas the ironic contrast can equally be a source of tragic emotion. Freud, in his *Der Witz und seine Beziehung zum Unbewussten* (1905), rightly emphasises the element of *Herabsetzung* or 'debunking' which must be present to produce the effect of ridicule: the comic author is aggressive and unmasks the pretence to superiority in his victim, destroying "the unity which exists between people's characters as we know them, and their speeches and actions, by replacing either the exalted figures or their utterances by inferior ones." In tragedy, the incongruity is there between the *grandeur* and the *misère*, as when Lear is reduced to "the thing itself—a poor forked animal"; but the initial greatness was a reality, so that its defeat is sensed as a terrible waste. These points are examined in the chapter on Racine.

18 Scene 3. Note the idea of 'irritation' plus 'delight' in debunking.

19 *Essais*, Book II, chapter 2: "De l'Ivrognerie".

20 Act I, scene 5.

21 Act III, scene 3.

22 *La Dramaturgie Classique en France*, (no date), p. 27.

23 Cf. A. Adam: *Histoire de la Littérature française au XVIIe Siècle*, t. II, 1951, pp. 27–8: "[Les Précieuses] se reliaient au vaste et lent mouvement qui, mis en branle par l'humanisme, poussait les idées et les mœurs vers une émancipation de l'individu, vers des formes de vie plus libres, plus raisonnables et plus humaines."

24 Cf. the definition of the term *visionnaire* given by Malebranche in his *Traité de Morale*, 1684, t. I, p. 211: "Par *visionnaire*, j'entends un homme dont l'attention détermine, à la vérité, le cours des esprits, mais elle n'en peut mesurer la force, ou retenir le mouvement. Ainsi le visionnaire pense à ce qu'il veut: *mais il ne voit rien tel qu'il est*. Car les traces étant trop grandes ou trop profondes, il ne voit rien dans son état naturel: il faut toujours rabattre quelque chose de ce qu'il dit. Tout le monde en ce sens est visionnaire à l'égard de certains sujets: ceux qui le savent le mieux sont les plus sages."

25 Bergson's *Le Rire* appeared in book form in 1900. The English translation by C. Brereton and F. Rothwell was published in 1911 (Macmillan). Together with George Meredith's *Essay on Comedy* (1877), it is reproduced in *Comedy*, edited by Wylie Sypher, Doubleday Anchor Books, 1956.

26 For a full survey of the *querelle*, see the chapter on *L'École des Femmes* in G. Michaut: *Les Débuts de Molière à Paris*, 1923. See also the Introduction to the edition of the play by W. D. Howarth (Blackwell, Oxford, 1963).

27 *L'École des Femmes de Molière*, 1939, pp. 297 and 314.

28 Scene 6.

29 "*L'École des Femmes*, tragédie burlesque?", *Revue des Sciences humaines*, 1960; see also chapter 8 of Hubert's book: *Molière and the Comedy of Intellect*, 1962.

30 Scene 5.

31 M. Hodgart, *op. cit.*, p. 124.

32 See my Introduction to *L'École des Maris*, Harrap, 1959.

33 Fragment 678 of Pascal's *Pensées* (ed. Lafuma; number 358 in Brunschvicg's edition). The Montaigne 'source' is the conclusion to the last of the *Essais*, Book III, chapter 13.

34 I have discussed Erasmus's *Folly* in "Érasme et Des Périers", *Bibliothèque d'Humanisme et Renaissance*, 1968, pp. 53–64.
35 Molière, *Homme de Théâtre*, 1950, Part III, chapter 6.
36 *Essais*, Book II, chapter 17. See my article: "The rôle of Chrysalde in *L'École des Femmes*", *Modern Language Review*, 1961, pp. 167–71.
37 *The Life of the Drama* (New York), 1965, pp. 53–4.
38 Baudelaire's poem *Les Aveugles* is an interesting example of the way an initially satirical reaction (the poet first finds the blind to be absurd—"vaguement ridicules") is transformed through self-recognition. See my analysis in *The Art of Criticism*, ed. P. H. Nurse, 1969, pp. 193–203.
39 *An Essay on Comedy*, ed. Wylie Sypher, pp. 42, 47.
40 *Essays of Elia*: "On the artificial comedy of the last century", first published in the *London Magazine*, 1822.
41 *Op. cit.*, p. 47.
42 *Structures de Tartuffe*, 1966, p. 37.
43 *Op. cit.*, p. 28.
44 *Mimesis*, trans. Willard Trask, Doubleday Anchor Books, 1957, p. 318.
45 *Op. cit.*, p. 545.
46 This quotation is taken from E. Cassirer: *The Platonic Renaissance in England*, trans. J. P. Pettegrove, 1953, pp. 163–4. I have also reproduced here several passages from my article: "Molière and Satire", *University of Toronto Quarterly*, 1967, pp. 113–28.
47 *Op. cit.*, t. III, p. 318.
48 *Op. cit.*, t. III, p. 315.
49 *Impressions de Théâtre*, t. IV, 1892.
50 *Op. cit.*, p. 540 sq.
51 *Cf.* the commentary of Elmire in lines 1357–8:

   ...On est aisément dupé par ce qu'on aime,
   Et l'amour-propre engage à se tromper soi-même.

52 *The Platonic Renaissance in England*, p. 171.
53 One question not touched on here is the satirical implications of the way Tartuffe was dressed in Molière's production of the play. G. Couton, in his article "L'État civil d'Armande Béjart", *Revue des Sciences humaines*, July–September 1964, gathers together the evidence which suggests that Tartuffe probably appeared in 1664 as a *petit-collet*—"un de ces gens qui, sans être tout à fait d'Église, sont candidats aux bénéfices ecclésiastiques." Couton concludes: "Tartuffe a sans doute fait son entrée avec le petit-collet; peut-être avec la soutane, ou la soutanelle. Il apparaissait certainement comme un diacre ou un sous-diacre; peut-être comme un prêtre... On comprend la fureur des dévots."
54 *La Vie de Molière*, 1929, pp. 165–7.
55 *Morales du Grand Siècle*, 1948, p. 172.
56 As with Tartuffe, so too with the *Pauvre*, Molière had to leave his religious status ambiguous, since the law forbade the representation of religious orders on the stage: "Défense aux joueurs de farces, bateleurs et autres de...se vêtir d'habits ecclésiastiques...à peine de prison et punition corporelle" (*Ordonnance d'Orléans*, art. 24 of the *Code Pénal*, titre VIII).
57 *Op. cit.*, t. III, p. 332.
58 *Œuvres de Molière*, ed. Despois et Mesnard, t. V. The author of the *Observations* calls himself "le Sieur de Rochemont, avocat en Parlement."
59 *Sur le « Dom Juan » de Molière*, 1967, pp. 91–2.

60 *Dom Juan ou Le Festin de Pierre*, ed. W. D. Howarth, Blackwell, Oxford, 1968, pp. xxix–xxxii. Howarth also supplies a very useful analysis of earlier dramatic versions of the theme.

61 This view is also put by W. G. Moore in *Molière, A New Criticism*, 1949, and in his article: "*Dom Juan* reconsidered", *Modern Language Review*, 1957, pp. 510–7.

62 *Molière et la Comédie Classique*, 1965.

63 Cf. Act I, scene 2, where Sganarelle says of Dom Juan: "Il se plaît à se promener de lieux en lieux, et n'aime point à demeurer en place."

64 *Op. cit.*, t. III, p. 343.

65 This *Lettre* is discussed by R. Robert in the article: "Des Commentaires de première main sur les chefs-d'œuvre les plus discutés de Molière", *loc. cit*. The text is reproduced in the *Œuvres*, ed. Despois et Mesnard, t. V. I quote it from the edition of *Le Misanthrope* by E. Lop and A. Sauvage (Éditions Sociales, 1963), which also contains a very substantial Introduction.

66 A. Adam, *op. cit.*, t. III, p. 344. For an outline of the history of critical reactions to *Le Misanthrope*, see G. Michaut: *Les Luttes de Molière*, 1925, pp. 203–10.

67 *Essais*, Book III, chapter 9 (ed. Plattard, 1947, Livre III, Vol. II, p. 77).

68 *Œuvres en Prose*, ed. R. Ternois, t. III, 1966, p. 16.

69 *Lettre sur les Spectacles*, ed. L. Brunel (5th edition, 1910), pp. 61–2.

70 *Op. cit.*, pp. 62–4.

71 *Cf.* L. Gossman: *Men and Masks*, 1963, p. 80: "The inauthenticity of the world is not a menace to him; on the contrary, it is the very source of all his satisfactions. It provides the basis of his own superiority and he spends all his time not in a real struggle to reach authenticity, but in endless efforts to have his superiority recognised by the very world of inauthenticity which he affects to detest. The absence of value in the world becomes, with Alceste, a matter of self-congratulation." Hence his characteristic reaction to the loss of his law-suit; it is quickly seized upon as a sign of his ultimate triumph:

> Ce sont vingt mille francs qu'il m'en pourra coûter,
> Mais pour vingt mille francs j'aurai droit de pester
> Contre l'iniquité de la nature humaine,
> Et de nourrir pour elle une immortelle haine.
>
> (1547–50)

La Rochefoucauld provides the perfect commentary when analysing *amour-propre*: "Il passe même dans le parti des gens qui lui font la guerre... il travaille lui-même à sa ruine; enfin il ne se soucie que d'être, et pourvu qu'il soit, il veut bien être son ennemi... Quand on pense qu'il quitte son plaisir, il ne fait que le suspendre ou le changer, et, lors même qu'il est vaincu et qu'on croit en être défait, on le retrouve qui triomphe dans sa propre défaite" (*Maximes*, ed. J. Truchet, 1967, pp. 284–5). The word we now use for such behaviour is 'masochism'.

72 Among the more recent expressions of this viewpoint, see P. Yarrow: "A Reconsideration of Alceste", *French Studies*, 1959, pp. 314–31.

73 *Molière et le Misanthrope*, 1951, p. 133.

74 See particularly the 'Commentaire et Notes' in the edition of *Le Misanthrope* by G. Rudler (Blackwell, 1952), pp. 124 sq. For example: "1281–84. Imprécations de tragédie (cf. *Horace*, 1301–1318), donc parodie. Le v. 1284 est d'ailleurs de comédie pure." Line 1311 recalls *Le Cid*, line 291: "Percé jusques au fond du cœur/D'une atteinte imprévue aussi bien que mortelle."

75 Reference has already been made above to the way Elmire exploited this ambiguity to deceive Tartuffe in Act IV, scene 5.
76 "Don Juan and Le Misanthrope, or the Esthetics of Individualism in Molière," *PMLA*, 1969, p. 569.
77 *Molière: Une Aventure Théâtrale*, 1963, pp. 404–5. Guicharnaud develops systematically the idea already sketched in A. Simon: *Molière par lui-même*, 1959, pp. 122–4: "Sa sincérité ne peut être mise en cause: elle est exactement ce qu'elle paraît. L'unique but de sa vie est le jeu. Elle est sans fatuité et sans illusion. A son piège seul se prend celui qui veut bien s'aveugler et joue à colin-maillard. Provocatrice comme Don Juan (mais son défi ne concerne que la vanité du mâle), comme lui elle est un être sans visage, donc sans masque. Survient Alceste. Pour se défendre, Célimène interposera entre elle et lui la cohorte des fâcheux."
78 *Op. cit.*, p. 476 (my italics).
79 *Op. cit.*, pp. 90–1.
80 *Fables*, Book I, number 7.
81 Lines 975–6. A similar statement of Sceptic relativism is made by Éliante in lines 711–30, describing the subjective judgement of lovers:

Jamais leur passion n'y voit rien de blâmable
Et dans l'objet aimé tout leur devient aimable.

The source of these lines is Lucretius's *De Natura rerum* which Molière is said to have translated, though no copy of his translation survives.
82 *Op. cit.*, pp. 429–30. In *Molière et Le Misanthrope*, pp. 261–68, René Jasinski illustrates the same conflict of opposing tendencies in one of the Sceptic treatises of La Mothe le Vayer: *Prose Chagrine* (1661). Like Alceste, the philosopher feels a strong rebellious *chagrin* against the world, but opposes to it a *sagesse* clearly derived from Montaigne: "Il faut acquiescer aux décrets du Ciel, se réjouir et non pas se chagriner de voir exécuter ses ordonnances, et songer que comme c'est folie de s'opposer à ce qui ne saurait être évité, il y a de l'injustice à disputer contre les lois que nous avons trouvées établies en venant au monde... A la vérité, les disgrâces de la vie sont bien plus fréquentes que les satisfactions... Mais puisque ces mêmes malheurs ne se peuvent éviter, étant si fort attachés que nous le disons à la condition de notre vie, pourquoi les augmenterons-nous par notre impatience et par un chagrin déraisonnable?"
83 *La Vie de Molière*, p. 108. Cf. also p. 109, referring to *L'École des Maris*: "Sganarelle est condamné, ainsi le veut le bon sens, ainsi l'a voulu Molière. Mais avant de s'évaporer dans l'explosion comique, il vivra, de tout son poids, de tout son saoul; et il vivra de la vie de Molière, de ses muscles, de son sang, de son élan. Il affirmera sa possession absolue de la femme, sa volonté féroce de ne comprendre que son propre langage, de s'envelopper dans ses propres incompatibilités. Il s'abandonnera à l'exquise et funeste paresse d'être absolument tout ce qu'il veut être, tout en sachant qu'il n'est rien de ce qu'il veut être."
84 For a fuller analysis of the links between Erasmus's *Folly* and *Le Misanthrope*, see my "Essai de définition du comique moliéresque", *loc. cit.*, pp. 16–19.
85 *Pensées*, ed. Brunschvicg, no. 320.
86 In his literary theory, Molière expresses the same distrust of the neo-Classical rationalism with its reverence for dogmatic rules. Cf. *La Critique*, scene 5: "Il y en a beaucoup que le trop d'esprit gâte, qui voient mal les choses à force de lumière..."; also scene 6: "Laissons-nous aller de bonne foi aux choses qui nous prennent par les entrailles, et ne cherchons point de raisonnements pour nous empêcher d'avoir du plaisir."

87 Cf. the same Sceptic argument in Pascal, *Pensées*, ed. Brunschvicg, no. 430, ed. Lafuma, no. 149: "*Incompréhensible.* — Tout ce qui est incompréhensible ne laisse pas d'être." My references to *Amphitryon* will make it obvious that I was quite out of sympathy with the Comédie Française production of the play in London, 1970, in which Robert Hirsch played Sosie as a raving lunatic. There is, of course, a strong farce element in the servant's rôle, but the more profound comic and moral perspective is really focused on Amphitryon, whose fits of jealousy, anger and self-righteous indignation make him very much a comic lover in the manner of Dom Garcie, Arnolphe and Alceste.

88 As J. D. Hubert remarked in *The Comedy of Intellect*, it is possible to look upon the servant-girl, Élise, in *Dom Garcie*, as Molière's first *raisonneuse*. She, too, always puts the Sceptic thesis, as in lines 153 sq.:

> J'admire cependant que le Ciel ait jeté
> Dans le goût des esprits tant de diversité
> Et que ce que les uns regardent comme outrage
> Soit vu par d'autres yeux sous un autre visage.

Cf. also lines 1182–3:

> Nous avons du Ciel, ou du tempérament
> Que nous jugeons de tout chacun diversement.

89 *L'Ombre de Molière*, 1674.

90 This is the traditional Sceptic-Epicurean view of the 'human comedy'; one of its earliest formulations is in Lucretius's *De Natura rerum*, while it is also found in La Mothe le Vayer, *Quatre Dialogues*, 1630: "Toute notre vie n'est, à le bien prendre, qu'une fable, notre connaissance qu'une ânerie, nos certitudes que des contes: bref, tout ce monde qu'une farce et perpétuelle comédie."

With the permission of Oxford University Press, I have reproduced in this chapter several pages from the Introduction of my edition of *Le Malade imaginaire* (1965).

CHAPTER FOUR

MADAME DE LAFAYETTE

Marie-Madeleine, comtesse de Lafayette (1634–1693)
Painting by Antoine Hoerse

Published in 1678, *La Princesse de Clèves* enjoys the reputation of being the first masterpiece in the history of the French novel, and certainly nobody would dispute Sainte-Beuve's verdict calling it "le premier en date des plus aimables romans". As such, its position in French literature is equivalent to that in English literature of Richardson's *Clarissa*, and the particular excellence of both novels has been spoken of in very similar terms. Just as Dr. Johnson wrote of *Clarissa* that it was the "first book in the world for the knowledge it displays of the human heart", so *La Princesse de Clèves* is commonly singled out for the extraordinary penetration of its psychological analysis. But what is still more important is that in each of these works the profound insights are controlled and moulded into an organic, imaginative whole by what Virginia Woolf called "the single vision . . . the immense persuasiveness of a mind which has completely mastered its perspective", and in both cases this is a tragic vision.

Thus, when Arnold Kettle speaks of Richardson as being the first truly tragic English novelist, placing his heroine in a dilemma from which, in terms of her own society, there is no escape, his formulation is essentially applicable to Madame de Lafayette and her heroine. Following an upbringing which has implanted in her the strictest principles and the cult of purity, the Princess is exposed by her creator to a corrupt world from which there is no escape, but in which one can only survive at the cost of compromise with that spiritual purity which is ultimately more precious than life itself to the heroine. In other words, Mme de Lafayette has re-enacted the eternal human confrontation between the ideal world of the human spirit and the fatal pressures of material reality which is, in some degree, at the centre of all human experience, but which is here taken to its tragic extreme. And it is this *aesthetic* purity with which the confrontation is carried out that gives the novel its Classical status, comparable to that achieved in the drama by Racine.

In the French novel, before Mme de Lafayette, there is ample reflection of the idealism which inspires the Princess, and, in its way, this idealism is a genuine facet of the sociological reality of the period. But it is only a partial view of things, and in that sense the bulk of seventeenth-century narrative fiction was more strictly composed of Romances, rather than Novels, if we adopt the familiar distinction made by Clara Reeves in her *Progress of Romance* of 1785:

> The Novel is a picture of real life and manners, and of the time in which it is written. The Romance, in lofty and elevated language, describes what never happened nor is likely to happen.

The same distinction was familiar to the French seventeenth century, as when Segrais wrote in *Les Nouvelles françaises* of 1657:

> Il me semble que c'est la différence qu'il y a entre le Roman et la Nouvelle — que le Roman écrit les choses comme la bienséance le veut et à la manière du Poète, mais que la Nouvelle doit un peu davantage tenir de l'histoire et s'attacher plutôt à donner des images des choses comme d'ordinaire nous les voyons arriver que comme notre imagination se les figure.[1]

Mme de Lafayette's work will in a sense emerge from the fusion of these traditions, and her masterpiece of 1678 provides the perfect illustration of the Lukács-inspired definition of the novel as a *genre* given by Lucien Goldmann in his *Pour une Sociologie du Roman*:

> Le roman [est] un genre épique caractérisé, contrairement à l'épopée ou au conte, par la rupture insurmontable entre le héros et le monde... dans un monde de conformisme et de convention.[2]

No doubt such a definition is altogether too sweeping for a *genre* which Henry James rightly called "the most independent, the most elastic, the most prodigious of literary forms", but the contention of the following analysis is that it is particularly appropriate to *La Princesse de Clèves*.

* * *

Whatever the similarities between *La Princesse de Clèves* and *Clarissa*, in at least one fundamental respect they differ, namely in the social background against which they are set. Critics such as Ian Watt, in his book: *The Rise of the Novel*, have linked the evolution of the English novel in its modern form with the emergence of a substantial, politically influential and self-conscious middle class, possessing sufficient culture and material wealth to impose its own tastes on the literary world; and it is essentially the ethos of this class which is reflected in Richardson's work.

In seventeenth-century France, however, while there was already an increasingly active urban middle class, its advent to political power and full self-consciousness was much slower. France remains much longer a semi-feudal society, dominated by the aristocracy: although there had been a civil war, the Fronde of 1648–53, in which elements of the Parisian bourgeoisie had come out in opposition to the monarchy, there was nothing of the well-defined ideology which characterised the Puritan opposition to the English Crown at the same period; and the eventual triumph of Mazarin and Louis XIV led to a long period of political stagnation during which the social scene was predominantly led by an aristocratic élite grouped round the Court, an élite summed up in the contemporary phrase: 'la Cour et la Ville'. It is the ethos of this select group which is reflected in the majority of the outstanding works of French Classical literature, written either by bourgeois artists depending on royal or aristocratic patronage (Molière, for instance, son of a *marchand tapissier*, and from 1665 leader of the Troupe du Roi) or by nobles like Mme de Lafayette or her intimate friend, La Rochefoucauld.[3]

Indeed, Mme de Lafayette's own background is the perfect illustration of the culture which moulds the literary masterpieces of the age. Born in 1634, Marie-Madeleine Pioche de la Vergne came of an unexalted Parisian noble family, which owed its high connections to her father's rôle as tutor to the nephews of the King's chief minister, Cardinal de Richelieu. Even from her early childhood in Paris she was in close contact with the fashionable literary world, for her house was visited by such distinguished figures as the poet Voiture and two of the leading salon hostesses, Mme de Sablé and Mlle de Scudéry. And once she herself reached the age of 16, when it was customary for a girl to frequent the *beau monde*— the same age at which her heroine, Mlle de Chartres, will emerge from the obscurity of her domestic background—she began visiting the more celebrated salons, the Hôtel de Rambouillet and the salon of Mlle de Scudéry.

From around this time, too, dates her entry to Court circles, for she was made a lady-in-waiting to Anne of Austria, the Queen Mother.

When she married in 1655, it was to a man considerably older than herself and a widower, the Comte de Lafayette; and though her husband was of nobler birth than herself and had important estates in Auvergne, he was beset by debts: not the least attractive aspect of what Marie-Madeleine brought to the marriage was therefore a sizeable dowry, thanks to the fact that her younger sisters had both entered convents and abandoned their share of the family fortune to her. This detail of the sociological pattern of the period in respect of marriage conventions will be echoed in Mme de Lafayette's work.

For some years Mme de Lafayette resided in Auvergne, but from 1659 onwards she was almost continuously in Paris, while her husband spent most of his time on the family estates. In the capital, she again re-established her social connections: her close friendship with Henriette d'Angleterre, known as Madame following her marriage to the King's brother, Philippe d'Orléans, is one of the factors that accounts for her frequent presence at Court— at the Louvre, at Fontainebleau and later at Versailles. The time she spent as courtier explains her authorship of two sets of memoirs, published after her death: the *Histoire d'Henriette d'Angleterre* (composed 1665–1670), and the *Mémoires de la Cour de France*, covering the years 1688–9.

When not at Court, Mme de Lafayette lived the life of a typical salon *habitué*: she was a regular visitor to the most prominent *ruelles* in the second half of the century—that of Mme de Sablé, for example, and the Hôtel de Nevers, run by Mme du Plessis-Guénégaud in the traditions of the Hôtel de Rambouillet. It was the latter that Racine attended, reading his *Alexandre*, and Boileau his *Satires*. At the same time, Mme de Lafayette was herself a hostess of distinction, and the most celebrated memorialist of the period, the Duc de Saint-Simon, said of her gatherings: "C'était un tribunal pour les ouvrages de l'esprit." This, in turn, explains her reputation among her contemporaries as "une des précieuses du plus haut rang et de la plus haute volée", and there is no doubt that the *préciosité* of the salon world left an indelible mark upon the literary genius of the author of *La Princesse de Clèves*.

When Somaize defined the *précieuses* as "celles qui se mêlent d'écrire ou de corriger ce que les autres écrivent",[4] he clearly points to the most obvious qualification of Mme de Lafayette to be counted among their number. But this literary activity was only one facet of more complex aspirations of salon society, aspirations which amounted to what another contemporary, the Abbé de Pure, called "une espèce de religion"[5]: namely, its quest for a more refined and spiritualised mode of existence, such as would enable its devotees to "se tirer hors du commun" and transcend their grosser physical appetites. The *précieux* cult of the intellect is echoed in the terms used by Mme de Sévigné to praise Mme de Lafayette shortly after her death: "Jamais elle n'a été sans cette divine raison qui était sa qualité principale"[6] and the essential idealism of the movement is well caught in the Abbé de Pure's reference to its ultimate goal: "de travailler les dons de l'esprit et les mettre si bien en œuvre qu'ils puissent arrêter les sens, élever le commerce de leurs plaisirs, et les rendre aussi spirituels que sensibles".[7]

It was this ideal that lay behind the sophisticated pleasures cultivated by the salons, particularly their preoccupation with ethical questions and psychological analysis. Hence the popularity of the *portrait*, a literary *genre* which ultimately reaches its highest form in the *Caractères* of La Bruyère in 1685, but which was already flourishing in the 1650s. One collection of such portraits was published in 1659, and originated in the salon of Mlle de Montpensier ("la grande Mademoiselle"): in it there was, for instance, a character-study of Mme de Sévigné done by Mme de Lafayette, and another such study of La Rochefoucauld, done by himself. It is in the latter that we find a statement of some of the most typical salon values: the premium placed upon moral analysis—"La conversation des honnêtes gens est un des plaisirs qui me touchent le plus. J'aime qu'elle soit sérieuse et que la morale en fasse la plus grande partie" —together with the pursuit of maximum lucidity and sincerity in the scrutinising of the self: "je me suis assez étudié pour me bien connaître, et je ne manque ni d'assurance pour dire librement ce que je puis avoir de bonnes qualités, ni de sincérité pour avouer franchement ce que j'ai de défauts".[8]

Without this sustained tradition of analytical expertise and the concomitant cult of sincerity, it would be difficult to account for some of the more fundamental qualities of *La Princesse de Clèves*.

But it was above all in the analysis and evaluation of love that the salon society excelled, and here, too, Mme de Lafayette's genius was deeply influenced. Running right through the literature of this *milieu* is the theme of the paradoxical ambiguity of love, holding the key both to the moral salvation and the damnation of man: potentially, it is the source of man's aspiration for the infinite, his desire to be reunited with God, whose beauty and goodness is reflected in the loved-one. In this neo-Platonic scheme of things, love is a spiritual perception, known in the salons as *l'amour-estime* or *l'amour-connaissance*. But the danger lies in the perpetual exposure of love to being tainted by other impure instincts which tend to convert the relationship between the sexes into something basically narcissistic and physical, so that the major problem for the *précieux* world was to establish social conditions in which the finer feelings could develop harmoniously, untouched by the material pressures of corrupt institutions. The reason why so many of the *précieuses* were ardent feminists, hostile to marriage, was precisely that they regarded marriage itself as an institution perverted by male tyranny: all too often, in a world where the arranged match was the rule, it served mainly to advance the political or economic interests of family dynasties, without any regard for the individual personality of those most intimately involved in the bond. When, at the age of 19, before her marriage, Mme de Lafayette wrote in a letter to Ménage: "Je suis si persuadée que l'amour est une chose incommode que j'ai de la joie que mes amis et moi en soyons exempts"[9], she was merely voicing an attitude highly characteristic of her *milieu*.

And yet it is essentially the idealistic view which predominates in the overwhelming bulk of the narrative fiction published in France before Mme de Lafayette began her career as a novelist. Just as, in the medieval period, the *roman* was primarily the vehicle of the aristocratic imagination, embodying in its tales the heroic ethos of chivalry and the code of the purifying *fin'amor* taken over from the Provençal lyric poets, so again, when in the late sixteenth century the *roman* is revived as a literary *genre*—and it is from about 1590 that the real vogue begins, literary historians showing that between then and the end of the seventeenth century over 1200 novels were published[10]—it still bears the mark of its old chivalrous heredity. Indeed, it is to a large extent the translations and reworkings of the old romances, such as the Spanish *Amadis de Gaule*, translated by Herberay des Essarts (1540–1576), which at first provide the framework of adventures for so many of the new tales, whose heroes' courage is inspired by the service of their lady.

Still more influential, perhaps, and reflecting the Renaissance return to Greco-Roman sources, was the third-century romance of the Greek Heliodorus: *Theagenes and Chariclea*, or *Ethiopian History*, translated into French by Amyot and published in 1547.[11] Such was the importance of this work that Guez de Balzac wrote in 1629 that almost all the French novels of his time were "des Héliodores déguisés". Its story of two young lovers who are separated by a host of misfortunes—storms at sea, shipwrecks, capture by pirates, being sold into slavery—but who remain perfectly constant in their love for each other until their final marriage is reproduced in innumerable French seventeenth-century variants.

But the most famous of all these early French *romans* is Honoré d'Urfé's *L'Astrée*, which appeared between 1607 and 1624, and which retained its popularity with the salon world right through the century—as is testified by the following reference by the Abbé de Longuerue: "M. de La Rochefoucauld a été toute sa vie fidèle aux romans. Tous les après-midi, il s'assemblait avec Segrais chez Mme de Lafayette, et on y faisait une lecture de l'*Astrée*".[12]

As its full title proclaims—*L'Astrée où par plusieurs histoires, et sous personnes de bergers et d'autres, sont déduits les divers effets de l'honnête amitié*—d'Urfé's novel has a pastoral setting and aims at illustrating a philosophical theory of love, based on the doctrines of neo-Platonism. During the countless discussions and analyses which interrupt the narrative, we get the characteristic definition of love as "un acte de volonté qui se porte à ce que l'entendement juge bon". For the hero, Céladon, cast in the rôle of *parfait amant*, love is the equivalent of a religious cult, demanding self-sacrifice to the highest ideals of perfection, and it is this dedication of service which proves the refining and purifying action of true love:

> L'amant ne désire rien davantage que d'être aimé; pour être aimé, il faut qu'il se rende aimable et ce qui rend aimable est cela même qui rend honnête l'homme.[13]

This formulates as clearly as possible the moral basis of the whole structure of the salon 'art de plaire' and its complex code of *bienséances*.

In their study of the influences which contributed to the growth of the *roman psychologique*, and, in particular, its greatest masterpiece —Mme de Lafayette's *Princesse de Clèves*—literary historians often stress that what was most important about *L'Astrée* was precisely its hint of the darker aspects of love—those less edifying elements in it which threaten the social order, just as in the medieval tale of *Tristan et Yseult* it was presented as primitively irrational and destructive. It is true that even d'Urfé's two protagonists, Céladon and Astrée, often behave in a way which invites a Freudian interpretation of their love as a *libido dominandi*, but as a rule it is in a much less direct manner that the book helps us to discover the way that led to Mme de Lafayette's triumph in finding the formula for the authentic psychological novel.

L'Astrée is, as already indicated, a pastoral novel and was in the tradition of another antique model, also translated by Amyot in 1559: Longus's *Daphnis and Chloe*. From this d'Urfé took over not only the theme of perfect love, but also the myth of a past golden age of innocence, set in a pastoral Arcadia, free from the evils bred by a more sophisticated urban or Court *milieu*. It is a world in which the discord sown by economic and political rivalries is still basically unknown, and its aristocratic inhabitants have voluntarily chosen it in preference to the Court, because it offers a "vie plus douce et accompagnée de moins d'inquiétudes". This is the *repos* which is always present as the ideal in the mind of Mme de Clèves, and it is always associated with flight from the intrigue-ridden society of the *beau monde*, in which she finds herself trapped, and where, according to Mme de Lafayette, "l'amour était toujours mêlé aux affaires et les affaires à l'amour".[14] It is significant, therefore, as M. Jacques Ehrmann has shown in his study of *L'Astrée*,[15] that the exceptional passages in which d'Urfé does describe a love that is unambiguously aggressive are almost all related to the courtly world: the grossest cases of sexual violence are those where the violator uses the political power of his rank to satisfy his lust.

What emerges from this brief analysis is that one major prerequisite for the creation of a genuine psychological novel lay in the discarding of the purely artificial *milieu* of the pastoral novel and the adoption of a realistically drawn background to provide the familiar framework of material contingencies within which any true human experience must be defined. However, it was not until the 1660s that this lesson was absorbed and translated into action; certainly, soon after 1630 the pastoral novel fell from favour as a *genre*, just as the dramatic *pastorale* virtually disappeared, but it was succeeded by other variants of the heroic romance. The most prominent examples of this later style are the novels of Mlle de Scudéry and her brother, in particular *Le Grand Cyrus* and *Clélie*.[16] Like nearly all the other *romans* produced between 1630 and 1660, they retain the stock novelettish ingredients of melodramatic incidents—battles, abductions, mistaken identities—and they attempt a superficial kind of evocation of a historical *milieu*, normally that of the ancient Roman Empire; but incongruously thrust into this material is a mass of sentimental analysis which has no organic connection with the narrative action.

Mlle de Scudéry prided herself on her skill in the salon art of character portraiture, as she makes clear when she draws her own portrait under the name of Sapho in *Le Grand Cyrus*:

> Sapho exprime si délicatement les sentiments les plus difficiles à exprimer, et elle sait si bien faire l'anatomie d'un cœur amoureux... qu'elle en sait décrire exactement toutes les jalousies, toutes les inquiétudes, toutes les impatiences, toutes les joies, tous les dégoûts, tous les mouvements, tous les désespoirs.

This she does in an interminable series of portraits, which are thinly disguised descriptions of her fellow salon *habitués*, but not only were these hopelessly out of place in the supposed historical *milieu* of ancient Rome (Mme de Lafayette herself was quick to point this out in her verdict on *Clélie*[17]); far more grave a fault was that they were never properly integrated into the action of the novel, and thus lacked any genuine imaginative life of the kind demanded by art. What M. Ehrmann says of *L'Astrée* is completely applicable here to Mlle de Scudéry's work:

> Dans l'*Astrée*, la *théorie* amoureuse avec toutes les arguties qu'elle comporte a une part beaucoup plus importante que l'*action* amoureuse: ce ne sont que raisonnements, déductions, abstractions, subtilités ver-

bales vidées de toute action. Le tragique n'y est plus vécu, il y est parlé. En devenant presque uniquement une rhétorique, la passion amoureuse est dissociée du réel. Ce phénomène est évident, non seulement dans l'*Astrée*, mais dans la plupart des romans contemporains, où la description de l'amour équivaut presque à la définition de l'amour.[18]

The real lesson, then, that had to be learned was that psychological analysis is not itself the stuff of creative literature: to become so, its insights must not be described, but enacted so as to create a dramatic action which fully involves the reader's imagination, whereby he shares the experience of the characters. And such a process is only possible where the novelist is dealing with essentially individualised characters—not abstractions—rooted in a precise social context. Here, in fact, lay the real nature of Mme de Lafayette's achievement.

Paradoxically, perhaps, such an achievement was only possible through the abandoning of the form that had hitherto borne the title of *roman*, and the adoption of another *genre* of narrative fiction, the *nouvelle*, as re-defined by writers in the 1650s such as Sorel and Segrais.[19] The *roman* is felt to be inseparably tied up with the world of make-believe, and when Mme de Lafayette herself does co-operate with Segrais in writing a *roman*—*Zaïde*, published 1669-71—it is typical of the *genre*. Set in ninth-century Spain, at the time of the struggle against the Moors, it is a long rambling tale, full of the conventional *romanesque* heroics and melodramatic intrigue, with only occasional glimpses of the penetrating insights into the tragic zones of human experience which will be explored in depth in *La Princesse de Clèves*.

In contrast to the *roman*, the *nouvelle* is equated with the 'histoire véritable', drawn from some real-life incident with historical credentials; and what R. Wellek and A. Warren say in their *Theory of Literature* is essentially true of the French literary scene:

> The novel develops from the lineage of non-fictitious narrative forms—the letter, the journal, the memoir or biography, the chronicle or history; it develops, so to speak, out of documents . . .[20]

Shortly after *La Princesse de Clèves* appeared, Mme de Lafayette thus wrote of it in terms which confirm the Warren-Wellek view:

> C'est une parfaite imitation de la Cour et de la manière dont on y vit; il n'y a rien de romanesque et de grimpé: aussi n'est-ce pas un roman, c'est proprement des mémoires...[21]

Long before 1678, however, Mme de Lafayette had herself helped to establish the *nouvelle historique* with her own first exercise in the new *genre*, *La Princesse de Montpensier* (1662), and this already shows the main features of her method of weaving together fact and fiction in the later masterpiece. Virtually all its characters, including the central figures of the husband and wife, the Prince and Princesse de Montpensier, really existed during the period covered by the story—the years 1566–72, during the reign of Charles IX. The heroine did in fact marry in 1566, when she was 16; the background of political and religious rivalries between the great aristocratic clans such as the Guises and the Bourbons is accurately transcribed; and the tale culminates in the massacre of Saint-Barthélemy, in 1572. Only the main love intrigue between the wife and a former suitor is invented together with the character of another hopeless suitor, Chabannes.

In *La Princesse de Clèves* the same approach is employed, but on an altogether larger and more impressive scale; and critics such as Henri Chamard and Gustave Rudler have shown the great range of meticulous historical research which went into the composition of the novel.[22] Documenting herself from histories of the Valois dynasty, such as Mézeray's *Abrégé de l'Histoire de France* (1668), Père Anselme's *Histoire de la Maison royale de France* (1674), or from recently re-edited sixteenth-century memoirs by Brantôme and Castelnau, she re-created with scrupulous authenticity the major historical events against which her tale is unfolded. The pages-long evocation of Court ceremonials—the ball, marking the nuptials of the King's daughter, Claude de France, with the Duc de Lorraine (during which Nemours and the Princess first meet); the tournament held to celebrate the marriage of another royal daughter to

Philip of Spain in 1559, during which Henri II was mortally wounded—these are all faithfully reconstructed from the sources. Indeed, for almost every rôle in the novel there are real historical models: even for such relatively insignificant figures as Nemours's sister, Mme de Mercœur; and the only complete inventions are the heroine and her mother, Mme de Chartres.[23] In all essentials, what emerges is that Mme de Lafayette's major concern, the triangular relationship between the husband, wife and lover, with all its moral and psychological complexities, is entirely the product of her own imagination, set against a substantially accurate historical back-cloth.

It has, of course, been pointed out by critics that, together with minor manipulations of historical chronology where the plot of the novel required them,[24] there is also a general tendency to idealise the sixteenth-century milieu in Mme de Lafayette's narrative, in so far as much of the coarseness revealed by Brantôme's account of the period is removed. But this is for the most part only a function of the aesthetic stylisation of the material: the choice of a past age serves the same purpose as in Classical tragedy, where the characters are 'distanced' and acquire a heightened seriousness that promotes the intensity of the tragic theme. The best comment on the nature of this *éloignement* is provided by Racine in the Preface to *Bajazet*:

> Les personnages tragiques doivent être regardés d'un autre œil que nous ne regardons d'ordinaire les personnages que nous avons vus de si près. On peut dire que le respect que l'on a pour les héros augmente à mesure qu'ils s'éloignent de nous: *major e longinquo reverentia*.

As in Racinian tragedy, therefore, the characters of Mme de Lafayette's work come with a ready-made poetic prestige that guarantees the aesthetic purity with which the moral issues are presented. It contributes to that atmosphere of *tristesse majestueuse* of which Racine spoke, and prepares our imagination to abandon its normal preoccupation with the trivial detail of conventional reality. Hence the extraordinary degree of abstraction which seems to be inseparable from the novelist's primary concern with moral conflicts. A striking example of this Classical refusal of concrete detail is to be found in the way Mme de Lafayette refers to the Prince de Condé. In reality, he was a hunchback, but with a characteristic use of litotes, he is referred to in the novel as having "un petit corps peu favorisé de la nature" (p. 3).

In general, Mme de Lafayette shows herself to be supremely unconcerned with physical appearances, whether she is dealing with people or places. There is a rare exception to the rule when we learn that the heroine has blond hair, but her "parfaite beauté" is summarily evoked in the most stereotyped of formulae:

> La blancheur de son teint et ses cheveux blonds lui donnaient un éclat que l'on n'a jamais vu qu'à elle; tous ses traits étaient réguliers, et son visage et sa personne étaient pleins de grâce et de charmes (pp. 7-8).

A similar vagueness is apparent in the description of her character: "elle avait le cœur très noble et très bien fait". Nemours, too, is "un chef-d'œuvre de la nature ... l'homme le mieux fait et le plus beau"; and of Clèves we do not even get this hint of his physical appearance, though we are told he is young and *magnifique*.

Much the same point can be made about the description of dress. We read that Nemours dresses exquisitely, but no detail is given. Mme de Lafayette manages to suggest a general aura of *magnificence*, yet only rarely do we come across any specific allusions, and even dress itself is more commonly referred to in such highly abstract terms as *ajustements*.[25]

Writing of this aspect of Mme de Lafayette's style, and in particular of her frequent recourse to hyperbole, M. Coulet says appositely:

> Le superlatif aristocratique, aussi fréquent dans la nouvelle classique que dans le roman baroque, y a un sens tout différent; au lieu d'exalter le mérite du héros, il suggère une grâce, une sensibilité que les mots ne peuvent préciser; il est le contraire de l'emphase, il traduit un mouvement de pudeur chez le narrateur; il a le même effet que les formules

généralisantes, les maximes par lesquelles l'histoire particulière est élevée au niveau du symbole et le jeu des passions au niveau de la fatalité.[26]

A comparable degree of abstraction is found in the novelist's manner of locating her action: it takes place amid the sumptuous splendours of the Louvre and other great residences, but the reader's imagination must supply the detail. When the narrative shifts to the country, to the country-house at Coulommiers, external nature is as if non-existent, apart from one fleeting reference after Nemours has spied on the Princess from a hidden position in the park: "Il s'en alla sous des saules, le long d'un petit ruisseau qui coulait derrière la maison . . .", but these are stock elements, as formalised as the traditional Classical garden.[27]

With places, as with people, what interests Mme de Lafayette is essentially the moral forces that lurk beneath the surface glitter in a world of which Mme de Chartres says, warning her daughter: "Si vous jugez sur les apparences en ce lieu-ci . . . vous serez souvent trompée: ce qui paraît n'est presque jamais la vérité" (p. 23). Very often, the external events of the novel—its succession of Court balls, receptions and tournaments—seem to have the air of set-pieces of historical description, indulged in for their own sake. Yet, in fact, they exist primarily to define the social pressures that govern the characters and constantly force them into each other's company at those critical moments when solitude is most urgently needed. Without such obligations of *bienséance*, which form the essence of the ethos of the courtier, the tragedy of the Princess would never have occurred. They are the equivalent of the conventional *romanesque* devices of the earlier heroic romance—the kidnappings, the abductions and shipwrecks—but whereas the latter were arbitrary interventions of *le hasard*, the imprisoning social ritual of *La Princesse de Clèves* is an organic feature of a precisely drawn historical milieu.

This point can be confirmed by a few characteristic extracts from the novel. Once the Princess becomes aware of her true feelings for Nemours, she sees that her only hope is to avoid his presence, a presence which paralyses her will: "connaissant que la seule présence de ce prince le justifiait à ses yeux . . ." (p. 108). Hence: "Elle jugea que l'absence seule et l'éloignement pouvait lui donner quelque force" (p. 142). Her mother gives her the same counsel: "retirez-vous de la cour, obligez votre mari de vous emmener" (p. 35). As long as she remains at Court her martyrdom continues, for Nemours is always there: "elle le vit chez la reine dauphine, elle le vit jouer à la paume avec le roi, elle le vit courre la bague, elle l'entendit parler . . ." (p. 21).

But the phrase which sums up her tragic predicament recurs like a leitmotif: "Elle n'était pas maîtresse de s'éloigner . . ." (p. 59). The decision is not hers, but her husband's, and for Clèves the first need is to save appearances, to satisfy the demands of convention:

> Je crois qu'il faut que vous reveniez aussi à Paris. Il est temps que vous voyiez le monde et que vous receviez ce nombre infini de visites dont aussi vous ne sauriez vous dispenser (p. 45).

Equally relevant to the tragic structure of the novel are the detailed references to the intrigues of the rival factions at Court: the Guise and the Montmorency dynasties, for instance, are both rivals for marital alliance with the offspring of the King and his allpowerful mistress, Diane de Poitiers, Duchesse de Valentinois ("L'un et l'autre parti avait toujours songé à gagner la duchesse de Valentinois"), and even peace treaties between the nations have as their main article a politically motivated match. Here again, the point is made that love is inseparable from the politico-social context, and without such a context the novel's psychological insights were doomed to imaginative sterility.

Of supreme concern to all the characters is their aristocratic pride of caste, their *gloire*, and it is as a pawn in this game of power-politics that Mme de Lafayette's heroine enters on her tragic course. It was from political motives that the Cardinal de Lorraine forbade the marriage between his younger brother, the Chevalier de Guise, and Mlle de Chartres. For all her moral idealism and insistence on the importance of love between husband and wife, Mme de Chartres is drawn into competing with tainted Court society on its own terms; she is, we are told, "extrêmement glorieuse", and her resentment at both the Cardinal's rebuff and the resistance of Clèves's father to his son's alliance with the girl produces in her a *dépit* which ill accords with her principles:

> Elle fut bien étonnée que la maison de Clèves et celle de Guise craignissent son alliance, au lieu de la souhaiter. Le dépit qu'elle eut lui fit penser à trouver un parti pour sa fille, qui la mît au-dessus de ceux qui se croyaient au-dessus d'elle (p. 13).

The essentially unemphatic nature of Mme de Lafayette's narrative tone tends to conceal the heavy significance of the sentence in which she indicates Mme de Chartres's share of responsibility in the Princess's subsequent tragedy:

> Dès le lendemain, ce prince [Clèves] fit parler à Mme de Chartres; elle reçut la proposition qu'on lui faisait et *elle ne craignit point de donner à sa fille un mari qu'elle ne pût aimer* en lui donnant le prince de Clèves.[28]

When, in the early pages of the novel, Mme de Lafayette décrit the nature of Court society (as opposed to her normal practice of dramatising her insights) she insists particularly upon the atmosphere of feverish intrigue and dissimulation, in which the courtiers pursue their ambitions:

> L'ambition et la galanterie étaient l'âme de cette cour, et occupaient également les hommes et les femmes. Il y avait tant d'intérêts et tant de cabales différentes, et les dames y avaient tant de part que l'amour était toujours mêlé aux affaires et les affaires à l'amour. Personne n'était tranquille, ni indifférent; on songeait à s'élever, à plaire, à servir ou à nuire...
> Toutes ces différentes cabales avaient de l'émulation et de l'envie les unes contre les autres: les dames qui les composaient avaient aussi de la jalousie entre elles, ou pour la faveur, ou pour les amants; les intérêts de grandeur et d'élévation se trouvaient souvent joints à ces autres intérêts moins importants, mais qui n'étaient pas moins sensibles. Ainsi il y avait une sorte d'agitation sans désordre dans cette cour, qui la rendait très agréable, mais aussi très dangereuse pour une jeune personne (pp. 11–12).

This analysis points to a secondary function of the choice of a sixteenth-century setting for the action of the novel: namely that, while providing the desirable degree of aesthetic *éloignement*, it was at the same time sufficiently close to Mme de Lafayette's own experience of the seventeenth-century Court for her to claim with justice that the novel was "une parfaite imitation de la Cour et de la manière dont on y vit". All the major descriptions of Louis XIV's Court that have come down to us fit the world of *La Princesse de Clèves*, and memorialists such as La Bruyère and Saint-Simon all stress the same political jockeying of the various *cabales* that surrounded the monarch. Here, for instance, is how Saint-Simon's *Mémoires* evoke the situation at Versailles:

> Chaque visage vous rappelle les soins, les intrigues, les sueurs employés à l'avancement des fortunes, à la force des cabales; les adresses à se maintenir et en écarter d'autres...[29]

And when Saint-Simon refers to the way every courtier had to learn to be a mind-reader in this society of masks, writing of "la promptitude des yeux à voler partout en sondant les âmes", he gives a further clue to Mme de Lafayette's solution to the problem of finding the perfect literary mould for a novel of moral analysis. In a society where all personal relationships are inseparable from political interests, every man must be constantly alert not only to the mental processes of those that surround him; he must also be equally watchful of himself, practising that "extrême défiance de soi-même" which Mme de Chartres urges upon her daughter. Hence the ease with which the long passages of self-examination fit into the structure of the novel, with its basic rhythm of public confrontations during which the heroine's emotional and moral development is made to take some fresh and irretrievable steps, followed by periods of temporary withdrawal into solitude when she can take stock of herself. One of the best, though completely typical, examples of this, comes after a particularly moving and lyrical passage, when Nemours and the Princess have spent time together composing a substitute letter on behalf of Mme la Dauphine—"elle ne sentait que le plaisir de voir M. de Nemours, elle avait une joie pure et sans mélange qu'elle n'avait jamais sentie"— and it is worth quoting at length in order to illustrate the nature of Mme de Lafayette's analytical method:

> Après qu'on eut envoyé la lettre à Mme la Dauphine, M. de Clèves et M. de Nemours s'en allèrent. Mme de Clèves demeura seule, et, sitôt qu'elle ne fut plus soutenue par cette joie que donne la présence de ce que l'on aime, elle revint comme d'un songe; elle regarda avec étonnement la prodigieuse différence de l'état où elle était le soir d'avec celui où elle se trouvait alors; elle se remit devant les yeux l'aigreur et la froideur qu'elle avait fait paraître à M. de Nemours tant qu'elle avait cru que la lettre de Mme de Thémines s'adressait à lui; quel calme et quelle douceur avait succédé à cette aigreur, sitôt qu'il l'avait persuadée que cette lettre ne le regardait pas. Quand elle pensait qu'elle s'était reproché comme un crime, le jour précédent, de lui avoir donné des marques de sensibilité que la seule compassion pouvait avoir fait naître et que, par son aigreur, elle lui avait fait paraître des sentiments de jalousie qui étaient des preuves certaines de passion, elle ne se reconnaissait plus elle-même. Quand elle pensait encore que M. de Nemours voyait bien qu'elle connaissait son amour, qu'il voyait bien aussi que, malgré cette connaissance, elle ne l'en traitait pas plus mal en présence même de son mari, qu'au contraire elle ne l'avait jamais regardé si favorablement, qu'elle était cause que M. de Clèves l'avait envoyé quérir et qu'ils venaient de passer une après-dînée ensemble en particulier, elle trouvait qu'elle était d'intelligence avec M. de Nemours, qu'elle trompait le mari du monde qui méritait le moins d'être trompé, et elle était honteuse de paraître si peu digne d'estime aux yeux même de son amant. Mais ce qu'elle pouvait moins supporter que tout le reste était le souvenir de l'état où elle avait passé la nuit, et les cuisantes douleurs que lui avait causé la pensée que M. de Nemours aimait ailleurs et qu'elle était trompée (pp. 82–3).

It was in particular this passage which was singled out for praise by Mme de Lafayette's contemporary, Valincour, for the extraordinary complexity of its psychological insights:

> Il n'y a rien de plus beau que toutes ces réflexions, et il faut avouer que l'auteur est admirable, lorsqu'il entreprend de faire voir ce qui se passe dans notre cœur. L'on ne peut mieux en connaître tous les divers mouvements, ni les exprimer avec plus de force et plus de délicatesse. Ces retours de Madame de Clèves sur elle-même, ces agitations, ces pensées différentes, qui se détruisent l'une l'autre, cette différence qui se trouve de ce qu'elle est aujourd'hui avec ce qu'elle

était hier, sont des choses qui se passent tous les jours au-dedans de nous-mêmes, que tout le monde sent, mais qu'il y a très peu de personnes qui puissent dépeindre de la manière dont nous le voyons ici.[30]

We will return later to the content of Mme de Lafayette's analysis, but for the moment, what this extract demonstrates most tellingly is her method. In the first place, one of its salient characteristics is the refusal to attempt any physical description of emotion, just as we saw there was no interest in drawing physical portraits, except in the most stylised form. Of course, this is perfectly appropriate in a milieu which explicitly frowns upon any emotional exhibitionism—and the scenes dealing with the deaths of both Mme de Chartres and Clèves are striking illustrations of the Stoic affiliations of the aristocratic code of *gloire*.[31] We are worlds apart, in *La Princesse de Clèves*, from the effusions of the novel of *sensibilité*, where characters "collapse in a dead faint, fall into paroxysms of weeping, interspersed with lamentations and heartrending cries" (Des Grieux, in *Manon Lescaut*), or "roll on the ground, biting the legs of the chairs" (Claire, in *La Nouvelle Héloïse*).

Yet, in spite of the calmness of the surface of things, reflected in the measured, unhurried rhythms of the prose and the sobriety of the vocabulary, *La Princesse de Clèves* can generate an unsurpassed intensity of emotion; and the secret of this achievement lies in the author's method of allowing the reader to experience directly the emotion by analysing the factors and the situation which give rise to it. In this way, we share the perspective of the novel's protagonists and supply from ourselves the emotional content of their experiences and thoughts. These thoughts are introduced in four different ways, three of which are found in the quoted passage. At times, Mme de Lafayette adopts the straightforward third-person narrative, but usually stresses by her choice of verbs that we have before us a subjective vision: "Elle regarda avec étonnement . . ."; or "elle se remit devant les yeux . . ." Very similar, and equally taking us directly into the immediate thought-processes of the characters, are the innumerable cases of the so-called *style indirect conjonctionnel*: "Quand elle pensait que . . ."; "elle trouvait que . . .".

A step further in the same direction of increasing subjectivity in the narrative is the transition to the *style indirect libre*, where the conjunctional phrase disappears. The device is usually regarded as a very modern one, practised on a large scale by Flaubert and leading to the 'stream of consciousness' techniques of the twentieth century, and first defined by William James. There are occasional hints of this in *La Princesse de Clèves*, and it is reasonable to interpret as such the italicised sentence in the following:

> Elle se remit devant les yeux l'aigreur et la froideur qu'elle avait fait paraître à M. de Nemours tant qu'elle avait cru que la lettre de Mme de Thémines s'adressait à lui; *quel calme et quelle douceur avait succédé à cette aigreur, sitôt qu'il l'avait persuadée que cette lettre ne le regardait pas.*[32]

The final stage of this movement towards complete subjectivity of narrative method is when the thoughts are transcribed in the *style direct*. Again, such passages are relatively rare in *La Princesse de Clèves*, but when they do occur they normally represent a supreme crisis of emotional conflict—as though the emotion has broken through all the customary barriers of repression. Such is the case, very clearly, in the lines that follow closely on the above-quoted passage:

> Elle trouva qu'il était presque impossible qu'elle pût être contente de sa passion. « Mais quand je le pourrais être, disait-elle, qu'en veux-je faire? Veux-je la souffrir? Veux-je y répondre? Veux-je m'engager dans une galanterie? Veux-je manquer à M. de Clèves? Veux-je me manquer à moi-même? Et veux-je enfin m'exposer aux cruels repentirs et aux mortelles douleurs que donne l'amour? Je suis vaincue et surmontée par une inclination qui m'entraîne malgré moi... »

Here, the broken rhythms of the prose contribute to accentuate the exceptional intensity of the inner conflict.

What is perhaps most paradoxical about this style is that, while using a highly abstract, restrained diction, it nevertheless proves so powerful to move us; but such effects are only achieved provided we are ready to co-operate with the author. She provides all the equipment but our imagination must work upon it. Thus, following the first major climax of the novel, after the scene of the *aveu*, when relations between Clèves and his wife are at their greatest point of strain, the novelist writes: "Il est aisé de s'imaginer en quel état ils passèrent la nuit" (p. 102). In what follows, however, there is no single hint of the physical scene, but only an analysis of the situation in which each of the protagonists finds himself. For instance, of Clèves, we read:

> M. de Clèves avait épuisé toute sa constance à soutenir le malheur de voir une femme qu'il adorait touchée de passion pour un autre.

Here is the unique blend of abstraction and analysis of the Classical artist: it is all the more apparent if one reduces the sentence to its most simple formulation: "M. de Clèves s'était épuisé à voir sa femme amoureuse d'un autre".

As in the Classical tragedies of Racine, the real action of *La Princesse de Clèves* lies in the inner world of conflicting passions and ideas, and this was what Valincour meant in 1678 when he said of the work that its *incidents* were often inseparable from its *sentiments*: "Ces deux choses sont quelquefois tellement liées ensemble qu'il est difficile de les séparer".[33]

* * *

Just as certain formal aspects of *La Princesse de Clèves* reveal a close similarity to the work of Racine, so too there is a distinctly Racinian quality in the content of the moral drama in Mme de Lafayette's novel; indeed, it was no accident that *La Princesse de Clèves* appeared little more than a year after the first performance of *Phèdre*, for both works can be seen to emerge from a common set of literary and social circumstances.

It has frequently been pointed out that a genuinely profound sense of the tragic in human destiny is a rare literary phenomenon because men cannot bring themselves to face squarely the terrible realisation of their own inner void. The whole burden of Pascal's analysis is along these lines, stressing the innate tendency of mankind to disguise from itself the ultimate *misère* of the human condition. What is particularly paradoxical, however, is that the rare moments in history when this tragic insight found a fully ritualised expression in the drama—in the Golden Age of ancient Greece, in Shakespearian England, and in the middle phase of Louis XIV's reign—have coincided with periods of apparently exceptional political and social stability, when the promise of achievement and progress seemed highest. The explanation of the paradox is possibly that it is only in such infrequent times of relative external stability that a society can afford to scrutinise itself in depth and abandon its normal existential preoccupation with constructing a less vulnerable pattern of values. What is certainly true is that the full experience of *misère* is only realised when set off against the potentialities for *grandeur*. In Sophocles, Shakespeare and Racine, this dual perspective is always present.[34]

It is in this sense that Mme de Lafayette's work represents, and depends on, the fusion of two traditions of thought. The world of *La Princesse de Clèves* still carries important echoes of the aristocratic idealism which has been evoked in the preceding pages— the aspiration towards a greater purity in personal relationships, the high premium placed on sincerity, and, above all, the cult of that mastery of the passions by the will which Descartes had defined as *générosité* and which was at the heart of the nobleman's concept of *gloire*. For M. and Mme de Clèves, these ideals retain their urgency and constitute the measure by which they judge themselves, yet what the novel essentially records is an experience of failure and *déchéance*; and, in this respect, it reflects the same collapse of the heroic tradition as gives Racinian tragedy its distinctive tonality.

Significantly, Racine and Mme de Lafayette were both closely connected with the same circles in which the heroic image of man was most tellingly challenged, notably those where the philosophical pessimism of Jansenism tended to prevail. Mme de Lafayette was a close friend of the Arnauld family, who dominated the Port-Royal community, and she regularly attended the Hôtel de Nevers, where, according to a contemporary witness, the abbé Rapin, "on enseigne l'évangile janséniste". And when, in 1670, Port-Royal produced an edition of the *Pensées* of its most outstanding moralist, Pascal, Mme de Lafayette expressed her admiration for the book. That is not to say she was a religious woman in the orthodox sense, but she apparently found in the Jansenist analysis of the human condition profound truths that evidently echoed her own convictions. In this, she was a sister-spirit to her closest friend from 1665 onwards, the Duc de La Rochefoucauld, whose *Maximes* also reproduced many of the central themes of Augustinian moral pessimism.

What Pascal and La Rochefoucauld both emphasize is that the rationalist image of man, presented by such idealist philosophies as Stoicism or Platonism, is essentially an illusion; the reality is that human beings are infinitely more complex, and their actions are seldom motivated by lucid, objective judgements. Reason is the plaything of a host of *puissances trompeuses*, so that, to adopt the expression of Mme de Lafayette, "ce qui paraît n'est presque jamais la vérité". According to the traditional view, the definition of such virtues as magnanimity, sincerity, generosity and courage, depended upon the concept of disinterestedness, our degree of merit being proportionate to the extent of our ability to master the passions and subordinate them to the objective sanctions of 'right reason'. Pascal and La Rochefoucauld undermine this notion of disinterestedness and concentrate on ferreting out the hidden self-interest that lurks behind our façade of social gestures. They draw a picture of the human ego which anticipates many more modern psychological theories, by insisting on the moral ambivalence of our activity; and the stress is on the *versatilité* and aggressiveness of the *moi*.

Inevitably, it was the neo-Platonic idealism with regard to love that bore the brunt of the attack. La Rochefoucauld compares love to a fever whose violence escapes our control, and concludes:

> Il n'y a point de passion où l'amour de soi-même règne si puissamment que dans l'amour, et l'on est toujours plus disposé à sacrifier le repos de ce qu'on aime, qu'à perdre le sien.[35]

Hence the strange intermingling of hatred with love, since love threatens the tranquillity of the self and leaves it vulnerable: "Plus on aime une maîtresse, et plus on est près de la haïr."[36]

It would be an exaggeration to suggest that these insights into the complex nature of the passions were unfamiliar to the generation of writers who dominated the literary scene before 1660, and it has already been shown that the salon-world's breviary of idealism—d'Urfé's *L'Astrée*—had its darker aspects. Even Corneille's early work, such as *Le Cid*, besides its more overt tributes to Stoic and neo-Platonic sentiments, frequently presents a less edifying picture of love-relationships than the manuals would suggest, and critics like Octave Nadal have indicated the very real vein of hostility that occasionally threatens to disrupt the pattern of Rodrigue and Chimène's love for each other.[37] Yet, it is principally after 1660 that creative literature exploits unambiguously the tragic potential of what Mme de Lafayette, in the opening sentence of her first *nouvelle*, *La Princesse de Montpensier*, calls "les désordres de l'Amour", and all three protagonists of *La Princesse de Clèves* illustrate the different facets of this theme.

The heroine's feelings for Nemours have all the ambivalence described by La Rochefoucauld: once she is conscious of her passion and the threat it poses to her peace of mind, "il s'en fallait peu qu'elle ne crût le haïr par la douleur que lui donnait cette pensée" (p. 34). Similarly, in her husband, when he finds his love is not reciprocated, it rapidly becomes "une passion violente et inquiète qui troublait sa joie" (p. 18). And once he has learned that he has a rival, he submits his wife to a ruthless inquisition to discover the identity of the unknown suitor, knowing that he is unjust, yet helpless to resist the aggressiveness in himself. One of the most painful episodes in the novel is the passage where the full acrimony between husband and wife erupts, when Clèves declares:

> Vous aviez donc oublié que je vous aimais éperdument et que j'étais votre mari? L'un des deux peut porter aux extrémités: que ne peuvent point les deux ensemble? Hé! que ne sont-ils point aussi, continua-t-il; je n'ai que des sentiments violents et incertains dont je ne suis pas le maître. Je ne me trouve plus digne de vous; vous ne me

paraissez plus digne de moi. Je vous adore, je vous hais, je vous offense, je vous demande pardon; je vous admire, j'ai honte de vous admirer. Enfin il n'y a plus en moi ni de calme, ni de raison... Je vous demande seulement de vous souvenir que vous m'avez rendu le plus malheureux homme du monde (p. 114).

As one would expect, it is in Nemours, the typical Court *beau*, that love is most visibly associated with the *libido dominandi*, and his behaviour towards the heroine frequently reminds us of Molière's Dom Juan and his celebrated declaration:

On goûte une douceur extrême à réduire, par cent hommages, le cœur d'une jeune beauté, à voir de jour en jour les petits progrès qu'on y fait, à combattre par des transports, par des larmes et des soupirs, l'innocente pudeur d'une âme qui a peine à rendre les armes, à forcer pied à pied toutes les petites résistances qu'elle nous oppose, à vaincre les scrupules dont elle se fait un honneur et la mener doucement où nous avons envie de la faire venir (Act I, scene 2).

Thus, when Nemours has overheard the confession by Mme de Clèves to her husband, and witnessed the full extent of her anguish, we read:

Il sentit pourtant un plaisir sensible de l'avoir réduite à cette extrémité. Il trouva de la gloire à s'être fait aimer d'une femme si différente de toutes celles de son sexe (p. 90).

Later on, he deliberately sows the seeds of suspicion between husband and wife, relishing their growing estrangement:

M. de Nemours, qui vit les soupçons de Mme de Clèves sur son mari, fut bien aise de les lui confirmer. Il savait que c'était le plus redoutable rival qu'il eût à détruire (p. 99).

This not only reminds us again of Dom Juan ("je me figurai un plaisir extrême à pouvoir troubler leur intelligence, et rompre cet attachement, dont la délicatesse de mon cœur se tenait offensé"), but also it confirms La Rochefoucauld's statement that the lover is "plus disposé à sacrifier le repos de ce qu'on aime qu'à sacrifier le sien".[38]

Once the Princess becomes aware of the way Nemours has behaved, she draws the bleak conclusion that men are discreet only so long as they are unsure of themselves; no sooner is their ego flattered than it acts with total disregard for the feelings of those they profess to cherish:

> Il a été discret, disait-elle, tant qu'il a cru être malheureux; mais une pensée d'un bonheur, même incertain, a fini sa discrétion. Il n'a pu s'imaginer qu'il était aimé sans vouloir qu'on le sût... J'ai eu tort de croire qu'il y eût un homme capable de cacher ce qui flatte sa gloire (p. 103).

The same theme has already been illustrated in the novel in the first of the 'digressions' which most earlier critics, with their too limited concept of formal unity, looked upon as spoiling the organic, Classical structure of the book:[39] but Mme de Chartres's story of the relationship between Henry II and Diane de Poitiers —a passion that only survived because the King could never be sure of his mistress's devotion—constitutes a vital element in the moral education of Mme de Clèves and prepares the ground for the later rejection of Nemours when she says:

> Mais les hommes conservent-ils de la passion dans ces engagements éternels? Dois-je espérer un miracle en ma faveur et puis-je me mettre en état de voir certainement finir cette passion dont je ferais toute ma félicité? M. de Clèves était peut-être l'unique homme du monde capable de conserver de l'amour dans le mariage. Ma destinée n'a pas voulu que j'aie pu profiter de ce bonheur; peut-être aussi que sa passion n'avait subsisté que parce qu'il n'en aurait pas trouvé en moi. Mais je n'aurais pas le même moyen de conserver la vôtre: je crois même que les obstacles ont fait votre constance. Vous en avez trouvé pour vous animer à vaincre, et mes actions involontaires, ou les choses que le hasard vous a apprises, vous ont donné assez d'espérance pour ne vous pas rebuter (p. 137).

It is here, in Mme de Clèves's reference to her "actions involontaires", that we have another direct pointer to the way Mme de Lafayette exploits the psychological insights already formulated by Pascal and La Rochefoucauld. Both of these moralists had attacked as presumptuous the claims made by the Stoics concerning the power of the will to enforce the dictates of reason, claims reiterated by Descartes in such neo-Stoic terms as: "La volonté est tellement libre de sa nature qu'elle ne peut jamais être contrainte... Il n'y a point d'âme si faible qu'elle ne puisse, étant bien conduite, acquérir un pouvoir absolu sur ses passions."[40] By constantly stressing the *involuntary* springs of action in her characters and showing how they are propelled by forces within themselves which they are powerless to control, Mme de Lafayette achieves her most characteristic tragic effects. Phrases which betray a lack of self-direction recur like a refrain throughout the novel:

> L'inclination qu'elle avait pour ce prince lui donnait un trouble dont elle n'était pas maîtresse (p. 50).
>
> Elle trouva qu'elle n'était plus maîtresse de ses paroles et de son visage (p. 59).
>
> Ce lui était une grande douleur de voir qu'elle n'était plus maîtresse de cacher ses sentiments (p. 63).
>
> Je n'ai que des sentiments violents et incertains dont je ne suis pas le maître (p. 114).

These are the kind of sentiments which build up the tragic resonance of the novel, producing the sustained lamentation for a lost glory, the sense of a fall from grace. In this respect we are again close to the tonality of Racinian tragedy, and one could apply to the protagonists of *La Princesse de Clèves* what Paul Bénichou has written of the world of Racine:

> Le propre de la passion, telle que la conçoit Racine, est qu'elle tend à posséder d'abord celui qui l'éprouve; elle est la négation de la liberté, la réfutation vivante de l'orgueil... Pour l'orgueil du moi, la passion coupable est un aveu radical de misère.[41]

I have already said that the basic structure of the novel is built upon the alternating phases of the Princess in society, where she comes face to face with Nemours, followed by a retreat into solitude, accompanied by self-analysis and moral judgement. It is this technique which highlights the tragic pattern, whereby instinct provokes actions which are subsequently condemned by the conscience. The Princess is again and again presented as the victim of those same subconscious forces as La Rochefoucauld had laid bare in his study of the mechanisms of *amour-propre*, summing up his thesis in the maxim: "L'esprit est toujours la dupe du cœur."[42]

This is the way Mme de Lafayette portrays the growth of the heroine's love for Nemours; it takes possession of her heart like a stealthy invader, and one of the first signs of her unconscious complicity with passion is that she ceases to be frank with her mother about her feelings:

> Elle ne se trouva pas la même disposition à dire à sa mère ce qu'elle pensait des sentiments de ce prince qu'elle avait eue à lui parler de ses autres amants; sans avoir un dessein formé de lui cacher, elle ne lui en parla point. Mais Mme de Chartres ne le voyait que trop... (p. 27).

The function of reason is repeatedly reduced to rationalising the demands of instinct, so that when the Princess hears that Nemours has spoken of the way a lover suffers if the woman he loves goes to a public ball, she seeks pretexts for not attending the ball given by the Maréchal de Saint-André: "Elle fut bien aise d'avoir une raison de sévérité pour faire une chose qui était une faveur pour M. de Nemours" (p. 30).

It is not until she hears from her mother that Nemours is reported to be in love with the Reine Dauphine—giving her her first cruel experience of jealousy—that she becomes fully conscious of her passion:

> L'on ne peut exprimer la douleur qu'elle sentit de connaître, par ce que lui venait de dire sa mère, l'intérêt qu'elle prenait à M. de Nemours: *elle n'avait encore osé se l'avouer à elle-même.*[43]

After the climactic scene of the *aveu*, when she is forced back into the presence of Nemours by her husband's insistence that social obligations must be met, she is, for all her efforts of will, helpless to conceal her feelings or control her reactions, constantly being betrayed by what the novelist calls "un premier mouvement", an impulse.

Feeding on these apparently incontrovertible signs of his wife's infidelity, Clèves's jealousy slowly undermines his health, and his death furnishes the central catastrophe of the novel. But, as in Racinian tragedy, the major concern of the author is to study the psychological repercussions of this catastrophe, and one is reminded of Racine's reply to those critics of his *Britannicus* who claimed that the play should have ended with the death of the eponymous hero:

> Pour moi, j'ai toujours compris que la tragédie étant l'imitation d'une action complète, où plusieurs personnes concourent, cette action n'est point finie que l'on ne sache en quelle situation elle laisse ces mêmes personnes.[44]

And, just as in Racine's *Phèdre* the tragic impact is so closely tied up with the process of self-recognition, followed by self-horror in the face of guilt (a process well illustrated by Bossuet's phrase: "Il faut aller jusqu'à l'horreur quand on se connaît"), so, in *La Princesse de Clèves*, the guilt-ridden reaction of Mme de Clèves to her husband's death accounts for some of the most moving effects achieved by the novel:

> Mme de Clèves demeura dans une affliction si violente qu'elle perdit quasi l'usage de la raison... Quand elle commença d'avoir la force de l' [=sa douleur] envisager et qu'elle vit quel mari elle avait perdu, qu'elle considéra qu'elle était la cause de sa mort, et que c'était par la passion qu'elle avait eue pour un autre qu'elle en était cause, l'horreur qu'elle eut pour elle-même et pour M. de Nemours ne se peut représenter (pp. 127–128).

And yet, in spite of this, the fact remains that Mme de Clèves, unlike Racine's Phèdre, never consciously yields to passion, nor does she, unlike Mme de Lafayette's other heroines in *La Princesse de Montpensier* or *La Comtesse de Tende*,[45] willingly embrace an adulterous relationship. When she confesses the truth of her feelings for Nemours to her husband, she presents this as an act of courage:

> L'aveu que je vous ai fait n'a pas été par faiblesse, et il faut plus de courage pour avouer cette vérité que pour entreprendre de la cacher (p. 88).

Again, later, when she is technically free to marry Nemours, she chooses to reject him, and many critics in the past have interpreted her as a 'Cornelian' figure, in whom we witness the final triumph of the will, enacting the sanctions of duty and reason. Thus, Charles Dédéyan, who has been one of the most recent writers to comment on the subject, says:

> Il s'agit de savoir qui vaincra en Mme de Clèves: la racinienne ou la cornélienne; la victime de la passion ou la femme du devoir...

And M. Dédéyan later concludes: "elle suit le devoir et la raison".[46]

As regards the motivation of the *aveu*, what radically distinguishes this action from the so-called 'Cornelian' pattern is that Mme de Lafayette presents her heroine as the victim of a growing panic which robs her of the lucidity necessary for any objective decision. After her virtually traumatic experience of jealousy, when she believed Nemours 'unfaithful' to her, and without her mother to turn to for moral support, she first gets the idea of confiding in her husband following his reaction to the Sancerre incident:

> Ce que M. de Clèves lui avait dit sur la sincérité, en parlant de Mme de Tournon, lui revint dans l'esprit; il lui sembla qu'elle devait avouer l'inclination qu'elle avait pour M. de Nemours.[47]

This idea is subsequently dismissed as a *folie*, but is again seized upon in desperation when Clèves has rejected her pleas to be allowed to stay away from Court; so that, although at the time she presents the *aveu* as an act of *courage* rather than of *faiblesse*, no sooner has Clèves left her than she has the premonition of disaster, realising that she has committed a profound error:

> Lorsque ce prince fut parti, que Mme de Clèves demeura seule, qu'elle regarda ce qu'elle venait de faire, elle en fut si épouvantée qu'à peine put-elle s'imaginer que ce fût une vérité. Elle trouva qu'elle s'était ôté elle-même le cœur et l'estime de son mari et qu'elle s'était creusé un abîme dont elle ne sortirait jamais. Elle se demandait pourquoi elle avait fait une chose si hasardeuse, et elle trouvait qu'elle s'y était engagée sans en avoir presque eu le dessein... (pp. 89-90).

It is this premonition that is eventually proved true by Clèves: "N'en doutez pas Madame,... vous vous êtes trompée; vous avez attendu de moi des choses aussi impossibles que celles que j'attendais de vous" (p. 114), and no character was ever further than the Princess from the stock reaction of the Cornelian hero assuming full responsibility for his deed with the words: "Je le ferais encore, si j'avais à le faire."[48] Indeed, once again, it is rather La Rochefoucauld who comes to mind when one analyses the true motivation of the *aveu*: "On est souvent ferme par faiblesse, et audacieux par timidité" (Maxime 11); and, as events show, the Princess finds that she too, in order to ensure her own *repos*, has sacrificed that of her husband. Seen in this perspective, the *aveu* is therefore a classic illustration of the Aristotelian formula for tragic irony: a deed performed with good intention recoils against the protagonist and is subsequently recognised as self-defeating, producing what the Shakespearian critic A. C. Bradley called a sense of "waste".[49]

When we turn to the final encounter between the heroine and M. de Nemours, we find a similar complexity of motivation behind her actions. What the episode demonstrates above all is the superbly organic way in which all the strands of the novel are gathered together and brought to bear on her decision to reject marriage. She speaks of the "règles austères que mon devoir m'impose", namely the duty towards her dead husband, for whose death she believes she and Nemours bear a deep responsibility.[50] And, when Nemours retorts that this a "fantôme de devoir", he is right in so far as she is haunted by a crippling sense of guilt at her own complicity. But Mme de Clèves herself is equally aware that more is involved than objective dictates of duty and reason, and she points to her deep-rooted fear of exposing herself again through marriage to the jealousy which had consumed her earlier in the novel:

> La certitude de n'être plus aimée de vous, comme je le suis, me paraît un si horrible malheur que, quand je n'aurais point des raisons de devoir insurmontables, je doute si je pourrais me résoudre à m'exposer à ce malheur... Ce que je crois devoir à la mémoire de M. de Clèves serait faible s'il n'était soutenu par l'intérêt de mon repos; et les raisons de mon repos ont besoin d'être soutenues de celles de mon devoir (pp. 137, 139).

It is this renewed emphasis on the psychological complexity of the heroine's behaviour which is more important than any reductive interpretation, and even in this Mme de Lafayette was true to La Rochefoucauld. For, although Gide attacked La Rochefoucauld for oversimplifying the nature of human motivation—comparing him unfavourably with Dostoievski—what the *Maximes* ultimately stress is precisely the fact that our ego is an impenetrable mystery which no one can neatly categorise:

> Rien n'est si impétueux que ses désirs; rien de si caché que ses desseins, rien de si habile que ses conduites, ses souplesses ne se peuvent représenter, ses transformations passent celles des métamorphoses, et ses raffinements ceux de la chimie. *On ne peut sonder la profondeur ni percer les mystères de ses abîmes: là il est à couvert des yeux les plus pénétrants...*[51]

The moral ambiguity which is a feature of Mme de Lafayette's presentation of character is, of course, best seen in the case of the Princesse de Clèves, who is the real focus of the novel, but the same technique is apparent elsewhere; and it has been commented on by Professor Jules Brody, when he writes of the way Nemours is portrayed: "Not even from the reader's omniscient vantage-point does Nemours's character ever really emerge with total clarity. Daring, cunning, and egotism mix constantly and randomly with self-effacement, submissiveness and ascetic devotion... Brantôme's exclusive insistence on aggressive sensuality [in Nemours] ... is absorbed here into a fuller, infinitely more complex picture. Equally irresistible as his historical model, he is also smooth, gentle, socially a 'catch', and so discreet, presumably, that none can penetrate the secrets of his heart."[52]

We are therefore back here to the question of narrative perspective which was discussed earlier: Mme de Lafayette's method is essentially similar to that of the contemporary drama, notably that of Racine, where the characters' actions and inner thoughts are presented without the intervention of an omniscient narrator to provide explicit interpretation. Only on very rare occasions does the narrator (referred to just once as "je", on p. 2) intervene to make a moral comment, and even then one notices how often the comment is guarded, the analytical judgement being restricted by some such expression as *peut-être*.[53]

While the narrative method of *La Princesse de Clèves* was no doubt considerably influenced by the drama (just as was the case with later novelists such as Dickens or Henry James[54]), Mme de Lafayette was at the same time respecting the convention of the *genre* of the historical novel within which she was working. We have already seen that she characterised her book as being "proprement des mémoires", and, as Sir Walter Scott says, it was part of the convention that a writer should accept a certain ambiguity when dealing with the motivation behind 'historical' events:

> The most marked distinction between a real and a fictitious narrative [is] that the former, in reference to the remote causes of the events it relates, is obscure ... whereas in the latter case, it is part of the author's duty to account for everything.[55]

Perhaps still more significant, however, is the fact that this convention was perfectly attuned to Mme de Lafayette's whole approach to the nature of the human *psyche*, an approach which, like that of La Rochefoucauld with which it shares so much common ground, seems to be derived from the tradition established by

Montaigne. Central to this tradition, with its roots in philosophical Scepticism, was the notion of the relativity of all phenomena, so that there was a fundamental refusal to consider character in terms of fixed and immutable essences. For this reason, it is quite appropriate to apply to Mme de Lafayette's narrative technique what the author of the *Essais* says of his own method of presenting himself:

> Je ne peins pas l'être, je peins le passage... C'est un contrôle de divers et muables accidents et d'imaginations irrésolues, et quand il y échoit contraires: soit que je sois autre moi-même, soit que je saisisse les sujets par autres circonstances et considérations.[56]

There is, in the final *dénouement* of *La Princesse de Clèves*, the same insistence upon the fluidity and contradictory nature of the human self, seen as being the plaything of Time:

> Tous ses sentiments étaient pleins de trouble et de passion... *Il y avait des moments* où elle avait de la peine à comprendre qu'elle pût être malheureuse en l'épousant... La raison et son devoir lui montraient, *dans d'autres moments*, des choses tout opposées, qui l'emportaient rapidement à la résolution de ne se point remarier et de ne voir jamais M. de Nemours.[57]

This is just one of the passages which confirm the point made by Mrs. Raitt in her perceptive discussion of Mme de Lafayette's techniques of psychological analysis:

> With the two main characters the author's analysis is always concrete and specific. The emotions of the Princesse are described in direct relation to a particular event and to a particular person, so that she always emerges clearly as an individual. Indeed, Madame de Lafayette takes the detailed precision of her analysis so far that we find it difficult to gain a general, consistent picture of the heroine at all. Her emotions and motives are noted according to their importance at any given moment and they may easily contradict what she was feeling a few pages before. In this way, Madame de Lafayette, without departing from her rôle as objective narrator of facts, suggests the chaos and indecision of the Princesse's mind as she favours first one course of action and then another—now desiring above all that Nemours should be a worthy object of her love and now thinking only of her duty to her husband regardless of whether Nemours is worthy or not. The author's narrative is simultaneous with the heroine's psychological waverings and Madame de Lafayette herself gives us no long view of

her heroine's dilemma, allows us no hint as to her own judgment of her character. Moreover, the Princesse's feelings reveal inconsistencies not only between two different occasions but at one and the same time, and again the author does not always indicate which motive has priority. She is described on the one hand in terms of lucid self-criticism, and on the other in terms of subconscious, unacknowledged desires. This sort of self-deception is especially noticeable in the final part of the novel after the Prince's death, when her two levels of consciousness are shown to change places: Mme de Clèves begins by refusing to acknowledge the survival of her love for Nemours, then acknowledges it with no intention of giving in to it, and finally gives in to it completely and refuses to satisfy it precisely because she cares too much to risk changing it in any way. Nowhere does Madame de Lafayette pinpoint this switch in her heroine's motives; she states each priority as she comes to it and leaves the Princesse's indecisiveness to emerge on its own. So we have the impression of really living the Princesse's final days in the world with her and not of observing them from some remote, omniscient viewpoint.[58]

Given this perspective, it therefore seems perfectly appropriate that the novel should retain in its *dénouement* something of the inconclusiveness which surrounds the episode when Nemours is rejected. Even the *refus* itself is not presented as an absolute, for it is mitigated by a suggestion of compromise when Mme de Clèves says, just before Nemours leaves her for the last time: "Attendez ce que le temps pourra faire" (p. 139). In the end, it is indeed Time which shapes the last stages of the drama: Nemours's passion fades ("Enfin, des années entières s'étant passées, le temps et l'absence ralentirent sa douleur et éteignirent sa passion"); and, while the final form of the *repos* which Mme de Clèves achieves virtually liberates her from Time through *détachement*, the author retains her sense of the complexities inherent in moral phenomena by carefully indicating the part played by the contingencies of Time—illness and physical decline—in bringing about her heroine's ultimate 'liberation':

> Cette vue si longue et si prochaine de la mort fit paraître à Mme de Clèves les choses de cette vie de cet œil si différent dont on les voit dans la santé. La nécessité de mourir, dont elle se voyait si proche, l'accoutuma à se détacher de toutes choses, et la longueur de sa maladie lui en fit une habitude (p. 143).

Hence the applicability to *La Princesse de Clèves* of what a Shakespearian critic, D. A. Traversi, wrote concerning *Troilus and Cressida* —namely, that its true tragedy lay in "the impossibility, the meaninglessness of constancy in a world where time dominates human relationships". For, at the bottom of the Princess's desperation lies the perception so tellingly voiced by Troilus:

> This is the monstruosity in love ... that the will is infinite, and the execution confined, that the desire is boundless, and the act a slave to limit (Act III, scene 2).

NOTES

1 1657; quoted from 1722 edition, I, p. 167.
2 N.R.F. (Collection: Idées), 1964, p. 24.
3 The debate as to the class affiliations of 'la morale de Molière' continues, but the best treatment of it is that of Paul Bénichou: *Morales du Grand Siècle*, N.R.F., 1948, pp. 156–218.
4 Preface to *Le Grand Dictionnaire des Précieuses*, 1661.
5 *La Prétieuse, ou Le Mystère des Ruelles*, 1656.
6 Quoted by Bernard Pingaud: *Mme de La Fayette par elle-même*, 'Écrivains de Toujours', 1959, p. 5.
7 *Op. cit.*
8 La Rochefoucauld: *Œuvres Complètes*, Bibliothèque de la Pléiade, 1964, pp. 3–6.
9 Quoted by Pingaud, *op. cit.*, p. 33.
10 Cf. R. C. Williams: *Bibliography of the XVIIth century Novel in France*, 1931. The author notes only two new *romans* in the period 1560–1590, but from 1592 to 1599 there are thirty-two, and five hundred and sixty-eight more from 1600 to 1661.
11 For a detailed study of this earlier period, see G. Reynier: *Le Roman Sentimental avant L'Astrée*, Armand Colin, 1908, and M. Magendie: *Le Roman français au XVIIe Siècle*, Droz, 1932.
12 Louis Dufour de Longuerue was a celebrated scholar who lived from 1652 to 1733.
13 See the abridged version in the Éditions 10/18, 1964, p. 52.
14 P. 11; all quotations from *La Princesse de Clèves* are taken from my critical edition (Harrap, 1971).
15 J. Ehrmann: *Un Paradis désespéré: l'amour et l'illusion dans L'Astrée*, P.U.F., 1963.
16 *Le Grand Cyrus*, 10 vols., published 1649–1653; *Clélie* appeared from 1654 to 1661. The other major writers of the *roman héroïque* include Gomberville (*Polexandre*, 1637) and La Calprenède (*Cléopâtre*, in twelve volumes, that appeared from 1647). For further details, see Magendie, *op. cit.*
17 Cf. Pingaud, *op. cit.*, p. 25: "Songez que le bel esprit des Romains... n'allait pas à disputer des questions tendres et galantes comme elles sont dans *Clélie*".
18 *Op. cit.*, p. 35. A similar point is well made by H. Coulet in *Le Roman iusqu'à la Révolution*, Collection U, 1967, where he says of Mlle de Scudery's

work: "Les analyses s'insèrent dans le roman héroïque sans le modifier; d'un côté une matière romanesque nouvelle, la psychologie elle-même, mais inerte et restant en marge de l'action, ne fournissant qu'un objet de conversation; de l'autre, la matière romanesque attendue, actions d'éclat, sentiments héroïques, intrigues compliquées, nombre infini de personnages qu'on connaît mieux par leurs portraits et par leurs propos que par leurs actes fantastiques" (p. 177).

19 For a fuller treatment of the development of the *nouvelle*, see F. Deloffre: *La Nouvelle en France à l'Age Classique*, Didier, 1967.

20 R. Wellek and A. Warren: *Theory of Literature*, Peregrine Books, 1963, p. 216.

21 Letter to the Chevalier de Lescheraine, April 7, 1678.

22 "Les sources historiques de *La Princesse de Clèves*" and "Les Épisodes historiques", in *Revue du XVIe siècle*, II, 1914; and "La Couleur historique dans *La Princesse de Clèves*", in *Revue du XVIe siecle*, V, 1917.

23 The book by Valentine Poizat: *La Véritable Princesse de Clèves*, Paris, 1920, suggests that the prototype for the heroine was Anne d'Este. Brantôme tells us that she was courted by Nemours while still married to the Duc de Guise, but she married Nemours after her husband's death. In general, there does not seem much substance to this argument.

24 The death of the Prince de Clèves's father is advanced by a year or so, thus circumventing his opposition to the marriage.

25 Among the few exceptions to the rule are those on pp. 56, 105, 106.

26 *Op. cit.*, p. 210.

27 Saint-Évremond sums up well the salon world's attitude to nature: "Un discours où on ne parle que de bois, de rivières, de prés, de campagnes, de jardins, fait sur nous une impression bien languissante, à moins qu'il n'ait des agréments tout nouveaux; mais ce qui est de l'humanité, les penchants, les tendresses, les affections, trouvent naturellement au fond de notre âme à se faire sentir: la même nature les produit et les reçoit, ils passent aisément des hommes qu'on représente, en des hommes qui voient représenter" (*De la Poésie*, in Œuvres, 1711, III, p. 47).

28 P. 16; the italics are mine.

29 Students can sample the *Mémoires* in various published extracts such as those of the Classiques Larousse (the quoted extract is on p. 56) or the Classiques Bordas (Harrap).

30 *Lettres à la Marquise *** sur le sujet de la Princesse de Clèves*, 1678, p. 199. As in all other quotations, I have modernised the spelling.

31 Cf. also Clèves's attitude to Sancerre's outburst of emotion: "Je lui dis que tant que son affliction avait eu des bornes, je l'avais approuvée, et que j'y étais entré; mais que je ne le plaindrais plus s'il s'abandonnait au désespoir et s'il perdait la raison" (p. 42).

32 For a further discussion of this question, see the important article by Jean Fabre, to which this chapter is indebted: "L'Art de l'analyse dans la *Princesse de Clèves*", *Travaux de la Faculté des Lettres de Strasbourg*, Paris, 1946, pp. 261–306. Also Claudette Delhez-Sarlet: "Style indirect libre et « point de vue »" in *Cahiers d'Analyse textuelle*, 6, 1964, pp. 70–80.

Another clear instance of the *style indirect libre* can be found on p. 103, lines 29–30: "Comment excuser une si grande imprudence... elle avait été touchée".

33 *Op. cit.*

34 See my analysis of *le tragique racinien*, in Chapter Two.

35 *Maximes*, 1678 edition, n° 262.

36 Maxime III.

37 O. Nadal: *Le Sentiment de l'amour dans l'œuvre de Pierre Corneille*, Gallimard, 1948; cf. the remarks on pp. 170–1, concerning Rodrigue's first interview with Chimène after the duel in which he has killed her father: "Rodrigue poursuit une dialectique qui rassemble les meilleurs arguments destinés à forcer les hésitations de Chimène... Ce procédé inquisitorial, conduit avec délice, n'est certes pas le fait de la tendresse, mais celui de l'amour-propre et de l'égoïsme amoureux... Il préfère savoir Chimène sienne quoique humiliée, plutôt que perdue pour lui, mais libre et fière." For evidence of a similar feeling of hostility in Chimène towards Rodrigue, see *Le Cid*, ll. 1509 sqq.

Other earlier exceptions to the heroic view of love include Rotrou's *Venceslas* with its 'Racinian' portrayal of the prince Ladislas (1647–8).

38 There is a hint of the same attitude on p. 58 after Nemours has stolen her portrait:

Il s'en faisait aimer malgré elle, et il voyait dans toutes ses actions cette sorte de trouble et d'embarras que cause l'amour dans l'innocence de la première jeunesse.

39 See J. W. Scott: 'The "digressions" of the *Princesse de Clèves*', in *French Studies*, 1957, pp. 315–22. For some further reflections on this notion of 'organic form', see my Introduction to *The Art of Criticism: Essays in French Literary Analysis*, Edinburgh University Press, 1969.

40 Article 40 of *Le Traité des Passions*, 1649. In contrast to this, there is the phrase used by the Vidame de Chartres which characterises the world of Mme de Lafayette's novel: "L'on n'est pas amoureux par sa volonté" (p. 73).

41 *Op. cit.*, pp. 138 and 141.

42 Maxime 102.

43 P. 32. The italics here and in other quotations from *La Princesse de Clèves* are mine.

44 *Britannicus*: "Première Préface", 1670.

45 In *La Princesse de Montpensier*, the climax comes when the heroine secretly admits her lover into her room; in *La Comtesse de Tende*, published posthumously in 1724, the heroine becomes pregnant by her lover. For more details, see Janet Raitt, *op. cit.*

46 Charles Dédéyan: *Madame de Lafayette*, Société d'Édition d'Enseignement Supérieur, 1956, pp. 188–197.

47 P. 59. When Clèves relates to his wife the Sancerre episode, he reports the advice he gave to his friend: "Je vous donne, lui dis-je, le conseil que je prendrais pour moi-même; car la sincérité me touche d'une telle sorte que je crois que si ma maîtresse, et même ma femme, m'avouait que quelqu'un lui plût, j'en serais affligé sans être aigri. Je quitterais le personnage d'amant ou de mari pour la conseiller et pour la plaindre" (p. 41).

It is this which first gives Mme de Clèves the idea of confiding in her husband. But the episode contains a warning which she misses: Sancerre lives to regret his confrontation with the truth, and the total irrationality and unpredictability of his behaviour foreshadow Cleves's own reaction.

48 Cf. *Le Cid*, l. 878 and *Polyeucte*, l. 1671. The same attitude, if not the exact words, recurs with many other Cornelian figures, such as Horace.

49 For a fuller discussion of this concept of the tragic, see Chapter Two.

50 There is a close similarity here with the end of *Le Cid*, where Chimène's reaction to the proposed match with Rodrigue is deeply affected by her guilty feelings for having become an accomplice in her own father's death, through loving his killer, cf. lines 1809–12. In both contexts, it is suggested that there is

no social stigma attached to such a match—Mme de Clèves specifically makes the point: "Le public n'aurait peut-être pas sujet de vous blâmer, ni moi non plus" (p. 137)—but the resistance is on more intimate grounds of conscience: it is "un devoir qui ne subsiste que dans mon imagination" (p. 139).

51 This extract is from the *maxime* which came first in the 1665 edition, but which was subsequently suppressed.

The same awareness of psychological complexity is expressed by other contemporaries, such as Père Rapin, in his *Réflexions sur la Poétique* of 1674: "Le cœur humain est un abîme d'une profondeur où la sonde ne peut aller, c'est un mystère impénétrable aux plus éclairés" (*Œuvres*, Amsterdam, 1693, pp. 138-41). This is what lies behind the expression used by Mme de Lafayette in the *lettre* (p. 65): "la *bizarrerie* de votre cœur".

52 Jules Brody: "*La Princesse de Clèves* and the myth of courtly love", *University of Toronto Quarterly*, January 1969, pp. 105-135. The quotation is from pp. 112-13.

53 For examples, see pp. 93, 112, 115, 119, 128 etc. Mme de Lafayette's oftennoted liking for the word *quasi* frequently performs the same function. The same tendency carries over into the language used by the characters: cf. Mme de Clèves's use of *peut-être* three times on p. 137.

It is rare to find Mme de Lafayette abandoning her authorial reserve with the obviousness seen in the following instances: "Il [le vidame de Chartres] fut surpris de la grande beauté de Mlle de Chartres, et il en fut surpris avec raison" (p. 7). The same expression recurs on pp. 17-18: "Et elle l'admirait avec raison". Another instance involving a specifically moral judgement is found on p. 128: "Elle se faisait un crime de n'avoir pas eu de la passion pour lui, *comme si c'eût été en son pouvoir*" (my italics).

On this point, it is worth consulting Helen Kaps: *Moral Perspective in 'La Princesse de Clèves'*, University of Oregon Books, 1968, which I only received after my chapter was completed. Miss Kaps's chapter on "The Narrator" contains the following statement which indicates the similarity of her views and mine:

If the narrator refuses to censure the characters' actions, he is all the more neutral where feelings, or emotions, are concerned. Emotions are neither right nor wrong, they simply *are*. Their existence is not to be judged, but to be explained; and that explanation stresses their complexity and the multiplicity of the causes which trigger them (p. 49).

54 Dickens's debt to eighteenth-century comedy and melodrama was analysed by Otto Ludwig in his "Romanstudien", *Gesammelte Schriften*, VI, 1891, p. 59 sq. Henry James's debt to Ibsen is discussed by Francis Fergusson in "James's idea of Dramatic Form", *Kenyon Review*, V. 1943, p. 495 sq.

55 Quoted by R. Wellek and A. Warren, *op. cit.*, p. 218.

56 Montaigne: *Essais*, III, 2: "Du Repentir".

57 P. 141 (my italics). Here, as in many other respects, I am reminded of Henry James's *Portrait of a Lady*, another work which fits the definition of the novel given by Goldmann. James's novel deals with the similar theme of the innocent heroine (from the New World) confronted with the corruption of society (in decadent Europe). The author speaks of having depicted his heroine as existing "in a state of bewilderment" (how well that fits Mme de Clèves's normal condition!). Like the Princess, James's lady ends by making a morally ambiguous renunciation of love.

58 Janet Raitt, *op. cit.*, ch. 3.

SELECT BIBLIOGRAPHY

(Only books are listed here; references to the more important articles in learned journals will be found in the notes at the end of each chapter.)

1. General critical works

ADAM, A.: *Histoire de la littérature française au XVIIe siècle*, 5 vols., Domat, 1948–56.
BÉNICHOU, P.: *Morales du grand siècle*, Gallimard, 1948.
BÉNICHOU, P.: *L'Écrivain et ses travaux*, Corti, 1967.
BRAY, R.: *La Formation de la doctrine classique en France*, Payot, 1931.
CRUICKSHANK, J. (ed.): *French Literature and its Background*, vol. 2: *The Seventeenth Century*, O.U.P., 1969.
DEMOREST, J. J.: *Studies in Seventeenth-Century French Literature*, Doubleday Anchor Books, 1966.
HOWARTH, W. D.: *Life and Letters in France: The Seventeenth Century*, Nelson, 1965.
LANCASTER, H. C.: *A History of French Dramatic Literature in the Seventeenth Century*, 9 vols., Johns Hopkins Press, 1929–42.
LOUGH, J.: *An Introduction to Seventeenth-Century France*, Longmans, 1954.
MAY, G.: *Tragédie cornélienne, tragédie racinienne*, University of Illinois Press, 1948.
MONGRÉDIEN, G.: *La Vie littéraire au XVIIe siècle*, Tallandier, 1947.
MOREL, J.: *La Tragédie*, A. Colin, 1964.
MORNET, D.: *Histoire de la littérature française classique, 1660–1700*, A. Colin, 1947.
MOUSNIER, R.: *Les XVIe et XVIIe siècles*, Presses Universitaires de France, 1961.
PICARD, R.: *Two Centuries of French Literature, 1600–1800*, World University Library, 1970.
PINTARD, R.: *Le Libertinage érudit dans la première moitié du XVIIe siècle*, Boivin, 1943.
ROUSSET, J.: *Forme et signification*, Corti, 1962.
SCHÉRER, J.: *La Dramaturgie classique en France*, Nizet, n.d.
SPINK, J. S.: *French Free-Thought from Gassendi to Voltaire*, The Athlone Press, 1960.
STAROBINSKI, J.: *L'Œil vivant*, Gallimard, 1961.
TURNELL, M.: *The Classical Moment*, Hamish Hamilton, 1947.
VEDEL, V.: *Deux Classiques français vus par un critique étranger: Corneille et son temps. Molière*. Champion, 1935.
VOLTZ, P.: *La Comédie*, A. Colin, 1964.

2. Corneille

(a) *Editions*

The standard edition of the complete works of Corneille is in the series: "Les Grands Écrivains de la France", edited by C. Marty-Laveaux, 12 vols., Hachette, 1862–8. A convenient recent edition is in the collection "L'intégrale", ed. A. Stegmann, Éd. du Seuil, 1963.

(b) *Critical Works*

BARNWELL, H. T.: *Pierre Corneille: Writings on the Theatre*, Blackwell, 1965.
BRASILLACH, R.: *Corneille*, Fayard, 1938.
COUTON, G.: *Corneille*, Hatier, 1958.
DOUBROVSKY, S.: *Corneille et la dialectique du héros*, Gallimard, 1963.
HERLAND, L.: *Horace ou Naissance de l'homme*, Éd. de Minuit, 1952.
HERLAND, L.: *Corneille par lui-même*, Éd. du Seuil, 1959.
LANSON, G.: *Corneille*, Hachette, 1898.
MAURENS, J.: *La Tragédie sans tragique: Le néo-stoïcisme dans l'œuvre de Pierre Corneille*, A. Colin, 1966.
MELVILLE-RIDDLE, L.: *The Genesis and Sources of P. Corneille's Tragedies from Médée to Pertharite*, Baltimore, 1926.
NADAL, O.: *Le Sentiment de l'amour dans l'œuvre de Pierre Corneille*, Gallimard, 1948.
NELSON, R. J.: *Corneille, His Heroes and their Worlds*, University of Pennsylvania Press, 1963.
YARROW, P. J.: *Corneille*, Macmillan, 1963.

3. **Racine**

(a) *Editions*

The standard edition of the complete works of Racine is in the series "Les Grands Écrivains de la France", ed. P. Mesnard, 8 vols., Hachette, 1865–73. A sound modern edition is that of R. Picard, 2 vols., Gallimard (Bibliothèque de la Pléiade), 1966–8.

(b) *Critical Works*

BARTHES, R.: *Sur Racine*, Éd. du Seuil, 1963.
BUTLER, P.: *Classicisme et baroque dans l'œuvre de Racine*, Nizet, 1959.
FRANCE, P.: *Racine's Rhetoric*, O.U.P., 1965.
GIRAUDOUX, J.: *Jean Racine*, Grasset, 1930.
GOLDMANN, L.: *Le Dieu caché. Étude sur la vision tragique dans les « Pensées » de Pascal et dans le théâtre de Racine*, Gallimard, 1955.
GOLDMANN, L.: *Racine*, L'Arche, 1956.
HUBERT, J.: *Essai d'exégèse racinienne: les secrets témoins*, Nizet, 1966.
JASINSKI, R.: *Vers le vrai Racine*, 2 vols., A. Colin, 1958.
KNIGHT, R. C.: *Racine et la Grèce*, Didier-Boivin, 1951.
KNIGHT, R. C.: *Racine: Modern Judgements*, Macmillan, 1969.
LAPP, J. C.: *Aspects of Racinian Tragedy*, O.U.P., 1964.
LE BIDOIS, G.: *La Vie dans les tragédies de Racine*, De Gigord, 1929.
MAULNIER, T.: *Racine*, Gallimard, 1936.
MAURIAC, F.: *La Vie de Jean Racine*, Plon, 1928.
MAURON, C.: *Phèdre*, Corti, 1968.
MOREAU, P.: *Racine, l'homme et l'œuvre*, Hatier, 1952.
MOURGUES, O. DE: *Racine, or The Triumph of Relevance*, C.U.P., 1967.
PICARD, R.: *La Carrière de Jean Racine*, Gallimard, 1956.
POMMIER, J.: *Aspects de Racine*, Nizet, 1954.
VINAVER, E.: *Racine et la poésie tragique*, Nizet, 1951.
WEINBERG, B.: *The Art of Jean Racine*, Chicago University Press, 1963.

4. Molière

(a) *Editions*

The standard edition of the complete works of Molière is in the series "Les Grands Écrivains de la France", ed. Despois and Mesnard, 13 vols., Hachette, 1873–1900. Useful modern editions are those of R. Jouanny, 2 vols., Garnier, 1960, and P. A. Touchard (L'Intégrale), Éd. du Seuil, 1962.

(b) *Critical Works*

ATTINGER, G.: *L'Esprit de la Commedia dell'Arte dans le théâtre français*, La Baconnière, 1950.
BRAY, R.: *Molière, homme de théâtre*, Mercure de France, 1954.
BRISSON, P.: *Molière, sa vie dans ses œuvres*, Gallimard, 1942.
FERNANDEZ, R.: *La Vie de Molière*, Gallimard, 1930.
GOSSMAN, L.: *Men and Masks: A Study of Molière*, Johns Hopkins Press, 1963.
GUICHARNAUD, J.: *Molière, une aventure théâtrale*, Gallimard, 1963.
GUICHARNAUD, J.: *Molière: A Collection of Critical Essays*, Prentice-Hall, 1964.
GUTKIND, C. S.: *Molière und das komische Drama*, Max Niemeyer Verlag, 1928.
HUBERT, J.: *Molière and the Comedy of Intellect*, University of California Press, 1962.
JASINSKI, R.: *Molière et Le Misanthrope*, A. Colin, 1951.
JASINSKI, R.: *Molière*, Hatier, 1969.
KOHLER, P.: *L'Esprit classique et la comédie*, Payot, 1925.
MICHAUT, G.: *La Jeunesse de Molière; Les Débuts de Molière à Paris; Les Luttes de Molière*, 3 vols., Hachette, 1922–5.
MOLAND, L.: *Molière et la comédie italienne*, Didier, 1867.
MONGRÉDIEN, G.: *La Vie privée de Molière*, Hachette, 1950.
MOORE, W. G.: *Molière: A New Criticism*, O.U.P., 1949.
MORNET, D.: *Molière*, Boivin, 1943.
ROMANO, D.: *Essai sur le comique de Molière*, A. Francke, 1950.
SCHÉRER, J.: *Structures de Tartuffe*, S.E.D.E.S., 1966.
SCHÉRER, J.: *Sur le Dom Juan de Molière*, S.E.D.E.S., 1967.
SIMON, A.: *Molière par lui-même*, Éd. du Seuil. 1957.

5. Madame de Lafayette

(a) *Editions*

The edition of the *Romans et Nouvelles* by E. Magne, Garnier, 1939 (1958), is perhaps the best known; a few textual errors in Magne's version of *La Princesse de Clèves* are corrected in my own critical edition, Harrap, 1970.

(b) *Critical Works*

ASHTON, H.: *Madame de La Fayette, sa vie et ses œuvres*, C.U.P., 1922.
BEYERLE, D.: *'La Princesse de Clèves' als Roman des Verzichts*, Hamburg U.P., 1967.
COULET, H.: *Le Roman jusqu'à la Révolution*, A. Colin, 1967.
DÉDÉYAN, C.: *Madame de Lafayette*, S.E.D.E.S., 1956.
DELOFFRE, F.: *La Nouvelle en France à l'âge classique*, Didier, 1967.
DURRY, M. J.: *Madame de La Fayette*, Mercure de France, 1962.
GODENNE, R.: *Histoire de la nouvelle française aux XVIIe et XVIIIe siècles*, Droz, 1970.

KAPS, H.: *Moral Perspective in 'La Princesse de Clèves'*, University of Oregon Books, 1968.
LE BRETON, A.: *Le Roman au XVIIe siècle*, Hachette, 1890.
MAGENDIE, M.: *Le Roman français au XVIIe siècle, de l'Astrée au Grand Cyrus*, Droz, 1932.
MAGNE, E.: *Madame de La Fayette en ménage*, Émile Paul, 1926.
MAGNE, E.: *Le Cœur et l'esprit de Madame de La Fayette*, Émile Paul, 1927.
PINGAUD, B.: *Madame de La Fayette par elle-même*, Éd. du Seuil, 1959.
POULET, G.: *Études sur le temps humain*, Plon, 1950.
RAITT, J.: *Madame de Lafayette and 'La Princesse de Clèves'*, Harrap, 1971.
REYNIER, G.: *Le Roman sentimental avant l'Astrée*, A. Colin, 1908.
TURNELL, M.: *The Novel in France*, Hamish Hamilton, 1950.